PERSPECTIVES ON HONG KONG S

Nuala Rooney

PERSPECTIVES ON HONG KONG SOCIETY

Benjamin K. P. Leung

HONG KONG
OXFORD UNIVERSITY PRESS
OXFORD NEW YORK
1996

Oxford University Press
Oxford New York
Athens Auckland Bangkok Bogota Bombay
Buenos Aires Calcutta Cape Town Dar es Salaam
Delhi Florence Hong Kong Istanbul Karachi
Kuala Lumpur Madras Madrid Melbourne
Mexico City Nairobi Paris Singapore
Taipei Tokyo Toronto
and associated companies in
Berlin Ibadan

Oxford is a trade mark of Oxford University Press

First published 1996
This impression (lowest digit)
1 3 5 7 9 10 8 6 4 2

Published in the United States
by Oxford University Press, New York

© Oxford University Press 1996

All rights reserved. No part of this publication may be reproduced, stored in a retrieval system, or transmitted, in any form or by any means, without the prior permission in writing of Oxford University Press (China)Ltd. Within Hong Kong, exceptions are allowed in respect of any fair dealing for the purpose of research or private study, or criticism or review, as permitted under the Copyright Ordinance currently in force. Enquiries concerning reproduction outside these terms and in other countries should be sent to Oxford University Press (China) Ltd at the address below

This book is sold subject to the condition that it shall not, by way of trade or otherwise, be lent, re-sold, hired out or otherwise circulated without the publisher's prior consent in any form of binding or cover other than that in which it is published and without a similar condition including this condition being imposed on the subsequent purchaser

British Library Cataloguing in Publication Data
available

ISBN 0-19-586535-9

Printed in Hong Kong
Published by Oxford University Press (China) Ltd
18/F Warwick House, Taikoo Place, 979 King's Road,
Quarry Bay, Hong Kong

Preface

This book originated from my concern about the lack of a standard comprehensive text on Hong Kong society. The two existing, highly acclaimed works on the topic—Lau Siu-kai's *Society and Politics in Hong Kong* (1982) and Ian Scott's *Political Change and the Crisis of Legitimacy in Hong Kong* (1989a)—are primarily attempts to explain the society's political change and political stability. As such, despite the valuable insights they provide on the culture, economy, and politics of the territory, both books leave vast areas still to be explored. While a full treatment of these topics has not been available, they have been the subjects of inquiry in the proliferating literature on Hong Kong society. Together, the available published works provide the basis for a comprehensive and critical examination of the constitution and dynamics of the society. The present work is an endeavour to put into one volume the contributions made by these authors to our understanding of Hong Kong society.

My basic aim for this book is to advance our knowledge of Hong Kong as a whole. The book begins with an attempt to fulfill this objective through a discussion of the territory's socio-economic and political development in Chapter 1, followed by an inquiry into the society's class structure in Chapter 2, and an overview of major aspects of the culture of the Hong Kong Chinese in Chapter 3. These chapters provide the background for the discussion of particular topics and issues in the remainder of the book. The aim of the subsequent chapters, however, is not only to throw light on individual aspects of the society, but also to enrich our understanding of the society as a whole through examining its parts and processes from a broad societal perspective. Thus, my discussion of the family in Chapter 4 is situated in the context of social change, and of the bearing of the family on Hong Kong's political stability, gender inequality, and economy. In Chapter 5, crime, deviance, and social control are examined with regard to industrialization, urbanization, the growth of new towns, as well as the society's political and class structures. Chapter 6 on social policy delves into the Government's guiding values and concerns, and its style of policy-making, in coming to grips with the changing composition and orientations of the population, and in maintaining the legitimacy of colonial rule. This is followed by a study in Chapter 7 of social conflict and social movements, which brings to light the impact of the 'China factor' on the genesis and the nature of major episodes of collective oppositional movements in Hong Kong. The final chapter addresses the much debated issue of democratization, and assesses the socio-economic and political factors that bear on political development in Hong Kong.

This book thus offers 'perspectives on Hong Kong society' both through the overviews of the first three chapters and the discussion of specific topics and issues in the other chapters. Some of these perspectives have been the subject of debates and critiques within the academic community, and I have tried to reflect the nature of the pertinent dialogues in the present volume. Other perspectives still await the critical scrutiny of future research. In such cases I have refrained from mounting critiques purely on the basis of my subjective judgment. Finally, I would like to point out that my orientation in this book has been to present the various perspectives and their associated research and critiques for the reader's critical examination and choice, rather than to identify certain perspectives as the only 'correct' ways to look at Hong Kong society.

BENJAMIN K. P. LEUNG
The University of Hong Kong

Contents

Preface	v
Tables and Figures	viii
1 Economy, Politics, and Society: Developmental Overviews	1
2 Social Class and Social Mobility	29
3 Culture and Society	49
4 The Family and Society	75
5 Deviance, Crime, and Social Control	94
6 Social Policy	115
7 Social Conflict and Social Movements	139
8 The Development Towards a Representative Government	162
References	182
Index	197

Tables and Figures

Table 1.1 Percentages of Hong Kong's Gross Domestic Product by Selected Industries, 1961–1991   7
Table 1.2 Distribution of the Hong Kong's Working Population Among Selected Industries, 1961–1991 (as percentage of the total working population)   7
Table 1.3 The Revival of Hong Kong's Entrepôt Trade with China, 1970–1989 (in US$ millions)   8
Table 1.4 Distribution of Hong Kong's Manufacturing Establishments and Employment by Size of Establishment (as percentage of total manufacturing establishments)   8
Table 1.5 Hong Kong Household Income, 1976–1991 (as percentage of total population)   10
Table 1.6 Educational Attainment of the Hong Kong Population aged 15 and over, 1976–1991 (as percentage of total population)   11
Table 1.7 Hong Kong's Working Population by Occupation, 1981–1991 (as percentage of total working population)   11
Table 5.1 Hong Kong's Crime Rates for Property Crimes and Violent Crimes, 1956/7 to 1989/90 (incidents per 100,000 population)   96
Table 6.1 Social Service Expenditure as a Percentage of Public Expenditure: Selected Years   135
Table 7.1 Trade Union Density and Level of Industrial Strikes in Hong Kong, 1946–1989   153
Table 8.1 Composition of the Hong Kong Legislature Towards 1997 and Beyond   176

Figure 5.1 Hong Kong Crime Rates per 100,000 Population for Property Crimes, 1956–1989   97
Figure 5.2 Hong Kong Crime Rates per 100,000 Population for Violent Crimes, 1956–1989   97

1. Economy, Politics, and Society: Developmental Overviews

THE aim of this chapter is to provide a general introduction to Hong Kong society through an examination of major developmental changes in the territory's economy, politics, and social structure. We shall use as the basis of our discussion several prominent studies which attempt an historical and social-structural analysis of the society. There are differences as well as overlaps in the conceptual orientations and historical coverage of these works. Our objective, therefore, is to examine the variety of developmental overviews available to us, rather than to forge a single overview of Hong Kong's character. To the extent that the pertinent studies offer different perspectives and insights on Hong Kong's developmental history, they broaden and enrich our understanding of the dynamics of the society. In our review of these works, we place the emphasis on how the Hong Kong economy has impacted on, and interacted with, aspects of the society to shape its social-political structure. We shall dwell mainly on Hong Kong's development since the end of the Second World War, but to lay the background for this discussion the chapter begins with a brief historical and sociological overview of early Hong Kong society.

Economy, Race, and Class in Early Hong Kong Society

When the island of Hong Kong became a British colony in 1841, it had an estimated population of 7,450, made up of villagers, boat people, visiting labourers, and vendors (*Hong Kong Government Gazette*, May 1841, cited in Endacott 1973: 65). Its excellent geographical advantages for trade—a good natural harbour and promixity to China—attracted British and European merchants. Following the merchants came labourers, artisans, and vendors of all kinds from nearby villages in China to take advantage of the newly created job opportunities. The population grew rapidly as a consequence, reaching an estimated 23,817 in 1845, 125,504 in 1865, and slightly over a quarter of a million by the end of the century (Endacott 1973: 65, 183, 262).

As a colony, the society was racially segregated between the British colonizers and the subordinate Chinese. As an entrepôt, its economically dominant group was the merchants, whose domestic needs and labour requirements were met by the exploited and underprivileged Chinese labourers. These racial and economic factors combined to enable the

British merchants to establish themselves quickly as a potent social-political force. Hong Kong society was structured initially along racial lines, with the Chinese merchants and Chinese labourers coalescing into one community, in juxtaposition to the British merchants and the colonial government. But these were transient configurations, the elementary ingredients on the basis of which a different social structure evolved and took shape by the beginning of the twentieth century.

This process of development, characterized by class formation and the eclipse of the racial cleavage by class division, is the subject of a celebrated work by W. K. Chan (see W. K. Chan 1991). Chan views the formation of classes in Hong Kong as coterminous with the making of the society, and he sees class alliances and class inequality as setting and upsetting the equilibrium of the nascent social structure.

Chan's study is an ingenious analysis of how the socio-economic and political conditions of early Hong Kong engendered class boundaries and culminated in class formation. His work carries important implications for our understanding of the subsequent development of Hong Kong's social structure. Socio-economically, the British merchants were doubly advantaged—they were of the same racial stock as the ruling élite and they controlled the economic life of the Colony—to reach the top positions of political power. This they did when two of their wealthiest members were appointed by the Governor in 1850 to the Legislative Council[1], a top policy-making body in Hong Kong. Wealth and political clout combined to set them off as an élite social group distinct from other Europeans and the Chinese community.

A primary factor instrumental in converting them from a loosely organized social group to a solidary social class was the social clubs founded by the Europeans to forge among themselves a feeling of community. The Hong Kong Club, established in 1846, was the most noteworthy and functional in this respect, but other similar organizations worked to the same effect. Membership was confined to Europeans of wealth and influence, serving thus to delineate a social demarcation between the British merchants and their less illustrious compatriots. Hierarchical positions in these clubs, with their attendant etiquette, rights, and obligations, formalized and stabilized the otherwise spontaneous activities of the Europeans, bringing a level of organization and predictability to the British merchants' actions. In this way, beginning as an economic grouping, the British merchants acquired class consciousness and solidarity. The entailing class structure and relations had a long-lasting impact on early Hong Kong society (Chan 1991: chap. 2):

A set of social relationships gradually evolved, which remained after individual traders went home, and were reproduced, modified, and strengthened by the next generation of traders.... They acquired a permanent character and continually shaped the way other organizations were created and other relations structured (Chan 1991: 35).

This shaping of 'other organizations' and 'other relations', Chan maintains, has to be understood in the context of racial segregation, which left the Chinese, merchants and labourers alike, to regulate and structure their community with little interference from the British. The evolution of organizations and relations within the Chinese community was very much an effect of the exclusive and discriminatory character of the British merchant class. Excluded from the social circle of the British merchants and denied the power and privileges of their British counterparts, the Chinese merchants sought to carve out their niche of status and influence among their compatriots. They used their wealth to establish and maintain their reputations and leadership roles through acts of charity and through instituting a system of social control within the Chinese community. The organizations and relations they built up in the process constituted the main structural features of the Chinese community, for the organizations turned out in time to be centres of power and control.

Among these organizations and mechanisms, the most noteworthy were the Tung Wah Hospital,[2] a charitable organization catering to the medical and welfare needs of the Chinese population, and the district watch force,[3] a local police force financed and controlled by the Chinese merchants. These institutions not only conferred on the Chinese merchants status and leadership within the Chinese community, but also helped to inculcate class consciousness and organization among them in the same way as the European social clubs did for the British merchants. This making of the Chinese merchant class was the prelude to their incorporation into the Colony's formal political power structure (Chan 1991: chap. 3). When that incorporation occurred, Chan goes on to argue, the society underwent another transformation in its fundamental structure and relations.

Three major factors led to the co-option of the Chinese merchants into the Colony's ruling élite. Politically, as leaders of the Chinese community, the Chinese merchants' absorption into the formal political system would be tantamount to dissolving a prospective stronghold of power and opposition among the Chinese population, and their presence in the higher echelons of government would buttress the legitimacy of colonial rule. Economically, advantaged by their long-established connections with businessmen in China and by their greater knowledge of the Chinese market, the Chinese merchants were emerging by the 1870s as an important economic force on whom the British often depended in their China trade. Culturally, an increasing number of the Chinese merchants were becoming conversant with the English language—a consequence mainly of their English education in the Colony's mission schools and government schools. The first Chinese was appointed to the Legislative Council in 1880; by 1941, fourteen members were Chinese. All appointees were successful businessmen, had an English education, and were associated with one or more of the élite organizations of the Chinese community, in particular the Tung Wah Hospital and the District Watch Committee (Chan 1991: 105–17).

The effect of these developments, in Chan's view, was a growing economic and political affinity between the British and Chinese merchants as the racial barrier between the two groups was gradually eclipsed by the burgeoning homogeneity in economic interests and political status. The mass of Chinese labourers, on the other hand, felt themselves increasingly alienated from their former allied leaders, the Chinese merchants. The rupture grew with a series of industrial strikes in the late nineteenth and early twentieth centuries, when the Chinese merchants sided with the British in their confrontations with the Chinese labourers. In the course of these struggles, the labourers had to defend and advance their interests through their own efforts. Labour unions and leaders rose and proliferated, culminating in the formation of the labouring class in the 1920s. According to Chan, in the early decades of the twentieth century the main social cleavage in Hong Kong was shifting from a racial division to a class division between labourers and merchants (Chan 1991: chap. 4). The historical marker of this change was the Seamen's Strike of 1922.

Chan views the Seamen's Strike as a class conflict. To back up his contention, he cites as evidence the joint efforts of the workers in the struggle and their denuniciation of their employers as capitalist oppressors and class enemies. The Chinese Seamen's Union acted in coalition with twelve major labour unions, and at the height of the struggle on 28 February 1922, nearly all the workers in the Colony went on a sympathetic strike (Chan 1991: 173). The strikers and their sympathizers called the employers 'unvirtuous capitalists' and 'capitalists carrying out wicked plans against the labouring class'.[4] The strike led to the formation of the labouring class: the resulting class alliances and antagonisms defined the structural features of Hong Kong society until its entrepôt economy collapsed and was superceded by an industrializing economy in the early 1950s.[5] Commenting on the impact of class formation on the social structure of early Hong Kong and on subsequent developments before the end of the Second World War, Chan writes:

Hong Kong was transformed into an organic, self-reproducing social entity comprising well-defined social groupings each with its own identity and each maintaining specific structural relations with the others.... Although it was still vulnerable to changes imposed by external events beyond its control, Hong Kong was structurally a more permanent society and had a greater ability to respond to outside challenges (Chan 1991: 209).

Industrialization: Major Changes in Economy and Social Structure

The Impetus for Industrialization

Hong Kong's industrialization arose in the context of a number of related but externally induced circumstances. The establishment of the People's Republic of China in 1949 and its participation in the Korean War the following year led to an embargo by the United Nations on trade with China. The embargo severely crippled Hong Kong's entrepôt trade, on which the Colony's economy had heavily depended. Hong Kong was forced to overcome this crisis by producing its own industrial products for export to overseas markets, beginning its development into an export-oriented industrial economy.

The prerequisites for this industrialization—the presence of capital, labour, technical know-how, and entrepreneurship—came with the influx of refugees from China, a by-product of the Chinese civil war and the ensuing victory of the Communists on the mainland. An official source in Hong Kong estimated in 1973 that the inflow of capital and entrepreneurship had given Hong Kong 'ten to fifteen years' start in industrialization over many other Asian countries'.[6] The majority of the entrepreneurs came from Shanghai, then the leading urban industrial centre in China. The accompanying influx of capital from mid-1946 to October 1948 allegedly amounted to sixty billion Hong Kong dollars,[7] and reached an annual average of around HK$300–600 million in subsequent years up to the mid-1950s (Szczepanik 1958: 142; Wong Siu-lun 1988a: 43–4). The importance of this capital inflow to Hong Kong's early industrialization is made apparent in economist Edward Szczepanik's assessment: 'Approximately one-third of investment was financed by internal savings, the remaining two-thirds by capital from abroad.'

Most of these entrepreneurs brought with them skilled employees from Shanghai, and Hong Kong's early industrial structure bore the imprint of these immigrants' Shanghai industrial heritage. Textile manufacturing was the first industry to develop and became the leading sector in Hong Kong's industrialization, accounting for around 48 per cent of Hong Kong's export value in 1956 and employing some 30 per cent of the workers engaged in manufacturing in 1957. Other industries soon developed, the most important of which in terms of their share in export value were clothing, electronic and electrical goods, and plastic products.[8]

Labour for these rapidly growing industries was forthcoming through the influx of refugees and through the Colony's natural population increase. A United Nations report estimated the number of migrants who reached Hong Kong between September 1945 and December 1949 to be 1,285,000. After that time, except for a short period of refugee inflow in 1962, natural increase accounted primarily for the territory's population growth from about two million in 1950 to just over three million in 1961 and four million in 1969 (Podmore 1971: 25–6). Hong Kong's industrialization benefited not only from the quantity, but also the quality, of its labour force. Apart from harbouring the refugee mentality of working hard to make a new beginning, the new arrivals were prepared to put up with harsh working conditions and low wages in the Colony, for the political and economic conditions in their homeland seemed even worse. The docility of the labour force, however, was also rooted to some extent in traditional Chinese culture. Joe England captured succinctly the relevance of these characteristics to Hong Kong's smooth transition to an industrial economy:

Familial traditions of obedience and loyalty to autocratic authority, a shared positive belief in hard work and economic gain, . . . the habit of giving face and avoiding confrontation wherever possible, have all played a part in mitigating conflict between capital and labour in Hong Kong (England 1989: 42).

We can see from the above discussion that circumstances external to Hong Kong not only provided the momentum for its industrialization, but also impacted on the character of its industrial labour force and industrial relations.

The Development of the Industrial Economy: A Profile

To understand the main contours of Hong Kong's industrial development, we may begin with J. Reidel's apt summary of the prominent features of the Colony's industrialization:

> Hong Kong (1) specializes in the manufacture of standardized consumer goods (2) for export (3) to high-income countries in the West, and at the same time, the Colony (4) relies on Asian countries for the provision of raw materials and (5) on Western countries for capital goods.... [T]he fact that the goods manufactured are highly standardized, requiring little 'research and development', means that Hong Kong entrepreneurs are left to do what they can do best: produce. These features, taken together, constitute what shall be called the 'Hong Kong model of industrialization' (Reidel 1973: 3).

The point most pertinent to our discussion is the reliance of Hong Kong's industrial economy on the demand of Western markets for inexpensive, hence fairly low-quality, consumer goods, the production of which require little technological innovation and capital investment. On the one hand, this explains the labour-intensive character of Hong Kong's manufacturing production, as well as the predominance of small and medium-sized industrial firms in the territory. These main features of the economy, as I shall argue later, have an important bearing on Hong Kong's social structure and political process. On the other hand, the volatility of overseas markets—subject to changes in consumer tastes and the protectionist policies of the importing countries—and market competition from other newly industrializing countries has meant that the survival and success of the Hong Kong economy depends on its ability to cope with uncertainties and fluctuations, and to develop in appropriate new directions. This challenge was intensifying in the 1970s, as Hong Kong adapted through a process of industrial diversification and by moving 'up-market' to adjust to the overseas change in demand for new and higher-quality products.

The economy's continuing viability and vitality, however, has to be understood primarily in terms of China's open-door policy, in place since the mid-1970s, and the concomitant expansion of the financial and service sectors in Hong Kong. These new developments have had two major beneficial effects on the local economy. The open-door policy has enabled Hong Kong's manufacturers to reap the benefits of low-cost production through relocating their industrial plants to the special economic zones in southern China, thus sustaining the competitiveness of their exports in the international market. At the same time, the increasing contribution of the financial and service sectors to economic growth and to employment has compensated for the declining role of the industrial manufacturing sector. The opening up of China has had the further effect of reviving Hong Kong's entrepôt trade. Tables 1.1, 1.2, and 1.3 provide the vital statistics on these changes.

Table 1.1 Percentage of Hong Kong's Gross Domestic Product by Selected Industries, 1961–1991

Industry	1961	1971	1981	1986	1991
Manufacturing	23.6	28.2	22.8	22.3	15.2
Wholesale and retail trades, restaurants and hotels	19.5	19.5	19.5	21.3	25.4
Financing, insurance, real estate, and business services	10.8	17.5	23.8	17.3	22.7

Sources: D. L. Zheng, 1987, *Modern Hong Kong Economy*, Beijing: China's Financial, Political and Economic Publisher, p. 123; Census and Statistics Department (Hong Kong Government), 1991, *Estimates of Gross Domestic Product: 1966 to 1990*, Hong Kong: Government Printer, p. 31; Census and Statistics Department (Hong Kong Government), 1993, *Annual Digest of Statistics*, Hong Kong: Government Printer, p. 116.

Table 1.2 Distribution of Hong Kong's Working Population Among Selected Industries, 1961–1991 (as percentage of the total working population)

Industry	1961	1971	1981	1986	1991
Manufacturing	43.0	47.0	41.2	35.8	28.2
Wholesale and retail trades, restaurants and hotels	14.4	16.2	19.2	22.3	22.5
Financing, insurance, real estate, and business services	1.6	2.7	4.8	6.4	10.6

Sources: Census and Statistics Department (Hong Kong Government), Census and By-census Reports, various years (Hong Kong: Government Printer).

The Development of the Economy: The Significance of Small and Medium-sized Industrial Establishments

A distinct feature of Hong Kong's industrial economy has been the predominance of small (with fewer than fifty employees) and medium-sized (with between fifty to 199 employees) industrial firms. As Table 1.4 shows, the share of these firms in the territory's manufacturing establishments and employment has been substantial and has increased during the course of industrial development. Their rise and proliferation have been a product of Hong Kong's unique socio-economic circumstances. Their mode of operation has been the major contributing factor to the resilience and adaptive capacity of Hong Kong's export-oriented economy.

Table 1.3 The Revival of Hong Kong's Entrepôt Trade with China, 1970–1989 (in US$ millions)

	1970	1981	1985	1989
Hong Kong's imports from China for re-export (percentage share of Hong Kong's total re-exports)	97 (20.2)	1,951 (26.2)	3,778 (28.0)	20,517 (54.3)
Hong Kong's re-exports to China (percentage share of Hong Kong's total re-exports)	6 (1.2)	1,438 (19.3)	5,907 (43.7)	13,268 (29.9)

Source: Yun-wing Sung, 1991, *The China–Hong Kong Connection*, Cambridge: Cambridge University Press, pp. 19–20.

Table 1.4 Distribution of Hong Kong's Manufacturing Establishments and Employment by Size of Establishment (as percentage of total manufacturing establishments)

Size of establishment (persons employed)	Establishment distribution				Employment distribution			
	1961	1971	1981	1991	1961	1971	1981	1991
1–9	38.9	51.9	65.4	72.3	6.0	6.9	13.3	17.8
10–19	28.6	19.1	15.6	13.6	8.4	7.5	10.9	12.0
20–49	18.2	15.5	11.1	9.6	15.1	14.0	17.9	17.3
50–99	6.7	6.6	4.7	3.3	12.4	13.2	16.2	14.9
100–199	4.0	3.9	2.0	1.4	14.7	15.7	14.4	12.6
200–499	2.5	2.1	0.9	0.7	20.3	18.6	13.7	14.0
500 and over	0.9	0.7	0.3	0.2	22.9	24.2	13.6	11.6

Sources: Census and Statistics Department (Hong Kong Government), 1990, *Annual Digest of Statistics*, Hong Kong: Government Printer, p. 38; Census and Statistics Department (Hong Kong Government), 1993, *Annual Digest of Statistics*, Hong Kong: Government Printer, p. 50; Victor Sit et al., 1979, *Small Scale Industry in a Laissez-faire Economy*, Hong Kong: Centre of Asian Studies, University of Hong Kong, pp. 25–6.

The proliferation of small-scale industrial firms, beginning in the 1950s, occurred in a context in which one attractive venue for social and economic advancement for the arriving refugees was to set up their own industrial enterprises. The opportunity was provided by the territory's rapid industrialization, and it was seized zealously by the Cantonese, who made up the majority of the refugee population and who have been described as 'ambitious and possessed with a "gambler's instinct", and [who] aspire very much to be their own boss' (Chau 1989: 178). The paucity of viable alternatives provided another driving force, as Wong Siu-lun observes: 'As immigrants, most of them were not proficient in English, which was the key to stable administrative or commercial careers. Thus they turned to small-scale industry for advancement' (Wong Siu-lun 1991: 24). The immigrants made up for their deficiency in capital by pulling together their familial resources to run small-scale family firms. Their recent experience of instability and turmoil in China, coupled with their uncertainty about the Colony's political future, also disposed them to produce goods with low capital requirements, short gestation periods, and high labour content so that they could recover their investment quickly (Chau 1989: 178).

These small enterprises have fitted well with Hong Kong's export-based economy, and they have proved to be ideal in coping with the uncertainties and fluctuations in overseas markets. With modest technological input and a small labour force, they can recover their overheads and make a profit in a few years, switching to another line of production in response to changes in market demand. At the same time, as these firms are geared to the production of simple items, they require little skill in their workers, facilitating the transfer of workers from one firm to another when the necessity arises. In this way they enhance the flexibility and adaptability of the economy.

Another way in which small firms add to the economy's flexibility is through the system of subcontracting, a strategy by which Hong Kong's larger manufacturing firms cope with the volatility of overseas markets. The seasonal nature of orders and unpredictable drops in demand, among other factors, render it unprofitable for these firms to expand beyond a certain productive capacity. Consequently, such firms are ill-equipped to meet rush or surplus orders. Yet, to compete successfully in the international market, they must demonstrate the capacity for quick and punctual delivery whatever the rush and size of the order. To do so, they subcontract orders as necessary to small and medium firms. In this sense, the smaller firms act as a buffer between the volatile export market and the larger firms.[9] The smaller firms must operate with a flexible workforce whose productive capacity, work schedule, and employment can vary with the vicissitudes of overseas markets.[10] These requirements, and the relatively short life span of the smaller firms, have meant that workers have had to change jobs frequently in response to changing circumstances, a factor which contributes to high labour mobility and the low cohesiveness of workers.

Economic Development and the Restructuring of Hong Kong Society: An Introductory Discussion

The first major restructuring of Hong Kong society occurred in the aftermath of the Second World War, as a result of a large influx of refugees from China and of Hong Kong's industrialization. The rapid population

Table 1.5 Hong Kong Household Income, 1976–1991 (as percentage of total population)

Monthly Household Income (HK$)	1976	1981	1986	1991
Under 2,000	69.4	28.6	9.7	4.8
2,000–3,999		38.3	25.4	7.3
4,000–5,999	27.0	16.8	23.5	12.8
6,000–7,999		7.4	14.4	13.8
8,000–9,999	2.4	3.4	8.6	11.5
10,000–14,999	0.7	3.2	10.1	19.9
15,000–19,999	0.2	1.0	3.7	11.1
20,000 and over	0.3	1.3	4.6	18.8
Total	100.0	100.0	100.0	100.0

Sources: Census and Statistics Department (Hong Kong Government), *1986 By-Census: Summary Results*, Hong Kong: Government Printer, p. 15; Census and Statistics Department (Hong Kong Government), *1991 Population Census Main Report*, Hong Kong: Government Printer, p. 62.

increase and economic transformation led to a truncation of the class structure of early Hong Kong society. As a number of writers (Lau 1992, Luk 1995, Leung 1994d) have noted, the refugees came with the traditional parochial and familistic orientation, an outlook that interfered with the formation of class consciousness and class identity. Moreover, as noted in our discussion of Chan's study (1991), class formation is a protracted process, and in the case of labourers, most often contingent upon confrontation with an antagonistic class.

As recent arrivals harbouring a 'don't rock the boat' mentality, the refugee workers had neither the time nor the confrontational disposition to form themselves into a class. The rise of new industries and the corresponding decline of old ones, such as shipbuilding and docking, which had been the stronghold of working-class solidarity, contributed further to the dissolution of working-class consciousness. The predominance of small-scale industrial estabishments and high labour mobility posed additional obstacles. In short, there are strong grounds for the assertion that industrial Hong Kong, up to at least the mid-1960s, was no longer structurally characterized by the class divisions and antagonisms which Chan (1991) considers to be the defining features of the society in the first half of the twentieth century. While the industrial proletariat swelled with industrialization, its members constituted a 'working class' only in the sense of a social category, rather than a social grouping with a distinct class identity and capable of concerted collective action.

Hong Kong society went through another structural change from the mid-1970s, when the increasing affluence of the community, the rising educational attainment of the population, and the expansion of the financial

Table 1.6 Educational Attainment of the Hong Kong Population Aged 15 and Over, 1976–1991 (as percentage of total population)

Educational Attainment	1976	1981	1986	1991
No Schooling/Kindergarten	20.2	16.2	14.1	12.7
Primary	39.7	34.1	29.3	25.1
Secondary	33.2	39.4	42.8	46.0
Matriculation	2.1	3.6	4.7	4.9
Tertiary:				
Non-degree courses	1.6	3.3	4.7	5.4
Degree courses	3.2	3.4	4.4	5.9
Total	100.0	100.0	100.0	100.0

Source: Census and Statistics Department (Hong Kong Government), 1993, *Annual Digest of Statistics*, Hong Kong: Government Printer, p. 203.

Table 1.7 Hong Kong's Working Population by Occupation, 1981–1991 (as percentage of total working population)

Occupation	1981	1986	1991
Professional, technical and related workers	6.0	8.3	8.7
Administrative and managerial workers	2.7	3.6	5.1
Clerical and related workers	12.2	14.6	18.6
Sales workers	10.3	11.7	11.5
Service workers	15.6	16.2	18.7
Agricultural workers and fishermen	2.1	1.9	0.9
Production and related workers, transport equipment operators, and labourers	50.4	43.3	36.2
Armed forces and unclassifiable	0.7	0.4	0.3
Total	100.0	100.0	100.0

Source: Census and Statistics Department (Hong Kong Government), *1991 Population Census, Main Report*, Hong Kong: Goverment Printer, p. 94. Note: Due to different occupational classifications used in the 1976 By-census, the 1976 statistics have not been reproduced in this table.

and service sectors (see Tables 1.5, 1.6, and 1.7) gave birth to what some writers have called the 'new middle class'.

Composed of better-educated and better-paid professionals, administrators, managers, and lower-level clerical and white-collar workers, the new middle class can be expected to differ from the class of manual labourers in lifestyle, attitudes, and social aspirations. Furthermore, a substantial portion of the new middle class were born and raised in Hong Kong, and they do not share the refugee experience and mentality of the older generations. The size of the new middle class cannot be accurately gauged, but with the society's continuing affluence and the rapid expansion of the economy's tertiary sector, they are judged to make up the majority of the population in the 1980s and early 1990s. Hong Kong has been evolving in the past two decades into a predominantly middle-class society. The character of this class—its social and political aspirations, its relations with the capitalist class and the working class, and its capacity for collective action—bears significantly on our understanding of contemporary Hong Kong society. We shall return to this theme later in this chapter and in the next chapter. We proceed now to examine some prominent studies of Hong Kong's evolving social and political structure in light of the discussion in this section.

Hong Kong as a Minimally Integrated Social-Political System

From the early 1950s to the mid-1970s, Hong Kong was a rapidly industrializing society with gross social inequalities. Other societies in a similar situation have been plagued by frequent outbreaks of social disturbance and political turmoil, yet Hong Kong was remarkably stable during this period of rapid social change. This puzzling and intriguing feature of Hong Kong's social development has been the subject of inquiry of several local studies (e.g. Miners 1975; King 1981b; Lau 1982; and Scott 1989a). Of these, Lau Siu-kai's work is arguably one of the most comprehensive and influential. With analysis based mainly on the author's research in the 1970s, Lau's study is an attempt 'to make sense of the social and political phenomena in Hong Kong in the last three and a half decades' (Lau 1982: 17).

In the process of explicating his inquiry, Lau articulated a social-structural model of Hong Kong, describing the society as a 'minimally integrated social-political system'. He justified this description as follows: 'An autonomous bureaucratic polity, an atomistic Chinese society, and weak linkages between them are the three principal structural features of Hong Kong. Because of this, Hong Kong can be characterized as a minimally integrated social-political system...' (Lau 1982: 157). This model has constituted the underlying conceptual framework, as well as the basis for contention, of subsequent local studies. The book's value and relevance are not time-bound, and it remains even today one of the most influential and widely read writings on Hong Kong society.

The Inquiry: The Social-Structural Basis of Political Stability

Lau makes clear his conceptual orientation early in his book:

The approach to political stability advocated in this book is a comprehensive framework focusing upon the polity and the Chinese society of Hong Kong, and their relationships with each other.... Basically, the approach to political stability advanced here is a structural approach (Lau 1982: 17).

The absence of any reference to class and class relations in this statement suggests that from the start Lau does not consider them to be pertinent to the understanding of the structure and dynamics of Hong Kong society. This implicit dismissal of the relevance of class, which he justifies later in the book with reference to empirical data, raises the question of what constituted the structural characteristics of Hong Kong society at the time—characteristics which might be said to account for the society's political stability. His answer, which constitutes his main thesis in the book, is that the basic structural components of the society were the bureaucratic polity and the Chinese community, and that their complementarity was the basis of social order and stability. Lau's structural approach to Hong Kong's stability is thus concomitantly an analysis of the fundamental social structure and relations of the society.

Description of the bureaucratic polity and the Chinese community as the basic components of the society implies that these two were by and large disparate entities each with its own characteristics. The phrase 'bureaucratic polity' here refers to Hong Kong's then-undemocratic political system, in which senior government bureaucrats, mostly of British origin, ruled over the politically under-privileged Chinese majority. In Lau's view, the few members of the Chinese élite in the top echelons of power —within the Executive[11] and Legislative councils, for example—were dependent on the Government for their political appointment and belonged to the same socio-economically privileged group as their expatriate counterparts. As a result, it may be expected that their views were largely subordinate to and commensurate with those of the government bureaucrats. For this reason, the bureaucracy had a virtual monopoly of policy-making, a situation that contributed to its political and social seclusion from the Chinese community. The bureaucracy's insulation rendered the Government insensitive and even oblivious to the interests and demands of the people it ruled. As a colonial government, moreover, it was inherently weak in legitimacy. Why then did the Hong Kong Chinese remain politically acquiescent? What might explain Hong Kong's political stability? Lau finds answers to these questions in the character of the territory's Chinese community.

In Lau's view, the orientations of the Hong Kong Chinese until at least the 1970s were the product of the interaction between cultural tradition and the Hong Kong experience. As refugees, mostly from pre-modern rural parts of China, who had arrived seeking a safe haven in a borrowed time and borrowed place, the population's traditional political apathy was reinforced by their quest for stability and quick material gains in the Colony. Lacking the support of the Government, which was both unwilling and unable to adequately provide for the needs of the rapidly expanding population, the arriving refugees had to rely on their family and kinsfolk for material support and economic advancement. This reliance disposed the Chinese community to place the material pursuits and interests of the family above other concerns, inculcating a mentality which Lau has termed 'utilitarianistic familism' (later re-termed 'utilitarian familism'; Lau and Kuan 1988), a modified revival of traditional Chinese familism in the exigencies of Hong Kong's socio-economic setting.

This familial orientation had important implications for the Colony's social and political structure. It bred an attitude of indifference and aloofness towards society, resulting in low civic consciousness and low social participation. In addition, by atomizing society into self-centred familial groups oriented primarily to the pursuit of wealth, it was a stumbling stock to the formation of social classes. Lau's research findings, based on a representative sample of the population, testified to this social-structural consequence of utilitarianistic familism. His findings indicated that the respondents had no clear or consistent idea about what constituted a class in Hong Kong, and that they tended to see the society as hierarchically structured by a gradation of wealth rather than by antagonistic classes. The overwhelming majority (91 per cent) of the respondents also did not see the wealth of the rich as having come from an exploitation of the lower social strata. Most (81 per cent) believed that the way for the poor to improve their livelihood was to rely on their own efforts, and only a small minority (5 per cent) advocated the collective efforts of the poor to fight for their rights (Lau 1982: 96–102). Lau sums up the implications of these findings as follows:

In short, social classes as structural forces in shaping interpersonal relationships and political actions are relatively insignificant in Hong Kong (Lau 1982: 98).

Utilitarianistic familism impacted on Hong Kong's social-political structure in another way as well. In fostering among members of the Chinese community an inclination to resort to the family for solutions to their problems, it absolved the Government to a significant extent of its responsibilities to society. In effect, the family functioned to depoliticize the Chinese community through resolving potential politically relevant issues within the familial context, and through rendering mobilization for collective political action difficult in the ensuing atomistic society. To Lau, this characterizing feature of the Chinese community provided the main explanation for Hong Kong's political stability. It was also one major explanation for the viability of the minimally integrated social-political system which Lau considers to be the defining structural characteristic of Hong Kong society at that time.

Over-arching Consensus and the Complementarity between the Bureaucratic Polity and the Chinese Community

The minimally integrated social-political system was partly the product of the familial system and depoliticizing sentiments within the Chinese community, and partly the outcome of a policy of depoliticization pursued by the Colony's government. Both in turn are ultimately attributable to the consensus shared by the Government and the Chinese community about the value of Hong Kong society. The nature of this consensus is well captured by Thomas W. P. Wong (1993):

If there is any consensus, akin to some Social Contract, among government and people, it is that for them alike, the business of Hong Kong is business, and not art, reflection, politics, religion (Thomas W. P. Wong 1993: 281).

Lau, in explaining the Government's depoliticizing policy, substantiates his argument with a quotation from Governor Alexander Grantham:

We cannot permit Hong Kong to be the battleground for contending parties or ideologies. We are just simple traders who want to get on well our daily round and common task (*Hong Kong Hansard* 1950: 41; cited in Lau 1982: 36).

This depoliticizing policy was reflected in the Government's 'positive non-interventionist' approach to the affairs of the Chinese community. In confining itself largely to the role of maintaining social order and the provision of vital goods and services for building up its legitimacy, the Government kept a low profile within the Chinese community. Hence, it reduced the possibility of provoking the Chinese public to take action against what they might perceive as undue intervention from an alien power. This policy, however, could work only under the conditions that the Chinese population were to a high degree self-sustaining, politically indifferent, and not politically mobilized. The structure and sentiments of the Chinese community, as we have seen, fulfilled these conditions. The confluence of factors fostered in the Hong Kong Chinese the view that a good government was one which provided a stable environment for the pursuit of economic gains. The legitimacy of the Government was gauged mainly in terms of its role in facilitating the accumulation of wealth rather than in terms of its constitution or its attention to the affairs of the society.

The unique circumstances of Hong Kong forged an overarching consensus between the Government and the Chinese community about the value of Hong Kong society. It was this consensus which enabled the two sides to function and 'fit' as largely segregated components of the same entity. Some linkages did exist between the polity and the Chinese community: for example, the members of the Chinese élite co-opted into the Executive and Legislative councils, the Kaifong (neighbourhood) Associations, the Clansmen Associations, and the linkage mechanisms, such as the Urban Council Ward and the City District Offices, installed by the Government in the 1960s. None of these persons or institutions, in Lau's view, were effective in bridging the communication gap between the Government and the Chinese community. The Chinese élites were too remote from the grass roots to be their recognized spokesmen; the Kaifong and Clansmen associations had declined in importance and could no longer function as adequate intermediaries between the Government and the general public; and the official linkage devices lacked the scale and authority to effectively attend to the needs of the masses. In any event, drastic changes in society and politics were in store for Hong Kong in the early 1980s, as Britain and China were preparing for negotiations concerning the territory's future. Lau concludes his book with a forward-looking note:

While the general configuration of the minimally integrated social-political system will be maintained, we can expect the closer integration of the bureaucratic polity and the Chinese society to usher in a new era in the history of Hong Kong (Lau 1982: 190).

Hong Kong as a Minimally Integrated Social-Political System: Continuities and New Directions in Development

Lau's portrait of Hong Kong society in the three-and-a-half decades after the end of the Second World War suggests that the stability or equilibrium of the society has depended on a delicate balance between the political style of the Government and the values of the Chinese community. It was a delicate balance because their peaceful co-existence had not been the outcome of deliberate mutual accommodation of the other's needs and interests, or the product of cooperative interdependence. The lack of communication and integration between the two major components of the society could be expected to reduce grossly the system's capability to maintain its equilibrium while meeting drastic changes or adapting to new challenges. With this inherently deficient system, Hong Kong has had to cope with momentous changes and challenges during the transition to 1997.

As stipulated in the Basic Law,[12] Hong Kong will become a special administrative region (SAR) of the People's Republic after 1997 under the sovereignty of China but with a high degree of autonomy. Since the mid-1980s, the preparation for self-government has been the top priority in Hong Kong's agenda for change. This preparation has proceeded by way of a development towards a more representative government, or in short, democratization. The process has brought about a closer integration between the polity and the society and altered the character of the society. The outcome of this change will depend greatly on the society's potential and capability to meet the challenge of a fundamental transformatioin in its social-political system. In Lau's view, this potential and capability have been constrained by the legacy of the past—the exclusive nature of the bureaucratic polity, the utilitarian-familistic orientation and political deprivation of the Chinese community, and the compartmentalization of polity and society. These limitations and the ensuing problems are readily apparent in the area of political leadership.

The Preparation for Self-Government and the Paucity of Political Leaders

That one prerequisite for autonomous government is strong political leadership is a truism that would apply with accentuated significance to Hong Kong under the sovereignty of China. Up until recently, however, nearly all of Hong Kong's political leaders have been senior government bureaucrats, most of British origin. The demise of colonialism in the territory would be expected to leave a vacuum in political leadership, but the Chinese community, long deprived of a role in government, is ill-prepared to fill this political gap. This is the fundamental problem identified by Lau in his thesis on the paucity of political leaders in Hong Kong (1990). His assessment of the leadership-generating potential of the Chinese community points to the effects of clearly seen legacies of the past:

Political leaders could not emerge or survive in the absence of a strong sense of community identification.... People in Hong Kong basically identified themselves with narrow familial and other parochial interests (Lau 1990: 9).

Nor has the social structure been conducive to the development of strong leadership. In making this point, Lau alludes to the predominance of small firms, high labour mobility, and an associated weak trade unionism, all of which mitigate against working-class consciousness and solidarity. The capitalists, he says, on the other hand, have been perceived by the Chinese public to be self-seeking and immersed in crass materialism, and as such not morally suited for political leadership. The middle class is individualistic, disunited, and devoid of class consciousness. He spells out the implications of these conditions for political leadership:

None of the existing social groups or strata in Hong Kong have been capable of establishing the kind of social, ideological or cultural domination or leadership ... that could be regarded as a viable alternative to colonial rule (Lau 1990: 11).

The loosely organized nature of the society, with its attendant lack of strong united leadership, has also paved the way to fragmentation in whatever leadership was being cultivated by the British and Chinese governments in the service of their respective vested interests. Those persons patronized by the colonial administration are not to be trusted by the future sovereign power; those groomed by the Chinese government are seen to lack a solid basis of legitimacy among the local population. The pro-democracy activists, furthermore, are not acceptable to the Chinese authorities. This leadership fragmentation is aggravated by the multiple channels of leadership recruitment that have been prescribed for the future SAR government. Until the year 2003, the legislature will be made up of three types of members: members elected by functional constituencies (constituted by the territory's major occupational groupings), members elected by the Election Committee (composed of 800 members from various socio-economic sectors), and members elected by geographical constituencies through direct elections. In short, the social-political heritage of the past, the political development during the transition, and the political system prescribed for the future all, in Lau's view, serve to hinder the growth of strong leadership in Hong Kong.

Democratization and the Utilitarian Nature of Political Participation and Political Attitudes

The legacy of Hong Kong's social and political development has also impacted on public political participation and on the public's attitudes towards the nascent political activists and groups that have emerged in conjunction with the society's democratization. This impact is at the heart of the arguments presented by Lau and his associates in their studies of Hong Kong's first two District Board elections (Lau and Kuan, 1983; Lau and Kuan, 1985) and in their survey studies of the Hong Kong people's political attitudes (Lau and Kuan, 1989; Lau, Kuan, and Wan, 1991; Lau, 1992). As a pioneering step in Hong Kong's development towards a representative government, the 1982 and 1985 District Board elections provided an acid test of the Hong Kong people's attitudes towards democracy and participation in democratic politics.

The outcomes were not encouraging. Voter turnouts were low (37.9 per cent and 33.5 per cent of the 1982 and 1985 registered voters, respectively),[13] and there was substantial evidence that the voters made their choices on the basis of the candidates' personal attributes rather than their organizational affiliations or political platforms. Lau and Kuan also observed on the basis of their empirical findings that the voters were 'pragmatic, self-oriented, and instrumental . . . and [paid] heed only to the kinds of material and concrete goods [the candidates] can be expected to deliver' (Lau and Kuan 1985: 36). In the authors' view, these were telltale signs that the opening up of the political system and even the 1984 Sino-British Joint Declaration[14] on Hong Kong's future failed to reorient the people from their familistic parochial concerns to broader socialpolitical issues. Political organizations perform important functions in a democracy, mobilizing the populace to participate in politics and articulating political goals and visions for the electorate's choice. Lau and Kuan argue that the Hong Kong voters' instrumentalist approach to politics and their tendency to 'personalize' politics rendered them largely impervious to organizational mobilization and oblivious to the larger goals and spirit of the democractic process.

The same instrumental orientation seemingly underlies the Hong Kong people's contradictory attitudes towards the territory's political leaders. A 1991 survey by Lau showed that a significant portion (49 per cent) of the respondents held the view that political leaders elected by the people would rule Hong Kong better than would the existing government (Lau 1991: 204). Yet as Lau's (1991) research findings also reveal, the level of the Hong Kong people's trust in their political leaders was low, much lower in fact than was their trust in government bureaucrats and the existing non-democratic political institutions.[15] It is worth noting in particular that their degree of trust in the pro-democracy leaders and pressure groups was significantly lower than was their trust in civil servants and the appointed members of the Legislative Council. Perceptions of a person's ability to rule and a pro-democracy stance were apparently not positively related to the Hong Kong people's level of political trust. Why was this so and what was the major contributing factor to political trust? Lau deduces an answer from the respondents' skepticism about political parties—half of his respondents opposed the formation of political parties in Hong Kong:

In the mind of the Hong Kong Chinese . . . political parties conjure up pictures of conflict, sectional interests, political repression, and corrupt government (Lau 1991: 205).

The corollary of this attitude is that what the Hong Kong Chinese treasures most is stability, harmony, and a benevolent and clean government. A government that meets these requirements, be it democratic or not, therefore merits the Hong Kong person's trust. Lau's survey findings indicate that many people felt that the emergent political leaders were suspect in this regard, and hence they had a low level of trust in them:

The Hong Kong Chinese do not base their political trust in institutions and groups on the latter's political orientations. . . . [They] seemingly adopt an instrumental approach to political leadership and it appears that they would trust those leaders who can deliver the goods which they treasure. These goods include economic prosperity, social stability, improvement in standard of living, and better opportunity (Lau 1991: 201).

Evidence indicates that the subsequent increased prominence of political groups and leaders in local politics has by no means bolstered political trust in them. Lau's (1992) later research findings, comparing the public's political trust in different kinds of political institutions and leaders, are similar to those of the earlier study. The author's summary statement in fact reveals a declining trend in the overall level of political trust: in comparison with just a year earlier, he wrote, 'today the people of Hong Kong trust their leaders even less' (Lau 1992: 141). It appears that political trust dwindled as the past consensus and ensuing harmony and stability so treasured by the Hong Kong Chinese seemed threatened by the divergent and conflicting views of the proliferating political parties and leaders.

A Summary of Lau's Thesis

In his 1982 book, Lau characterizes Hong Kong society as composed of two largely segregated segments: a bureaucratic polity with a monopoly of political power, and a politically apathetic and atomistic Chinese community whose main concerns are the material interests of the family. The depoliticizing strategies of the colonial government and the depoliticizing proclivities within the Chinese community have contributed to the territory's political stability and social order. Lau's analysis suggests that the structure and functioning of Hong Kong society from the end of the Second World War to the late 1970s were moulded by the political style of the Government, the character of the Hong Kong Chinese, and the relationship between these two entities. This social-political structure, Lau says, underwent significant changes with Hong Kong's political development, beginning in the 1980s, towards a more representative form of government.

If, however, this development has reduced the seclusion of the bureaucatic polity and narrowed the communication gap between the Government and the people, it has not successfully alleviated the latter's entrenched yearning for stability and prosperity and its instrumental approach to government and politics. The utilitarian ethos of the Hong Kong Chinese remains the old wine in a new bottle of a changing political system. The Hong Kong Chinese have been less than enthusiastic in political elections, unconcerned about higher political goals, and distrustful of nascent political groups and leaders. If they value democracy, it is because they see it as a means to preserve their old way of life. In this sense, in the popular ethos if not in its formal structure, Hong Kong remains very much a minimally integrated social-political system.

Yet democratization is inevitably also a process of politicization. In Hong Kong's case, given the instrumental bent of its people, politicization has taken the form of rising popular expectations. The primary concern, it appears, is for the Government and political leaders to deliver goods and to satisfy the immediate interests of the people. In order to win in elections, political leaders will have to dwell primarily on the immediate needs of the populace, rather than on higher and long-term political goals. With the added factors of the paucity and fragmentation of the political leadership and the Hong Kong people's low level of trust in their political leaders, these concerns suggest that a strong united leadership, characterized by sophisticated political vision, is not likely to emerge soon in Hong Kong. Given the type of political system that has been prescribed for the SAR government, moreover, the situation is not likely to improve after the transfer of sovereignty in 1997.

Legitimacy and Its Crisis: The Impetus and Pattern of Political Change in Hong Kong Society

Lau Siu-kai (1982), as we have seen, explains political stability in the rapidly modernizing colonial society of Hong Kong in terms of the political acquiescence of the Chinese community and its complementarity with the non-interventionist policy of the colonial government. Another highly acclaimed treatment of these issues, published in the late 1980s, is by political scientist Ian Scott (1989a). Scott's work supplements Lau's explanation by offering an historical study of how the Hong Kong government has sought to resolve legitimacy crises and to re-establish order and stability through the introduction of political changes. Scott's study is couched in the context of Hong Kong's economic development and its concomitant impact on social structure and political order from the beginning of the colonial period to the late 1980s. As such, Scott's book is at the same time a comprehensive examination of the interrelationships between the changes in Hong Kong's economy, social structure, and political system.

The Entrepôt Economy: The Co-option of Élites and the Making of Hong Kong's Political Power Structure

Acquired by Britain primarily as a base for trade with China, the Colony of Hong Kong was from the beginning run to serve the interests of its British merchants. Scott calls the Colony's government in the 1840s and early 1850s a minimal state with its functions restricted to the promotion of business enterprises and the bare minimum of the maintenance of law and order. Even the small amount of spending thus incurred was resisted by the merchants, who called for a reduction in rates and in government expenditure, and 'in effect for the colony to be abandoned' (Scott 1989a: 39). The merchants were so crucial to the economic well-being and hence the viability of the Colony that their challenge impacted on the Government as a crisis of legitimacy. The Government resolved the crisis by co-opting two prominent members of the British merchant houses into the Legislative Council in 1850, with the consequence that thereafter the Government's policy-making was subject to the legitimate scrutiny of the merchants.[16] Its autonomy suffered a further set-back when in the 1890s the merchants' increased economic clout prompted them to demand an even greater role in the governance of the Colony. This second crisis of legitimacy was resolved through the Government's appointment of members of the business élites into its highest advisory body, the Executive Council.[17] The ensuing political power structure became a long-lasting feature of Hong Kong society:

Rule by small committees with interlocking memberships of bureaucrats and businessmen became an essential characteristic of government. Government's decisions were legitimized by the consensus reached by different élites within what had become a closed system.... This structure of authority persists in present-day Hong Kong in inappropriate circumstances (Scott 1989a: 60).[18]

This first major political change in colonial Hong Kong initiated a tradition in which a small exclusive circle of élite individuals, sharing a similar outlook and complementary interests, ruled over a politically powerless and economically underprivileged population. Business interests prevailed over those of the subject population, and government played but a minimal role in the provision of social services. The third crisis of legitimacy occurred in the mid-1960s in this context of gross inequality.

Industrialization and Its Discontents: Rebellion and Reform

Hong Kong's industrialization effected changes in the society which eventually taxed severely the coping capacity of its obsolete political system. The industrial proletariat was fast expanding, but both the government sector and business interests did little to improve its working conditions and standard of living. The workers' continued deprivation amidst the growing affluence of the industrial economy heightened their awareness of the Colony's social inequality and injustice. Scott observes:

The state remained unreformed; the structure of colonial authority stayed in place; and the people continued to be isolated, distant and sometimes resentful of their government and the privilege and wealth it represented (Scott 1989a: 80).

Signs of discontent first surfaced in 1956 in the form of riots 'probably fuelled by resentment over social conditions' (Scott 1989a: 77).[19] It was, however, the riots of 1966 and 1967, particularly the latter events, which testified to the pervasiveness of popular dissatisfaction with the Colony's social-political system and which most profoundly challenged the legitimacy of the Government. The 1966 riots originated from a peaceful protest against a fare increase by the Star Ferry Company, but they rapidly escalated into violent attacks on the police and extensive looting and destruction of property. The rioters consisted mainly of poorly paid, poorly educated, and inadequately housed young workers. Scott deduced from the identities of the rioters that 'the causes of the riots lay in social and economic conditions which were, in turn, a product of the colonial regime's political and class structure' (Scott 1989a: 92).

If the 1966 Star Ferry riots, which were confined to certain overcrowded areas and lasted only a few days, reflected little more than isolated and disorganized opposition, the disturbances in the following year were a six-month protracted confrontation that plunged the whole territory into conflict and turmoil.[20] Precipitated by minor labour disputes, spurred on by the Cultural Revolution recently begun on the mainland, and spearheaded by local pro-Communist trade unions and organizations, the 1967 riots were a frontal attack on Hong Kong's colonial government and capitalist system. Despite the aims of some of the events' organizers, Scott argues, the 'communist cause' was of merely circumstantial importance. The underlying cause was the Government's failure to address a fundamental issue in industrial capitalism:

The problem was that the political structure was unable to cope with demands from the working class or to give institutionalized expression to them (Scott 1989a: 78).

The reforms introduced by the Government in the aftermath of the riots were targeted at rectifying this problem, and they launched a new era in Hong Kong's social-political development. These reforms were of three main types. First, the Government introduced policies and institutions for the purpose of bridging the gap between the Government and the Chinese community and establishing procedures for addressing grassroots grievances. The City District Officer Scheme introduced in 1968, the Community Involvement Plan and the ensuing Mutual Aid Committees of the early 1970s, the establishment of the Independent Commission

Against Corruption (ICAC) in 1974, and the Official Languages Act of the same year, under which Chinese was recognized as an official language, were notable examples in this category.[21]

The second type of reforms, prompted by the Government's recognition that improved industrial relations were the key to future stability, consisted of the enactment of new labour legislation, in particular the Employment Ordinance of 1968, which provided a basis for the more equitable treatment of workers and a platform for the extension of increased benefits to workers. The third type of reforms consisted of measures for the vastly expanded provision of public goods and services. They included the Ten Year Housing Programme of 1972 and the related New Towns Policy, the extension in 1978 of free primary education to an additional three years of free compulsory secondary education, and the greatly increased public expenditure in the 1970s on social welfare and medical and health services. Despite these reforms, the hard-won legitimacy of the Government was soon put to the test again. This challenge came in the early 1980s amidst the Sino-British negotiations on Hong Kong's future.

Economic Restructuring and the Transition to 1997: The Loss of Governmental Autonomy

Throughout the colonial period, the resilience of Hong Kong's system of governance had rested on the Government's capacity to promote stability and prosperity in the presence of a generally acquiescent population, and to resolve occasional legitimacy crises through the introduction of changes in the political structure. Hong Kong's economic transformation beginning in the mid-1970s produced a more affluent, better-educated, and sizeable middle class who began to demand—as a political right and as a way to safeguard its interests and lifestyle after 1997—a greater role in the governance of the territory. The legitimacy of government and the territory's social stability from the early 1980s onward would hence hinge on the capacity of the Government to cater to the political demands of the middle class.

In response to the demands of the middle class, the Government in 1985 incorporated for the first time into the Legislative Council members elected by the newly established functional constituencies, as well as members indirectly elected through District Board electoral colleges. But this political reform proved inadequate as a measure to pacify the middle class, for the resulting political system was still very much biased in favour of entrenched Government supporters and members of the economic élites.[22] The subsequent demand of middle-class liberals to rectify the situation through the introduction of an element of direct election to the 1988 legislature was frustrated by the objections of the Chinese government whose intention to retain as much as possible Hong Kong's political power configuration beyond 1997 was then connived at by the British authorities.

The Chinese and British governments conceive the transfer of power to be from one executive to another without any fundamental change in existing power relationships. This would effectively exclude the middle class from any decision-making role (Scott 1989a: 246).

For their part, members of the middle class expressed their dissatisfaction at the time through protests or emigration, but Hong Kong's government, incapacitated by the overriding decisions of the two sovereign powers, was unable to resolve the ensuing legitimacy crisis by simply introducing the required political changes. This fourth crisis of legitimacy is in Scott's view different from the previous occasions in that it occurred in conjunction with the Government's loss of autonomy. As a result, the Hong Kong government faced the prospect of declining popular trust and support in the final phase of its colonial administration.

Economy, Social Structure, and Politics: Scott's Analytic Perspective on Stability and Change in Hong Kong

Scott's analysis of political change in Hong Kong is simultaneously a study of the changes in the society's economy and in its social structure. His underlying conceptual framework implicitly takes the economy and its transformation as the prime impetus for changes in the social and political spheres. Each phase of economic development left its impact on the social structure by way of shaping its class configuration, which in turn generated its corresponding class-related challenges to the Government, whose response resulted in political change. Thus, the flourishing entrepôt economy in early Hong Kong consolidated the mercantile capitalist class, whose demand for a share of governmental power led to their incorporation into the Colony's formal political structure. The industrializing economy of the 1950s and 1960s bred a large working class, whose turbulent protests against existing social inequalities forced the Government to reform its out-dated political system. The rapid growth of the economy's tertiary sector in the 1980s gave birth to the new middle class, whose demands for political participation generated a crisis for which the Government, soon to lose power altogether, had no adequate solution. Each class, as it were, has had its day in exerting pressure on the Government to bring about political change.

From Scott's perspective, political change in Hong Kong has not been effected on the initiative of the Government. Rather, it has come about as a consequence of the Government's ad hoc attempts to resolve crises through the absorption of social and political discontent. This absorption has been pursued primarily through political institutionalization: opposition has been incorporated into existing political institutions, as was the case in the early co-option of business élites, or altogether new political institutions or channels have been established to absorb the discontented elements, as was seen in the aftermath of the 1967 riots and in the failed attempt in the 1980s to contain the political aspirations of the middle class. This political institutionalization is political change, and its outcome is restored legitimacy and political stability.

Scott's explanation of political stability (and instability) is strikingly similar to that of Samuel Huntington in his celebrated book, *Political Order in Changing Societies* (1968). Huntington holds the view that in modernizing societies, political participation is often the means by which people express the discontents and frustrations generated during the process of socio-economic development. Whether political participation will result in the politics of disorder depends on the local government's capacity to absorb it through political institutionalization. He conveys the idea succinctly by means of the following equation[23]:

$$\frac{\text{Political Participation}}{\text{Political Institutionalization}} = \text{Political Instability}$$

This equation also summarizes the main thrust of Scott's thesis. In Hong Kong, the challenge to the Government's legitimacy came in the form of political participation, and political change by way of political institutionalization resolved the first three legitimacy crises and restored order and stability. Inadequate institutionalization during the final crisis, however, installed in the society a potent force of instability. For this reason, Scott describes the middle class as 'the primary source of instability' (Scott 1989a: 267) and 'the major dissident group' (Scott 1989a: 273) in Hong Kong since the mid-1980s.

Conclusion

This chapter draws from three important studies of Hong Kong to illuminate major aspects of the society's development. Both Chan's (1991) and Scott's (1989a) works situate their analyses of Hong Kong's social-political development against the background of the territory's economy. Chan's study of early Hong Kong society is an attempt to illustrate how the merchants' economic control and power interacted with the racial factor in shaping the Colony's class and political structure. By the 1920s, in Chan's view, the defining characteristic of Hong Kong's social-political structure was the cleavage and opposition between the capitalist and the labouring classes. We have argued that Hong Kong's experiences during the early years of its industrialization worked against the development of class consciousness. As yet unanswered are questions of the extent to which Hong Kong's social structure and political process during the first one or two decades of industrialization should be best understood in terms of class divisions and class antagonism.

It is in respect to the question of the importance of class divisions that Scott's and Lau's (1982) studies diverge. The class and social inequalities inherent in Hong Kong's colonial capitalism, in Scott's view, were together the major contributing factor to the three large-scale episodes of working-class insurgency in the 1950s and 1960s. The territory's changing economic structure since the 1970s, on the other hand, has led to the rapid expansion of a new middle class whose dissatisfaction with the political system has rendered it the main source of instability in the 1980s and 1990s. It is in terms of Hong Kong's changing economy and class structure that Scott undertakes his analysis of the corresponding political changes and challenges which the territory has encountered in the past few decades.

Lau, in contrast, by and large dismisses the pertinence of class in the study of Hong Kong society. He conducts his analysis of stability and change in the society on the basis of the characteristics and depoliticizing strategies of the bureaucratic polity and of its complementarity with the ethos of the Hong Kong Chinese. The territory's future political development, he maintains, will continue to be handicapped by this political legacy. Since the publication of his study, Lau has been criticized by a number of writers for overlooking class differences within the Chinese community and hence misrepresenting the Hong Kong Chinese as a homogeneous and amorphous social entity. These writers have also attacked Scott's reference to class as casual and devoid of conceptual rigour and empirical support. The next chapter examines these writers' arguments and their attempts to articulate a class perspective on Hong Kong society.

Notes

1. In early colonial Hong Kong and throughout much of Hong Kong's history, the Legislative Council and the Governor formed the territory's legislature. The Legislative Council was the legislative body which scrutinized, debated, reviewed, and ratified legislative proposals by the executive branch of the Government. When the Governor gave his assent to what had been agreed upon by the Legislative Council, a legislative proposal became law.

2. From its founding in 1870, the Tung Wah Hospital offered a wide range of free services and financial assistance to the Chinese community. These services included medical treatment, repatriating the coffins of the poor to their hometowns for burial, financial aid for the poor and destitute, relief for victims of disasters, and free education. In addition, the Tung Wah directors assisted in the settlement of disputes among the Chinese and in organizing public campaigns such as the Save-Water Campaign of 1916. For a detailed historical study of the Tung Wah Hospital, see Sinn 1989.

3. The district watch force was established in 1866. Its management committee became an officially constituted body, the District Watch Committee, in 1891 and served as an advisory body to the Government on the affairs of the Chinese community. One early observer described the committee as follows: 'In reality the Committee is the Chinese Executive Council of Hong Kong and is consulted on all matters affecting them' (Chan 1991: 112).

4. These descriptions were reported in a local English-language newspaper, *The South China Morning Post*, 24 and 31 January 1922 (cited in Chan 1991: 182).

5. Chan mentions a number of influential events in the intervening years, including the Canton–Hong Kong strike-boycott of 1925–6, the economic recession of the 1930s, and the Japanese occupation of the territory in the first half of the 1940s. He comments: 'Despite the scale of these events, Hong Kong was able to cope with them because they happened at a time when the colony's social structure had already taken mature shape; in a sense, Hong Kong was able to "stand on its own feet"' (Chan 1991: 209–10).

6. Commerce and Industry Department (Hong Kong Government), 'Memorandum for the Trade and Industry Advisory Board: Land for Industry', p. 2 (cited in Wong Siu-lun 1988a: 2).

7. The figure of sixty billion dollars was the estimate of the financial agency of the Chinese Nationalist government in Hong Kong. Some journalists believed

the figure to have been grossly exaggerated and put it at four to five billion Hong Kong dollars.

8. In 1956, 1966, and 1976, respectively, the major industries' percentage shares in Hong Kong's export value were: clothing (21%, 40%, 45%), textiles (48%, 16%, 9%), electronic and electrical goods (8%, 11%, 15%), and plastic products (1%, 13%, 9%) (Census and Statistics Department 1968; Sit and Wong 1989: 17, table 2.2).

9. Subcontracting is also a form of division of labour between larger and smaller firms. The large firms explore external markets, take overseas orders, handle the import and export of goods, design the products, and produce the more complicated parts. Production of the more simple items, apart from surplus orders, is subcontracted to the smaller firms for production or part-processing. For a detailed account and empirical study of the subcontracting system, see Sit and Wong (1989, chap. 13).

10. In the local context, a flexible labour force is attained most often through the use of female workers, part-time workers, and outworkers, many of whom are employed on a piece-work basis. The flexibility of female labour owes much to the fact that in Hong Kong paid employment for women, particulary working-class women, is widely considered to be supplementary to housework. Female workers can be hired, especially for part-time work or outwork, or 'returned' to housework as circumstances require. Outwork is work outside the factory premises and is usually done at home. Part-time workers and outworkers are employed on a temporary basis. As home-based production, outwork also reduces the small firm's overhead costs. For a detailed study of outwork in Hong Kong, see Lui (1990: 187–215).

11. The Executive Council is the equivalent of the Governor's cabinet. It is the body which the Governor consults when making legislative and policy proposals to be scrutinized and made into law by the Legislative Council. The Executive Council consists of Official Members and Unofficial Members. The Official Members are senior civil servants, while the Unofficial Members are members of the public. Appointment to the Executive Council is made by Britain's Secretary of State on the recommendation of the Governor.

12. The Basic Law stipulates the basic policies which will govern the running of Hong Kong after its return to China's sovereignty in 1997. It was prepared in the second half of the 1980s by the Basic Law Drafting Committee. All members of this Committee were appointed by the Chinese Government; they consisted of representatives from China and representatives from Hong Kong. The Chinese Government formally promulgated the Basic Law on 4 April, 1990.

13. The figures are even lower when expressed as a percentage of the number of qualified voters. The 1982 and 1985 figures would be around 12 per cent and 17 per cent, respectively.

14. The Sino-British Joint Declaration is a signed agreement between China and Britain regarding China's basic policies towards Hong Kong after 1997. This Joint Declaration was signed in 1984, after two years of negotiations between the Chinese and the British Governments. The most important stipulations in the Joint Declaration are:

• After 1997, Hong Kong will become a Special Administrative Region of China.

• The Hong Kong Special Administrative Region will be autonomous save in foreign and defence matters.

• The Hong Kong Special Administrative Region will have its own form of government and retain its existing laws.

• Hong Kong's existing socio-economic system, and all Hong Kong's basic freedoms, will remain.

• Hong Kong people will govern Hong Kong.

15. Lau's study shows that 52.2 per cent of the respondents in the territory-wide sample said that they trusted the Hong Kong government, while 60.2 per cent said they trusted or strongly trusted the civil servants. Figures of support for other political institutions were 52.5 per cent for the appointed members of the Legislative Council, 64.1 per cent for the elected members of the Legislative Council, 39.9 per cent for the leaders of the democratic movement, 40.7 per cent for pressure groups, 31.3 per cent for the Hong Kong branch of the New China News Agency, and 35.7 per cent for business leaders.

16. 'The merchants regarded themselves, or their representatives on the Legislative Council, as legitimate guardians of the public purse.... The merchants' complaints in the 1840s had successfully established that the colony would be run in their general interests' (Scott 1989a: 58). The entry of the British merchants into the Legislative Council was followed much later by the appointment of its first Chinese representative in 1880.

17. The first unofficials, two prominent businessmen, were appointed to the Executive Council in 1896. The first Chinese unofficial was appointed to the Executive Council in 1926.

18. For a detailed account of the interlocking relationships within this closed ruling élite, see Davies (1977). Davies uses the term 'the power élite' (adapted from Mills 1956) to describe the territory's closed, cohesive ruling group composed of government bureaucrats, wealthy businessmen, and high-status professionals. Professionals were not part of the ruling élite in Scott's portrait of colonial Hong Kong's early political authority structure.

19. Scott only mentions the 1956 riots in passing, despite the magnitude of the disturbances, and his attribution of their possible cause to resentment over social conditions is questionable and not substantiated by empirical evidence. For a more detailed account and explanation of the events, see Chapter 7.

20. For a detailed account and interpretation of the 1966 and 1967 riots, see Chapter 7.

21. For a detailed and critical account of this category of reforms, see Chapter 8.

22. The reformed Legislative Council of 1985 was composed of twelve functionally elected representatives, twelve representatives elected through an electoral colleage made up of members of the District Boards and the Urban and Regional councils, ten official members who were senior Government bureaucrats, and twenty-two members of the public appointed by the Government. Five of the twelve functional constituencies were given to the commercial, industrial, and financial sectors where, because of the constitution of the electorate, the elected representatives were predominantly members of the economic élites. The remaining functional constituencies were given to labour (two seats) and the professions—legal, education, medical, engineering, and social services—whose members were elected by trade unions and the relevant professional bodies. In respect of the electoral college, the presence of Government-appointed members on the District Boards and the Urban and Regional councils biased the outcome of elections to the Legislative Council in favour of the Government. Scott comments: 'As a consequence of these and other provisions, a substantial majority of the 56-member legislature owed their presence to government largesse. Of the remainder, many were [members of] traditional economic elites' (Scott 1989a: 277).

23. Huntington in fact expresses his thesis in the form of three equations; only the last is cited here because it is most pertinent to our discussion. See Huntington (1968: 55).

2. Social Class and Social Mobility

THE term *social class* is used by sociologists to denote a large-scale grouping of people sharing some socio-economic characteristics which have a strong influence on their lives.[1] Such socio-economic characteristics include ownership of property, income, education, and occupation. Sociologists following in the Marxist tradition generally use the ownership of property—or what they call the ownership of the means of production—to divide people in society into the propertied class and the property-less class. They hold the view that the propertied class (capitalists, for instance) exploit and oppress the property-less class (the industrial proletariet, for instance) and that such exploitation and oppression inevitably generate class conflict. Sociologists subscribing to the Weberian tradition, in contrast, often use income, education, and occupation as the main criteria for separating people into different classes. They do not think that class conflict is inevitable, although they believe that differences in income, education, and occupation tend to produce class differences in lifestyle, attitudes, and orientations which may lead to conflict between classes. The term 'social mobility', on the other hand, refers to the movement of people between different socio-economic positions. If we conceptualize these socio-economic positions as class positions, then the study of social mobility is tantamount to the study of class mobility.

The analysis of the structure and dynamics of post-war Hong Kong society in terms of social class and social mobility is a relatively recent development, having emerged in the context of critiques of previous studies of the society. Its proponents attempt to articulate a fresh perspective on Hong Kong society through rectifying what they consider to be gaps and misconceptions in past studies. This chapter is an assessment of the extent to which they have succeeded in this endeavour.

The Background: The Irrelevance of Social Class in Hong Kong?

The most emphatic dismissals of the relevance of social class in the study of Hong Kong society appeared in two scholarly works of the early 1980s: Lee Ming-kwan's 'Emergent Patterns of Social Conflict in Hong Kong Society' (1982)[2] and Lau Siu-kai's *Society and Politics in Hong Kong* (1982). Lacking the support of rigorous empirical data and hence essentially conjectural in nature, Lee's thesis is that since the early 1970s, the fluidity of Hong Kong's social structure—characterized by abundant opportunities for social mobility—and the existence of a large and expanding heterogeneous middle class, have rendered Marxist notions of class and class conflict inapplicable to the society. His main contention is this: Hong Kong's phenomenal economic growth and its meritocratic capitalist system provided plentiful opportunities for social advancement, obviating in effect class boundaries and distinctions and creating at the same time a large heterogeneous middle social stratum of professionals, administrators, and clerical workers who had no class consciousness or class interests. In this situation, Lee maintains, the individual's identity and affiliation were lodged in occupational groups and interest groups rather than in social classes. Social conflict in Hong Kong therefore was no longer a 'Marxian' class struggle between an exploiting capitalist class and a dominated working class. It was, instead, a competition among the various occupational and interest groups for the society's resources.

Social change during the last few decades has ... pre-empted class conflicts.... It will no longer be realistic to describe Hong Kong as a 'class society'.... The last decade saw the beginning of a new pattern of social conflicts, which assume the form of 'interest group politics' (Lee Ming-kwan 1982: 30–1).

While Lee's thesis is in essence an application of a then standardized critique of orthodox Marxist theory to the local situation,[3] Lau's contention is based on empirical research (Lau 1982: 87–119). Lau's survey findings, discussed in the previous chapter, led him to the following conclusion:

When social relationships are viewed primarily in pecuniary terms..., when opportunities for upward mobility are seen as available, and when the wealthy are admired as people who have earned their success..., then class consciousness and class antagonism would be low.... In short, social classes as structural forces in shaping interpersonal relationships and political actions are relatively insignificant in Hong Kong (Lau 1982: 98).

It is arguments such Lee's and Lau's which became the main target of the critique contained in several ground-breaking studies of the late 1980s and early 1990s. Some of these studies evolved later into an ambitious attempt at building a class perspective on Hong Kong society.

The Critique: The 'New Middle Class' Debates

The debates on the status of the territory's middle class, published in a volume of collected essays titled *Class Analysis and Hong Kong* (Cheung et al. 1988),[4] revolve around the issue of whether Hong Kong's new middle class is sufficiently homogeneous in its interests and orientations to constitute a distinct and potent social and political force. In spirit, these debates are a reaction against Lee and Lau's denial of the significance of class in Hong Kong's social relationships and politics. The new middle class in question refers to that middle stratum of the local population—mainly professionals, administrators, skilled technicians, and clerical workers—who have worked their way up from the working class in the past two or three decades. This new middle class, Cheung Bing-leung (1988: 9–26) argues in the opening essay of the volume, shares a number of socio-economic characteristics: a grass-roots origin, Western-style education in local schools, and exposure to the social-political protests and movements in Hong Kong in the late 1960s and the early 1970s. From this similarity in background and life experiences, Cheung infers a similarity in the outlook of the new middle class, who in his description are liberal–democratic in political orientation, sympathetic to the plight of the underprivileged, and supportive of egalitarianism. Hong Kong's recent social-political development bears clearly the imprint of their class characteristics. Their predominance and success in pressure-group politics and electoral politics, in Cheung's view, testify to the coming of age of the new middle class and the pioneering and indispensable role they play in Hong Kong's current development.

This attempt at 'resurrecting' class, however—in this case the new middle class—is based on an inference which is not based on empirical research and hence of dubious validity. Even assuming a similarity in background, can we, as Cheung does, infer from this a homogeneity in class outlook and action, a homogeneity that also distinguishes it from other classes? This is the heart of the problem of class analysis and the bone of contention among the contributors to the volume. Thus, Lui Tai-lok (1988a: 27–48), in the volume's second essay, points out that Cheung's conception of the new middle class embraces occupational groups (for instance, professionals and clerical workers) whose life experiences, interests, and orientations differ. The attribution of homogeneity to this class is therefore unwarranted. Lui further argues that the predominance of middle-class personnel in politics is not sufficient grounds for inferring that the new middle class as a whole is enthusiastic about political participation.

Lui's objections have implications that go beyond the pertinent debates. Underlying his first objection is a call for a rigorous and unambiguous conception of class as a prelude to class analysis. His second objection raises the thorny issue of the basis on which we can judge orientations and actions as class-specific. The first objection informs Lui's later collaboration with Thomas W. P. Wong in their comprehensive research project on social mobility and social class. The second objection finds a preliminary response in Wong's contribution (1988: 125–70) to the volume under discussion. In Wong's view, the political involvement, and by extension the orientations and actions, of some active middle-class members are an indicator of the potentiality of their class as a social and political force. He reasons that the active few typically precede the majority in awareness and action. As such, their interests and actions can be considered class-specific. From this, Wong concludes that a central task in class analysis is to investigate those conditions which facilitate or obstruct the transformation of the class consciousness and actions of the few into those of the majority. This endeavour is the subject of one of Wong's later studies (Thomas W. P. Wong 1993).

The essays in *Class Analysis and Hong Kong* are essentially conceptual discussions. They do not offer solidly based, empirical evidence to show that members of Hong Kong society can be differentiated one from another in terms of class interests and actions. But in debating the concept of Hong Kong's new middle class, and of class in general, these essays prepared the ground for Wong and Lui's comprehensive empirical studies of class structure and class mobility in Hong Kong (Thomas W. P. Wong 1991; Wong and Lui 1992a, 1992b; Thomas W. P. Wong 1993).

From Critique to the Articulation of a Class Perspective: The Class Basis of Social Orientations and Social Actions

Wong and Lui's treatise (1992a) on the necessity of bringing class back into the study of Hong Kong society is predicated mainly on their critique of allegedly flawed analyses in the writings of Ian Scott (1989a) and Lau Siu-kai (Lau 1982; Lau and Kuan 1988).[5] The flaw is identified early in their discussion:

The common deficiency of these analyses lies in their non-structural approach to 'social structure'. 'Society', or better, the 'Hong Kong Chinese society', is... perceived as some amorphous entity (Wong and Lui 1992a: 2).

Underlying this indictment is Wong and Lui's contention that class and class differences are the fundamental constituents and features of Hong Kong's social structure. The omission of these from analysis, allegedly a characteristic of the writings of Scott and Lau, results in an 'amorphous' portrait of the society. Scott's allusion to class, in Wong and Lui's view, does not excuse him from this critique, as his analysis in this respect is not based on empirical data on class sentiments and orientations, but is rather conducted 'vaguely and non-structurally... and in broad anecdotal terms' (Wong and Lui 1992a: 18).[6] Lau (1982), on the other hand, conceived of Hong Kong Chinese society as a homogeneous community characterized culturally by the utilitarian-familistic ethos and structurally by the familial resource networks which together generated a depoliticized population. What is lacking in Lau's study, Wong and Lui argue, is an enquiry into whether such ethos and networks were class-related and how they might differ among different classes. The same inadequacy persisted in Lau's subsequent writings, as they were approached fundamentally under the influence of his earlier conceptual framework.[7] This critique of Scott and Lau laid the groundwork for Wong and Lui's reconstruction of Hong Kong's social structure.

The feasibility of this reconstruction depends on the applicability of the concept of class to the local setting; the worthiness of the product, in the light of its critique, hinges on its capacity to illuminate the areas that remained shadowy and uncharted in previous studies. Wong and Lui seek to affirm both of these intentions on the basis of research findings from a randomly sampled population of 1000 male heads-of-household in Hong Kong. Applying the Weberian conception of class,[8] they take occupation as the basis for the demarcation of classes. They explain:

Our class map is constructed on the assumption that occupation, in its ability to distribute benefits and generate identity, is... a pivotal axis in our society.

Occupation, with its twin components of market situation and work situation, thus forms the cornerstone of our structural understanding of Hong Kong society (Wong and Lui 1992a: 23).

The resulting class map consists of seven classes corresponding to the authors' rank-ordering of Hong Kong's occupational groups into seven major categories.[9] To validate this class demarcation, they compare the sampled respondents' 'subjective' self-assigned class membership with the 'objective' class positions assigned to them on the class map. Their findings testify to the feasibility of their class approach:

When asked if they feel themselves belonging to a class, 79% of our respondents said 'yes'.... When we crosstabulate the subjective class membership with the objective class position, we find a fairly 'congruent' picture (Wong and Lui 1992a: 26).

In light of these findings, the crux of the inquiry becomes: Do class positions differentiate their respective incumbents in terms of social orientations and social actions? Or, in short, Does class matter? Wong and Lui's research findings indicate that compared with the higher classes, the lower classes were more likely to see conflicts between classes as inevitable, to hold the view that employers have to exploit workers in order to make profits, and to believe that the average wage-earner receives less than he contributes.[10] Regarding the domain of actions, the authors seek to find out if the ways in which the respondents would handle certain problems in life differed in terms of class positions. The findings show that members of the higher classes would solve the problems more often through the market (such as borrowing from banks to pay the down payment for a flat, hiring a maid for child care, and moving if their existing living environment deteriorates) than would members of the lower classes, and that in finding a job, members of the lower classes would rely more often on the resource network of relatives and friends.[11] The authors conclude with implicit allusion to Lau's (1982) conceptual approach:

It is more truthful to reality ... to see that, instead of having a uniform, across-the-board accommodative mechanism, familistic-network in character, depoliticizing in effect, there are in fact different class-based (or at least class-related) mechanisms at work ... with different types of resources involved (Wong and Lui 1992a: 40).

The data the authors used to advance their thesis cannot but give the impression that the study represents perhaps only a preliminary effort at procuring an alternative structural understanding of Hong Kong society. There is no discussion of how the classes relate to make up social structure and condition the society's functioning, nor is there a rigorous and convincing demonstration that the class-based orientations and actions bear significantly on the society's stability, conflict, and change. The authors delivered less than what they set out to achieve.[12] But some of the

Social Mobility and Class Structure

Wong and Lui's (1992b) next work on Hong Kong's class structure is a conceptually sophisticated, technically daunting, and lengthy treatise on social mobility. This study supplements and advances their previous thesis (Wong and Lui 1992a) in several respects. It demonstrates, on the basis of the research which also informed their previous work, that the Hong Kong people's social-mobility opportunities, or life chances,[13] differ with the person's class position. In this sense, it offers additional evidence about the 'structural' or constraining effect of class. This evidence on class-based differential mobility opportunities also provides the groundwork for their explanation of the class differences in social orientations and social actions which they cited in the previous work.

Their argument in connection with class position is this: If class positions benefit some and disadvantage others in terms of life chances, and if owing to the lack of mobility opportunities people tend to be confined to their class position over a protracted period of time, this can be expected to inculcate in class members orientations and actions that reflect entrenched class-related privileges and constraints. The argument is then taken a step further: Such class-based orientations and actions are the stuff for class formation; they are the platform for the articulation of class consciousness, the advancement of class solidarity, and mobilization for collective class action. In short, the social-mobility study generates the empirical substance for the authors to address the significance of class as 'structure' (structuring life chances and orientations) and as a social-political force (class formation and the associated collective action). It serves as the theoretical axis of their class analysis.

However, the social-mobility study is concomitantly an inquiry of how 'open' is Hong Kong's social structure (or class structure in the present context). Is Hong Kong a society of abundant opportunities,[14] as some writers (e.g. Lee 1982) and the general population consider it to be, or is this belief only a delusion? Comparing the occupational status of the respondents with that of their fathers, Wong and Lui discovered that the intergenerational *total mobility*, a measure of the total rate of movement of the respondents away from the class position of their fathers,[15] came to 55.2 per cent. Part of this mobility (12.6 per cent), the authors point out, was constituted by *structural mobility*, or intergenerational changes in the society's occupational structure. In Hong Kong's case, such changes in occupational structure had taken place since the mid-1970s, and in creating more administrative, managerial, and professional jobs, had expanded the 'room at the top' and 'structurally' enabled more people to attain higher class positions.[16] The social mobility that results after the effect of structural mobility is deducted is *circulation mobility*, which came to 42.6 per cent. The authors comment:

On the whole, we may judge from the data that there is much mobility within the society, and in a very loose sense, one may say that our society has a high degree of openness (Wong and Lui 1992b: 44).[17]

The question that follows from these results is: Who has been able to make the best use of these mobility opportunities? This is a question about the equality (or inequality) of opportunity. The authors discovered in their ensuing investigation that class position made a difference. Referring to the seven hierarchically ordered classes in their class map, they observed that the chance of respondents from a background in Class 1 (that is, the highest service class) to attain a Class 1 position themselves was more than eight times that of those respondents from a Class 7 (that is, the lowest, manual working class) background.[18] As for respondents from the intermediate class backgrounds (Classes 3 to 5), their chance of reaching the top class position was about three times that of respondents from the lowest class background. In general terms, the authors thus express the class-related differences in upward mobility opportunities:

Professionals and top managers (class 1) have a large and largely uncontested competitive edge over the clerical and personal workers, just as the latter group outcompetes the unskilled manual workers (class 7)(Wong and Lui 1992b: 54).

Two caveats should be inserted here as additional information for understanding the authors' ensuing discussion. First, in commenting on the barriers within Hong Kong's class structure, the authors observe that 'the non-manual and manual break is quite substantial' (Wong and Lui 1992b: 70), implying that manual workers were still by and large 'trapped' within their working-class position. This entrapment could be expected to have both social and political ramifications. Second, the authors point out that 'about 60% of class 1 are upwardly mobile newcomers . . . due to the expansion of the "room at the top"' (Wong and Lui 1992b: 50). This last point reflects the heterogeneity of this class and bears on its capacity for class formation.

That the relative immobility of the manual working class impacts on their social and political orientations is attested to by the findings concerning the respondents' views on work, politics, and exploitation. Immobile manual workers, in comparison with those few of their class peers who had moved to the higher service classes and with members of the intergenerationally stable service classes, were far more likely to see their job as just a means of earning a living (93 per cent in contrast to about 43 per cent for members of the two other groups), to profess an inability to understand politics (65 per cent compared to 26 and 21 per cent respectively for the other two groups), and to see workers as being exploited by their bosses (46 per cent compared to 17 and 24 per cent respectively for the other two groups).[19] The authors infer from these findings, particularly the last set relating to the issue of social justice, that the 'significant differentials in the chance for upward mobility among the different classes . . . [are] an important, perhaps the fundamental, source for social instability' (Wong and Lui 1992b: 62). The implicit argument seems to be that the predicament of the manual working class, and their lack of upward mobility opportunities, generate social frustrations (for example, perceptions of the meaninglessness of work and the inability to understand politics) and discontents (seeing themselves as the exploited) which render them an inherently destabilizing social force. However, the potential of the manual workers for class formation and collective class action is left unexamined in the authors' study.

The issue of class formation is addressed with reference to the two classes at the top which the authors in analysis collapse into a single service class. With upwardly mobile newcomers making up a substantial component of its members, the service class exhibits anomalies in sociodemographic characteristics and identity. For instance, in comparison with the intergenerationally stable members, the newcomers were more likely to have been born outside Hong Kong, to have started their first job as a manual worker, and to have received fewer years of formal education than did their class peers. This heterogeneity of the service class is also reflected in class identity: 62 per cent of the stable group described themselves as 'middle class', whereas 65 per cent of the newcomers saw themselves as belonging to the 'working class'. Yet in other respects, such as views on the meaning of work, social stability, and employer–employee relationships, the two groups closely resembled each other. The evidence suggests that while differences in class origin were conducive to internal diversity in class identity within the service class, the similarity in existing class position tended to foster homogeneous social and political attitudes. This finding raises an intriguing question: What is the prospect of class formation for the service class, that is, of forging a common class identity and acting as a coherent social-political force? This question bears centrally on our understanding of Hong Kong's current development, as the service class is expanding quickly and plays an increasingly important role in the society's economic and political life. Three notable recent studies (So 1993; Lui 1993; Thomas W. P. Wong 1993) have made these developments the subject of their inquiry.

Class as a Social-Political Force: The New Middle Class

One theme common to all three of these studies is that the capacity of the service class, which the authors refer to as the 'new middle class', for class formation and collective action depends both on the internal characteristics of this class and on the society's current development. The argument is that while internal characteristics, such as the degrees of homogeneity and cohesiveness, bear significantly on the potential of the new middle class as a collective actor, this potential is modified by the impact of ongoing events on the interests, ideologies, and organization of this class. Hong Kong's development towards a representative government and its relationship with China during the transition to 1997 constitute the context in which the three studies adjudge the significance of the new middle class as a social-political force.

Of the three studies, Alvin So's (1993) is the most optimistic about the prospect of the new middle class emerging as a coherent and potent political force. His thesis revolves around two major contentions. First, the political uncertainty of the post-1997 era prompts the members of the new middle class to organize themselves politically to safeguard their free, privatized, and privileged lifestyle. In addition, they perceive Hong Kong's democratization as their opportunity to usurp power from the colonial administrators and the capitalist class, and so to establish themselves within the government before the transfer of sovereignty.

In sum, it is the 1997 issue which helps to hasten the formation of the HK new middle class. Without this incentive, it is doubtful whether the HK new middle class could overcome its individualism and privatized life style and transcend its narrow professional struggles to a class-specific movement for democratization (So 1993: 236).

So is at the same time aware of a split within the new middle class—a split which detracts from the group's capacity to act as a coherent political force. He sees this split as constituting two class segments different in ideology and political affiliation. The corporate segment, located in the capitalist sector and consisting of salaried empolyees such as managers, accountants, and technicians, shares the interests and perspectives of the capitalist class and is politically conservative in orientation. The service segment, on the other hand, is located in the state and nonprofit sectors and is comprised of salaried employees such as teachers, social workers, journalists, and state administrators. Not subject to profit-seeking and closer to the public in their work, members of this segment are more concerned with the provision of goods and services to the citizens and more egalitarian and liberal–democratic in orientation. The thrust of So's arguments suggests that he views Hong Kong's current political development as conducive to the narrowing of the differences between these two segments and hence to the formation of the new middle class as a potent political force. This note of optimism, however, is not echoed in the two other studies under discussion here.

Unlike So, Lui (1993) cautions against putting too much weight on the politicizing influence of Hong Kong's democratization on the new middle class. In the first place, members of this class have attained their present position through economic rather than political channels under an undemocratic capitalist system. This development process has meant that the socio-economic advancement of the new middle class has been tied to the success of the capitalist class. Tied thus to the capitalist class and faced with the quiescence of Hong Kong's working class, the members of the new middle class have not found it necessary to organize themselves politically to defend or advance their interests. Their prevailing concern, in Lui's view, has been and remains to preserve as much as possible the society's existing social-political organization—an orientation which aligns the new middle class politically with the capitalist class and even puts it in agreement with the Chinese government.

To take the political activism of a few middle-class liberals as a reflection of the ethos of the new middle class, as some writers have done, is, in Lui's accounting, a mistaken inference. Lui sees such political activism to be a continuation of the pertinent individuals' past involvement in student movements and community politics, and as such not a general characterizing feature of the new middle class. The society's recent wave of emigration, involving mostly middle-class personnel, testifies to the preference of members of the middle class for an individualist rather than a collectivist political solution to the problem of 1997. The new middle class is politically realistic in choosing this option:

Nor would the strategy of political participation help to further its interests before and after 1997. Politics in the transitional period will inevitably be conditioned by the diplomatic moves between the British and the Chinese Governments and compromises among different social classes. Anticipating that it is unlikely for any class (including the new middle class) to become politically dominant, the strategy of retreat sounds sensible (as the least costly) to the new middle class (Lui 1993: 266).

The question does not stop here, however, for a few politically active and successful middle-class liberals could eventually succeed in forging an identity and political organization among their fellow class members. This is the polemic set out in Thomas W. P. Wong's thesis (1993) on the prospect of middle-class formation in Hong Kong. The gist of Wong's inquiry is this: Does Hong Kong's current political development facilitate or obstruct the aforementioned prospective formation of the new middle class as a social-political force? His analysis leads him to a pessimistic conclusion. He identifies the main impediment to be the absence of a distinct and coherent class identity among the middle-class political leaders. Noting, with reference to Lau and Kuan's work (1985), that the common practices of local aspirant politicians place a 'premium on individual achievements, personal traits or sheer media publicity' (Thomas W. P. Wong 1993: 291), Wong considers Hong Kong's electoral politics to be divisive of middle-class political leadership. The institution of functional constituencies in the electoral system further fragments the budding middle-class leadership through tying their electoral support, and hence their accountability, to their respective occupational or functional categories. The situation was aggravated by the June Fourth Incident of 1989, which had the effect of dividing the middle-class leaders along lines determined by their orientations to China. Wong argues:

Whether it is a matter of leadership, organizational veracity or ideological commitment, the middle class component in the present political situation gives no strong indication that it could forge, by means of organizational capacity and political struggles, collective identities and consciousness conducive to middle class formation (Thomas W. P. Wong 1993: 294).

There are additional features of the middle class as a whole that stand in the way of its class formation. A sizeable number of its members have but newly ascended from working-class backgrounds and they still harbour old memories and identities. Wong testifies to the presence of these class 'residues' with reference to his survey findings (Thomas W. P. Wong 1991) indicating that a large proportion of the administrators/managers and professionals surveyed perceived themselves as belonging to the working class. In this connection, to the extent that the new middle class members have attained their present positions through familial efforts, the old familial utilitarian ethos of 'security and survival'[20] is likely to prevail over whatever orientations have emerged with their newly acquired class positions. In Wong's view, there is hardly a distinct middle-class identity and, as a result, it is unlikely that the middle class will act as a more or less unified social-political force in the foreseeable future.

Class as a Social-Political Force: The Capitalist Class

It is evident from the studies of W. K. Chan (1991: chap. 2) and Ian Scott (1989a: chap. 2) that the mercantile capitalists and later the industrial and financial capitalists together formed the hegemonic class in early colonial Hong Kong.[21] The Government's co-option of leading capitalists by including them in policy-making institutions—an indication of its recognition of the capitalists' political clout—was later interpreted by Ambrose Y. C. King (1981) as a strategy of administrative absorption of politics.[22] King's analysis is couched not in terms of class and class power, but of élites who were 'men with a power base' in the community, and of the Government's depoliticization of élites through co-option. The idea of depoliticization suggests that once co-opted, the élites, capitalists or not, became subordinate and subservient to the Government's prerogatives. The thesis was reinforced by Lau's (1982) depiction of Hong Kong's political system as a bureaucratic polity:

The administrative bureaucracy in Hong Kong, consisting of officials directly or indirectly appointed by the British Crown, ... lays down the rules of the political game in Hong Kong, and it almost always is the winner. Other political actors, as individuals or as groups, are inducted into the polity primarily upon the initiative of the bureaucracy, and hence they are dependent on it for maintaining their political privileges.... [N]o social or economic groups are able to 'capture' the bureaucracy to serve their own partisan interests (Lau 1982: 26, 28).

As a buttress for the above contention, Lau observes additionally that final decision-making power rests officially with the bureaucracy. In short, the bureaucracy's monopoly of power has been based on its political patronage of élites and on constitutional fiat. This thesis is the subject of Benjamin K. P. Leung's critique in his 'Power and Politics: A Critical Analysis' (1990a), which attempts to demonstrate that the power of the capitalist class is boosted rather than neutralized through the government's policy of élite co-option.

Leung's main contention is that élite co-option is a reflection of the political partnership between the Government and the capitalist class in which the latter is not necessarily the junior party. Using the composition of the 1982 and 1987 Executive Council as an illustration, supplemented by reference to the membership of the Legislative Council, Leung shows that the co-opted élite members were predominantly chairpersons and directors of Hong Kong's largest capitalist enterprises. He attributes this gross bias to the Government's dependence on capitalist enterprises for revenues (in the form of profit tax) and for the society's economic well-being and attendant stability. What is good for the capitalists, as it were, is also good for the Government. That being the case, the government bureaucrats' formal decision-making power seems secondary to the power of the capitalists, which is derived from their control over economic resources. The crucial question, in Leung's view, is not who formally makes the decisions, but who and what shapes the views of the decision-makers. This 'who and what' extends beyond the few capitalist representatives in the policy-making bodies; it epitomizes the common interests and power of the capitalist class in Hong Kong.

Leung seeks to demonstrate this commonality through a detailed analysis of the scope of connections between the seven capitalist representatives on the 1982 Executive Council. Each representative held multiple company directorships; the total amounted to an impressive seventy-one directorships of forty-five enterprises, which included many of Hong Kong's twenty largest public companies.[23] The scope of interests represented was extended further through the mechanism of interlocking directorships: a company interlocks with other companies by incorporating their directors into its own highest level of management in order to coordinate its interests and perspectives with theirs. Hongkong Bank, the largest public company in Hong Kong and represented by two members of the 1982 Executive Council, serves as a good illustration. It was linked at that time to 22 of the top 50 public companies in Hong Kong through interlocking directorships. In effect, nearly one-half of the top fifty public companies had, via the two Hongkong Bank representatives on the Executive Council, an official channel through which to communicate their views.

When the analysis of commonality was limited to directors of the top ten public companies, the data showed that Hongkong Bank had interlocks with seven of the remaining nine. Moreover, representatives of these eight interlocking companies among the top ten together occupied four of the nine Unofficial (that is, appointed) seats on the Executive Council. Leung did not pursue his investigation on interlocking directorships in respect to the other companies directly represented in the Executive Council. But one can construe from the case of Hongkong Bank that the total extent of interlocking would be huge, and hence that the bearing of capitalist interests on the Government's policy-making activities was pervasive. Leung concludes:

The nature of the data does not permit the conclusive claim that the Hong Kong government is run in the interests of the big resource controllers who therefore are the real power-wielders. More direct information, at present unavailable, on the actual process of policy-making within the government is needed. But . . . there is solid ground for maintaining that government policy-making is significantly subject to the constraint of big business (Benjamin K. P. Leung 1990a: 22).

Leung's observations pertain to the capitalists in Hong Kong in the early and mid-1980s. Two subsequent studies have maintained—as a consequence of changes in the patterns of resource control employed by local capitalists (Gilbert Wong 1991) and concomitant with Hong Kong's development towards a representative government (Wong Siu-lun 1993)—that the political power of the capitalists has in recent years declined substantially. Gilbert Wong attributes this decline mainly to the increasing diversification in capitalist resource control during the period between 1976 and 1986. Seeing the network of interlocking directorates as a reflection of the centrality of resource control, he discovered a concentration of such control in 1976 by a small number of non-Chinese, mostly British, business families or organizations, notably the Kadoorie, Swire, Jardine, Hutchison, and Wheelock Marden groups. This concentration of economic control had a significant impact on Hong Kong's power configuration, as was evidenced by the predominance of the relevant business representatives in the territory's highest policy-making bodies.

Wong's analysis concurs up to this point with that put forth by Leung,[24] but this pattern of economic and political domination began to change in the late 1970s when local Chinese entrepreneurs took over the ownership and control of a number of the established British business corporations.[25] This trend culminated in the dispersal of capitalist economic control and the resultant weakening of the political clout of the capitalists:

The network in 1986 is much more differentiated into separate business groups. Unlike in the previous years, there is not a large tightly knit group that encompassed a large number of companies and that linked up the Chinese and non-Chinese business groups (Gilbert Wong 1991: 149).

This decline in the power of the business class has occurred at a critical point in Hong Kong's political development, when various social forces are competing for political leadership during the transition to 1997. In an article that complements Gilbert Wong's work, Wong Siu-lun (1993) considers the implication of this decline for the political future of the business class. The trend towards disintegration of the business community, in Wong Siu-lun's view, has been reinforced by the inherently diversified structure of Hong Kong's capitalist economy. Supporting his argument by reference to the wide variety of business enterprises in the territory—the well-established British *hongs*, the large Chinese family firms, the small and medium Chinese factories, and the proliferating China-funded corporations—Wong observes:

Structurally, the economy is differentiated into various clusters of capital that are dissimilar in their social and organizational compositions.... Their diversity, though contributive to economic flexibility and vitality, is not conducive to political unity and cohesion (Wong Siu-lun 1993: 491).

The rise to prominence of local Chinese entrepreneurs aggravates the situation, as 'they tend to keep politics at arm's length' and 'in coping with political uncertainties, they prefer individual solutions rather than collective action' (Wong Siu-lun 1993: 494). The capitalists are further plagued by the public's lack of trust in the territory's business leaders. Citing empirical evidence from his and other scholars' survey researches, Wong notes that a large portion of the local population, and intellectuals in particular, are sceptical of the integrity of businessmen and consider them as having excessive political influence in Hong Kong. In their internal organization, mobilization, and electoral politics, the capitalists are thus seriously disadvantaged. Wong concludes with a call for setting up channels, of which functional representation and the electoral college are good examples, to ensure the adequate and indispensable representation of the business class in Hong Kong's democratizing political system.

The worry that the capitalists are losing their political influence is probably unwarranted. Benjamin K. P. Leung's recent papers on class and politics (1994a, 1994d) maintain that instead of suffering a set-back in power, the capitalists are on their way to consolidating themselves as the hegemonic class in post-1997 Hong Kong. The increasingly close economic and political ties between Hong Kong's capitalists and the Chinese government, which have been the product of China's economic reforms and open-door policy since the late 1970s, have fostered the growth of the capitalists as a dominant economic and political bloc under the patronage of the future sovereign power. Leung writes:

Control over [Hong Kong's] economy . . . and contribution to China's economic development have now made the capitalist class China's valuable partner in Hong Kong's future governance. This partnership is being mutually courted and consolidated through visits to Beijing, and through China's conferment of status and recognition on major local capitalists by appointing them into committees and positions with important social and political bearing (Benjamin K. P. Leung 1994a: 211).[26]

A systematic and rigorous sociological study in this respect is still to be undertaken, but Leung's recent, as yet unpublished, research findings on the background of local appointees to the Basic Law Drafting Committee provide a preliminary illustration. Of the four committee vice-chairpersons appointed by China to represent the Hong Kong people, three were among Hong Kong's wealthiest and most influential capitalists. Together these three held a total of 35 directorships, many of which were in Hong Kong's largest business concerns and which covered such varied domains as transport and public utilities, banking and finance, property development, manufacturing, commerce and trading, and the mass media.[27] Furthermore, of the 23 committee representatives from Hong Kong, eight (or 35 per cent) were wealthy businesspeople; in stark contrast, labour had only one representative.

More recently, China's announcement on 28 December 1995 of the Preparatory Committee line-up (with ninety-four Hong Kong members and fifty-six officials from mainland China) bears further testimony to Leung's contention. As the embryo of the leadership in post-1997 Hong Kong, the profile of the ninety-four members of the Hong Kong team is an illustration of the types of people being prepared by China to be the power élite of the Hong Kong Special Administrative Region. In this connection, a leading Hong Kong English-language newspaper comments:

More than 50 [of the 94 members] have strong business backgrounds with a major stake in the economy, both here and on the mainland. Clearly China is anxious to offer these people a direct say on the handover to ease doubts about the future... and keep their capital in the territory (*South China Morning Post*, 29 December 1995).

Another local newspaper, *Ming Pao* (28 December 1995), provides more details. According to its analysis, twenty-one of the businesspeople on the Preparatory Committee hold leading positions in Hong Kong's public companies, the total capital assets of which amount to 36 per cent of the market value of all the territory's public companies. 'The Preparatory Committee', *Ming Pao* states, 'carries the strong message of "businesspeople ruling Hong Kong"'. Considering the tremendous import of the Basic Law and of the Preparatory Committee for post-1997 Hong Kong, one can justifiably consider the cases cited above to be powerful testimonies to the recognition and influence which China has been bestowing on the capitalists in preparation for their future political role.

Class as a Social-Political Force: The Working Class

One conspicuous feature of Hong Kong's working class is its acquiescence in the midst of a capitalist society marked by gross income and political inequalities.[28] Despite the deprivations which manual workers face at work and in their lives outside the workplace, the number of industrial strikes (commonly taken as a reflection of working-class discontent and of labour's capacity for collective action against management) in Hong Kong is surprisingly low by international standards.[29] A number of writers (England 1979, 1989; Turner 1980; Benjamin K. P. Leung 1991b) have viewed this working class non-militancy as an incidence of the traditional Chinese passive orientation to politics, subservience to authority, and proclivity to non-aggression and compromise in interpersonal relationships. They further maintain that the refugee experience with its attendant 'don't rock the boat' mentality, the rivalry between left-wing and right-wing workers and their affiliated labour unions, and high labour mobility are additional major contributing factors to the passivity and weakness of the working class as a political actor.

Members of the working class, however, were the main participants in the three large-scale disturbances that have occurred in post-war Hong Kong. While these few outbreaks of working-class hostility are not sufficient to force a qualification of the thesis outlined above, they constitute the grounds for an inquiry into the factors which would provoke a usually quiescent and dormant collectivity into bellicose action. Such an inquiry holds the promise of illuminating the contingencies which would activate the working class as a potent social-political force, and such a desire serves as the guiding thread of our present discussion. We shall be examining in detail the three disturbances in question in the chapter on social conflict and social movements (Chapter 7), and so we highlight here only those elements that illuminate the present inquiry.

The 1956 riots were in essence a violent manifestation of the power struggle within Hong Kong's labouring class. The events were characterized by targeted attacks launched by the right-wing, pro-Guomindang trade unionists and their supporters against the property and personnel of pro-Communist trade unions and organizations. The Government-appointed commission of inquiry described the riots as the pro-Guomindang labour faction's 'attempt to win a dominant position in the labour world' (Hong Kong Government 1956: ii). The 1966 so-called Star Ferry riots were, strictly speaking, 'issueless riots', as the majority of the rioters, according to the report of the commission of inquiry appointed by the Government to investigate the disturbances, knew little or nothing about the causes of the rioting and acted in a spontaneous and uncoordinated manner (Hong Kong Government 1967). But political struggle was again the defining feature of the 1967 disturbances in which, under the influence of the Cultural Revolution then in full force on the mainland, left-wing trade unions and their sympathizers engaged in a protracted and violent confrontation with the colonial government and capitalist management.

We can discount the 1966 riots as an example of working-class mobilization for collective action, as there was no evidence of planning or organization among the riot participants. The other two episodes share one common feature: both reflected the influence of the politics of mainland China. The 1956 turmoil was an incidence of partisan political rivalry between Guomindang supporters and Communist sympathizers, while the 1967 disturbances were primarily an extension of the Cultural Revolution. This suggests that China's politics, be they partisan politics or the politics of anti-imperialism and anti-capitalism, could provoke the otherwise acquiescent Hong Kong working class into belligerent collective action, and that the potency of the working class as a political actor is or was contingent on political events in China and on Hong Kong's relations with China.

Partisan political affiliations have also created within the working class disunity and internal strife, characterizing features of Hong Kong's working class as a social-political force in recent years. China's policy, pursued since the early 1970s, of peaceful co-existence with Western capitalist countries has been the main factor contributing to working-class non-militancy in Hong Kong since 1967. One asks: Will this trend of working-class quiescence be reinforced or reversed in the transition to 1997 and beyond?

In two pertinent articles, Benjamin K. P. Leung (1993, 1994a) attempts an informed speculation to resolve these issues. He maintains that China's cooperative relationship with Hong Kong's capitalists in recent years, coupled with its guiding influence on the orientation of the local dominant, left-wing trade unions, has had the effect of substantially reducing the animosity of the workers towards capitalist management. China's united-front strategy has further forged bonds among Hong Kong's pro-China trade union leaders, major capitalists, and professional and administrative élites by way of appointing them to political bodies and advisory committees. It seems that a political melting pot is being formed in which the territory's residual class animosities are boiled down to become an allegiance with the future sovereign power. Leung observes in conclusion:

This will significantly dampen the class consciousness and militancy of the working class and grossly reduce the prospect of working class formation in Hong Kong (Benjamin K. P. Leung 1993: 56).

Conclusion: Does Class Matter?

We began this chapter with two studies which questioned the relevance of a class-based analysis of Hong Kong society on the grounds that the territory's people have not been particularly class-conscious and that what collective actions have been seen in Hong Kong were not themselves class-based. Subsequent studies, especially the social mobility research of Thomas W. P. Wong and Lui Tai-lok, have attempted to bring the subject of class back into the discussion by demonstrating empirically that the life chances of Hong Kong people, as well as certain important aspects of their social and political orientations, differ with their class positions. In this sense, class is a significant structural force in the society. These studies assert in effect that class analysis is more than just a study of class as a political actor; it is in its more fundamental inquiry an exploration of the class-related differences and inequalities that may constitute the basis of collective action.

The issue of class formation—the formation of class as a collective political actor—follows in the footsteps of the social-mobility study. In this respect, it seems ironic that having castigated Lau Siu-kai for portraying Hong Kong as a homogeneous and amorphous society, Thomas Wong in his study of middle-class formation depicts the new middle class as harbouring memories and orientations reminiscent of those shared by the larger society. His citation from another writer to buttress his argument about the improbability of middle-class formation brings him close to Lau's position:

There are no class inhibitions in this place. Almost everyone shares the memory of old hardships, if only by heredity, and almost everyone has similar aspirations (Thomas W. P. Wong 1993: 295, citing from Morris 1989: 196).

Wong, of course, is not attempting to deny the existence of class differences in Hong Kong society, but he does suggest that there are across-the-board similarities, such as the familistic ethos, the strong achievement motivation, and the individualist orientation, among Hong Kong Chinese. Lau Siu-kai has dwelt on these similarities in his portrait of the Chinese community in Hong Kong.

From the survey in this chapter of studies treating the effect of 'class' on Hong Kong society, it seems that the capitalist class is the one most able to stand the test of time as the territory's influential political actor. While the emerging economic and political relationships between Hong Kong and China seem to deter working-class formation, they are apparently conducive to fostering the capitalists as the society's hegemonic class. He who pays the piper calls the tune: this adage appears to be as true for Hong Kong's future as it has been for its past.

Notes

1. Most textbooks on introductory sociology contain a discussion of the concepts of class used by the Marxists and the Weberians. I am providing in this paragraph only a brief explanation of these concepts. For a more detailed account, see, for instance, Haralambos and Martin (1991: 36–45) and Giddens (1993: 216–29).
2. Lee reiterates his position in *Hong Kong Politics and Society in Transition* (Lee Ming-kwan 1987c); see, especially, chapter 3.
3. Such a critique is best exemplified in Dahrendorf (1959), from which Lee apparently derived the theoretical basis for his analysis.
4. The book's title is, strictly speaking, a misnomer, as the essays collected within it address primarily the issue of Hong Kong's new middle class, rather than Hong Kong's class structure.
5. Wong and Lui also include John Rear's 'One Brand of Politics' (1971) in their critique, but their focus is on Scott and Lau. Moreover, although Wong and Lui refer to several of the works of Lau and his associates, the main targets of their critique are Lau's *Society and Politics in Hong Kong* (1982) and Lau and Kuan's *The Ethos of the Hong Kong Chinese* (1988) and for this reason I list only these two works in the text.
6. Wong and Lui single out Scott's discussion of the middle class as an illustration of the deficiency in his 'class analysis'.
7. In this respect, Wong and Lui's interpretation of Lau's later writings concur with my own thoughts on the subject. See Chapter 1 for a discussion of the conceptual continuity in Lau's writings.
8. Weber described class as a group of individuals who share a similar position in a market economy and by virtue of that fact receive similar economic rewards.
9. The primary components of the seven ranked occupational categories, or classes, are:
Class 1. Higher-grade professionals, administrators, managers, and large proprietors.
Class 2. Lower-grade professionals, administrators, and managers.
Class 3. Routine non-manual employees and personal service workers.
Class 4. Small proprietors, and artisans.
Class 5. Lower-grade technicians and supervisors of manual workers.
Class 6. Skilled manual workers.
Class 7. Semi-skilled and unskilled workers, and agricultural workers.
For details of this classification, see Wong and Lui 1992a: 23–6.
10. For the percentage distribution of the responses of the different classes, see Wong and Lui (1992a: 30, table 4).
11. This reproduces only a small part of the authors' findings. For a detailed account of the coping strategies of different classes, see Wong and Lui (1992a: 31–5).
12. Wong and Lui clarified the objectives of their study: 'We are thus proposing an alternative framework of study on the question of politics and society, and more specifically on the issue of political stability . . . whereas Lau has "brought back sociey", in his own way, into the discussion of politics and political stability, we have tried to bring back social structure' (Wong and Lui 1992a: 21–2).
13. The term 'life chances' refers to a person's chances to obtain the things he or she desires, such as wealth, higher education, and a good job, and to avoid the things he or she dislikes, such as poverty, poor education, and an uncongenial job. Sociologists have generally found that the higher classes have better life chances than do the lower classes.

14. This inquiry is the subject of Tsang Wing-kwong's social mobility study, which was conducted independently of Wong and Lui's social mobility project. Unlike Wong and Lui's study, which was based on their survey data from a sample of 1,000 respondents, Tsang used materials from the Hong Kong 1981 census and 1986 by-census. Tsang's findings are on the whole similar to Wong and Lui's, showing that the occupational (or class) position of the father had a significant impact on the mobility opportunity (or life chances) of the son. Tsang uses the term 'economic class' to refer to an occupation-cum-class position, and the term 'social class' to refer to a class demarcated by life chances different from those of other classes. In the light of this terminology, his study is a demonstration of the conversion of 'economic class' to 'social class' in Hong Kong. Tsang also applies Weber's concept of social enclosure to describe Hong Kong's class structure, arguing that entry to the more privileged classes is largely closed to members of the less privileged classes.

Tsang's study is not discussed in the text partly to avoid the overlap with Wong and Lui's study and partly because the latter work is of greater theoretical importance. Tsang's work is solely a study of the mobility opportunities of different classes; Wong and Lui's relates differential class mobility theoretically to the value orientations of different classes and to the issue of class formation. For a rigorous exposition of the concepts, methodology, and empirical findings of his social mobility study, see Tsang (1994).

15. Information on the father's class position was obtained through a question that asked the respondent what his father's occupation was when the respondent was fourteen years old.

16. See Chapter 1 for a detailed discussion of Hong Kong's economic transformation since the mid-1970s and its impact on occupational and social structure.

17. The authors add that Hong Kong's high mobility rate 'is not particularly striking or unique. Similarly high rates are found in Tokyo, Chicago, Taiwan, [and] Scandinavia' (Wong and Lui 1992b: 44).

18. Class background refers to the occupational position, and hence the class position, of the respondent's father.

19. For a more detailed reporting of the findings, see Wong and Lui (1992b: 58–9, tables 19–21).

20. To back up his argument Wong states, with reference to Janet Salaff's *Working Daughters in Hong Kong* (1981), 'The distinct impression left by Salaff's study is that a lot of the middle class families have just barely left their working class background' (Thomas W. P. Wong 1993: 295). The phrase 'security and survival' comes from Salaff: 'There are particular features of [Hong Kong's] political and economic systems that encourage the inward-drawing family actions for security and survival' (Salaff 1981: 45).

21. In referring to the dominant economic and political clout of the capitalists, Scott writes: 'In the 1890s ... [the] economic basis of Hong Kong had become more sophisticated: a local capitalist class was emerging. Although trade was still the raison d'etre for the colony, financial institutions and manufacturing concerns were of growing importance. Leading British businessmen were increasingly vocal in their claim for a share in government' (Scott 1989a: 59).

22. For an explanation and detailed discussion of the 'administrative absorption of politics', see this volume's Chapter 8, under the heading 'The Background: The Administrative Absorption of Politics'.

23. The ranking was based on the total assets owned by individual companies. A public company is any company incorporated in Hong Kong which has more than fifty shareholders and the shares of which are freely traded through a stock exchange or similarly regulated body.

24. Gilbert Wong comments: 'This overlap of political and economic power lends support to a "class" theory of business groups postulating that the business groups are a manifestation and vehicle of domination' (Gilbert Wong 1991: 139).

25. As illustrations, Gilbert Wong mentions K. S. Li, who acquired control over the Hutchison Group, Green Island Cement, and Hong Kong Electric in the late 1970s and early 1980s, and Y. K. Pao, who took over Hongkong and Kowloon Wharf in 1980 and the Wheelock Marden group in 1984.

26. Examples include appointments to the Basic Law Drafting Committee, the Special Administrative Region's Preparatory Working Committee, and appointments as advisors on Hong Kong affairs and as delegates to the mainland's National People's Congress and Political Consultative Conference. A commentary on such appointments in one of the territory's most popular magazines, *Next Magazine* (26 February 1993, p. 31), observed: 'A rare feature emerges from Beijing's announcement last week of appointees to the Political Consultative Conference. A large number of Hong Kong's top-ranking and secondary-ranking rich people are on the list of appointments. All at once they have chosen "to turn left". This list and the list of appointments to the second batch of advisors on Hong Kong affairs have been in preparation for some time. Appointments are targeted mainly at Hong Kong's wealthiest people and their second generation.... Many who have been approached have gladly accepted the appointment'.

27. The three vice-chairpersons in question were Y. K. Pao, David K. P. Li, and Ann Tse-kai. The businesses involved include: Kowloon Motor Bus, Hong Kong Telephone, Cathay Pacific Airways, Hong Kong and China Gas, and Kowloon–Canton Railway (transport and public utilities); Hongkong Bank, Bank of East Asia, Hang Seng Bank, and World Finance International (banking and finance); China Entertainment and Land Investment, Manor House Holdings, and Chinese Estates and Finance (property development); Windsor Industrial (manufacturing); Hutchison Whampoa and Inchcape Enterprises (commerce and trading); and Hong Kong Television Broadcasts and South China Morning Post (mass media).

28. In 1981 and 1991, the poorest 20 per cent of Hong Kong's households received only 3.2 per cent and 3.0 per cent, respectively, of the society's total household income; in contrast, the richest 20 per cent received 35.2 per cent and 37.3 per cent. Politically, Hong Kong's labouring class has no representative in the Executive Council and has been grossly under-represented in the Legislative Council.

29. England writes: 'industrial conflict, as expressed through working days lost or the number of strikes and lock-outs, is not one of Hong Kong's problems. During the ten-year period from 1978 to 1987, there was an average annual loss through disputes of only 6.4 working days per 1,000 employees, one of the lowest averages among industrialized countries' (England 1989: 216).

3. Culture and Society

SOCIOLOGISTS generally use the word *culture* to mean 'a design for living', 'a way of life'. This chapter is about the Hong Kong way of life and how it has evolved as a product of the interaction between traditional Chinese culture and the experience of living in Hong Kong. The Hong Kong way of life is also the way Hong Kong people think and act. In undertaking this inquiry, we shall make reference to research findings on the orientations and behavioural characteristics of the Hong Kong Chinese in respect to their work, politics, and popular culture, and we shall examine research findings concerning their attitudes towards the relationship between the individual and society. In addition to our attempt to articulate a portrait of the Hong Kong person as an embodiment of Hong Kong culture, we shall seek to explain in terms of this portrait some of the most renowned features of the society, in particular its political stability and economic prosperity.

Chinese Culture and the Hong Kong Experience

Hong Kong in the nineteenth century was largely a society of so-journers. Both Europeans and Chinese came to the island to make fast and easy money for a better life in their respective countries of origin, and few members of either group regarded Hong Kong as their permanent home. Hong Kong's significance to them was, as one writer puts it, as 'a land of economic opportunites, not a place for emotional or spiritual commitment' (Luk 1995). Rigid racial and social barriers by and large precluded cultural exchange between the colonizers and the colonized (see W. K. Chan 1991: chap. 2), and each group identified with and followed the cultural norms and practices of its own home country. In short, because of the sojourner mentality and racial segregation, there was no true indigenous Hong Kong culture in the nineteenth century. However, developments within the Chinese community and in its relationship with the British colonizers lay the foundation for the evolution of a Hong Kong culture in later years. To understand this development, we need first to make a cursory examination of the traditional Chinese culture which the Hong Kong Chinese brought with them from their homeland.

The traditional Chinese way of life was founded on the Confucian belief that social order was part of the cosmic order and that the social ideal was to attain the harmony which was held to be inherent in the cosmos. Social harmony, in turn, rested on three related elements each of which allegedly had its basis in the cosmic order. Donald Munro describes these elements thus:

> The first element is a collection of occupational positions, every one having its own 'job description'. Second, there is a hierarchical relationship between these positions. Third, a formalized code of behavior, variously affecting the occupants of each place in the hierarchy, ties the whole together; the social virtues are realized by individuals who abide with this code (Munro 1969: 23).

In other words, order in traditional Chinese society was based on the individual's dutiful participation in a hierarchical, morally sanctioned division of labour. Several salient features of the Chinese culture can be derived from this conception of social order. First, the individual's moral worth is assessed primarily in terms of his contribution to social order and harmony through discharging his 'prescribed' occupational responsibilities. Traditional Chinese morality was oriented towards the collectivity: the collectivist interest of social order and harmony took precedence over the potentially disruptive interest of the individual. This moral standard applied to rulers as well as to laymen.

Second, the hierarchical division of labour meant that politics was solely the business of the government, and that for the purpose of maintaining social order, the government was entitled to intervene into every sphere of society without any restriction. Political apathy, subservience to governmental authority, and the state's domination over civil society were characterizing features of the traditional Chinese political culture. Third, the pursuit of wealth, viewed as a reflection of selfishness and avarice and as such not conducive to the collective interest of social order, was deemed unworthy of the person of virtue. Merchants, for instance, were usually looked upon with contempt for being exploitative, selfish, corrupt, and immoral. Finally, social conflict was considered a violation of the natural normal state of order and harmony and hence to be avoided as much as possible. The above account of some noteworthy features of traditional Chinese culture is obviously highly selective and condensed, and suffices merely as a parsimonious background for our discussion of the evolution of the Hong Kong culture.[1]

We may note at the start of this discussion that for the first century or so of the Colony's history, the Chinese population, whether original inhabitants or immigrants, consisted almost entirely of peasants, labourers, and merchants. The agrarian–landlord and scholar–official classes, the primary upholders and disseminators of Confucian morality and virtues in traditional China, did not exist in Hong Kong. The implication of this situation for the territory's cultural evolution is insightfully captured by Lau Siu-kai and Kuan Hsin-chi:

> Confucian influence lingers on, but this is contingent more on the natural influence of social customs and family socialization than on any institutional underpinnings (Lau and Kuan 1988: 34–5).

Given the make-up of the Hong Kong Chinese population, these 'social customs and family socialization' patterns were primarily those of the struggling masses whose concerns were security and survival rather than the grandiose Confucian ideals of moral cultivation and self-perfection as a preparation for serving the country and the people. This down-to-earth, pragmatic strain in the ethos of the Hong Kong Chinese was reinforced and boosted by the ascendance of the Chinese merchants as the leaders of the Chinese community towards the end of the nineteenth century. Unlike the élites in traditional China, whose claim to leadership was based on education in the Confucian classics and on moral excellence, the merchants' leadership was predicated on wealth and its ensuing political clout and social influence. The circumstances of Hong Kong thus fostered a cultural climate in which economic pursuits and the acquisition of wealth, whether for survival or status attainment, became the most valued goals of the population. Amorality, materialism, and a pragmatic, pecuniary orientation eventually prevailed over Confucian ethics in the evolution of the Hong Kong culture.

Nor did the drastic social and economic changes in Hong Kong in the 1950s bring about a fundamental transformation in the ethos of the Hong Kong Chinese. Having experienced the Chinese civil war and the war with Japan, and having then fled from Communist rule in their homeland, the refugees came to the Colony to seek a safe haven. They arrived at a time when the territory's economy was adjusting to the challenge of sudden industrial growth, when wages were low and working conditions deplorable, and when the Government was both unwilling and unable to look after the needs of a quickly expanding refugee population. In such circumstances, family and kinsfolk became the primary sources of social and economic support for the individual, contributing to and reinforcing the apolitical, pragmatic familistic orientation which Lau Siu-kai has termed 'utilitarianistic familism'. The ensuing 'minimally integrated social-political system', characterized on the one hand by the Government's monopoly of power and non-interventionist stance in social and economic matters, and on the other by the Chinese community's proclivity to shun politics and to resolve their problems through individual efforts and family and kin support, left its imprint in the attitudes of the Hong Kong people.

The Hong Kong experience as we know it today has its roots in the society's political and economic transformations beginning in the early 1970s. Politically, the institutionalization of government-sponsored élite–mass linkage mechanisms in the late 1960s and 1970s, the establishment of bodies facilitating political participation at the district level in the early 1980s, the introduction of elected elements at the central policy-making level since the mid-1980s, and the controversies regarding the 1997 hand-over of sovereignty have had the cumulative effect of politicizing a previously politically apathetic community.

Paralleling the gradual opening up of the political system has been the Government's adoption of a more active role in the provision of welfare and social services. This in turn has raised the population's expectation of what they are entitled to get from the Government, thus accentuating the trend in politicization. Economically, Hong Kong's industrial restructuring has created more room at the higher levels of the occupational structure and vastly improved opportunities for upward social mobility. To what extent, then, have such changes in the Hong Kong experience transformed the ethos of the Hong Kong Chinese? How does the Hong Kong person today compare with that of some thirty years ago? In the following, we seek answers to these questions through analysis of the values and orientations of the Hong Kong Chinese in several major aspects of their lives.

Individual and Society: The Moral Outlook of the Hong Kong People

We noted above that in the peculiar circumstances of Hong Kong, traditional Chinese morality, characterized by the Confucian principle of conscientious fulfilment of one's station in life in service of the collective interest, was overshadowed by a materialistic and individualist ethos which places the self-interest of one's family above the common weal of society. But this utilitarianistic familism, as the author who coined the term noted (Lau 1982), has since the 1970s been steadily declining in prominence in the life of the territory. This decline has come about as a result of the Government's enlarged role in providing social services, which increasingly have superseded the welfare function of the family.

Despite the increase in social supports available from outside the family group, the individualistic and materialistic element in the Hong Kong character has remained. Lau (1983) called the ensuing ethos 'egotistical individualism', and his empirical findings lend support to this epithet. In a study (Lau and Kuan 1990) of the Hong Kong people's attitude towards *laissez-faire* economic policies, the data reveal on the one hand strong public support for the non-interventionist economic policies of the Government, and on the other widespread popular demands that the Government look after the basic needs of the people. More specifically, the respondents expected the Government to play an active role in solving personal and family problems and to provide a job and a place to live for everyone. The current system of public welfare, they said, was insufficient. The authors observe:

Overall, public support for laissez-faire was substantial.... [Yet] Hong Kong people strongly expect the government to perform all the economic functions that, if actually done, would result in a highly interventionist government and a tightly regulated market (Lau and Kuan 1990: 769).

In the authors' view, this contradiction in attitudes bespeaks both the Hong Kong people's acceptance of the Government's economic policies for their role in the territory's economic success, and the respondents' conception of a good government as a paternalistic one catering to the needs of its subjects. The consistency underlying this apparent contradiction is thus a pragmatic, utilitarian orientation towards the government's role. The contradiction also reflects the two sides of the Hong Kong people's utilitarian (or egotistical) individualism: support for the individual's freedom to pursue economic goals with minimal intervention from the government (hence support for *laissez faire*), and an emphasis on the individual's material well-being (hence the welfarist conception of government). Elsewhere, Lau and Kuan's (1988) research findings testify to the persistence of the pecuniary orientation which had long been a facet of the Hong Kong people's materialist, utilitarian ethos: 85 per cent of the respondents in their 1985 survey sample either agreed or strongly agreed that the most important personal goal was to make as much money as possible without breaking the law.

The continuing prevalence of utilitarian individualism raises a number of intriguing questions about the Hong Kong people's view of morality. First, does the materialism and self-interest rampant in Hong Kong's brand of utilitarian individualism denote an amoral orientation? Or is such an individualism rooted and buttressed by a belief in the intrinsic and inviolable right of the individual to self-development and self-perfection—an individualism which has been termed ethical or moral individualism in Western philosophy? There is also the question of whether the people of Hong Kong subscribe to the view that the pursuit of self-interest cumulatively contributes to the collective good and hence is moral in effect even if not necessarily moral by conscious intent. Our inquiry represents little more than a preliminary effort to chart the moral outlook of the Hong Kong people. The scarcity of research data and studies in this respect imposes limits on the scope and depth of our discourse.

The discussion begins with Lau and Kuan's pertinent research findings (Lau and Kuan 1988: 49–50) which show that most people in Hong Kong would neither stick to their moral principles in disregard of consequences, nor abandon moral principles in order to attain desired personal goals. The majority (63.9 per cent) of the respondents chose to modify their moral principles if adherence to them would bring adverse consequences. Lau and Kuan call this preferred moral option of the Hong Kong people 'situational morality', meaning that the notion of what is morally right or wrong is flexible, varying according to situations, and as such not predicated on universalistic moral principles applicable to all individuals irrespective of conditions.

This finding suggests that the Hong Kong brand of individualism is not moral individualism, a point substantiated further by Lau and Kuan's research results (Lau and Kuan 1988: 51). The majority of their respondents (69.3 per cent) subscribed to the view: 'The rights possessed by a person in society are not in-born. It is because of his good performance that society gives him the rights as rewards.' This brings up the question of what counts as good performance (and by extension bad performance) in the eyes of the Hong Kong people. As their moral judgement is guided not by in-born individual rights but by a person's performance, the question should lead us to an understanding of their situational morality.

We may get a part of the answer to this question from Lau and Kuan's empirical findings (1988: 51): the Hong Kong people would not hestitate to deny rights to persons in situations where their behaviour constitutes a menace to the social order. This implies that performance which threatens the social order is considered bad; the corollary is that performance which upholds the social order is deemed to be good. We can infer that an important ingredient of the Hong Kong people's morality is situated in their predilection for order and stability, and this inference prompts us to a related inquiry: Do the people of Hong Kong perceive the pursuit of individualistic and materialist interests as conducive or deleterious to the maintenance of the social order? In other words, What is the Hong Kong people's moral judgement on utilitarian individualism?

Thomas W. P. Wong provides perhaps the appropriate response when he writes:

For the Hong Kong people... as long as there is room for their individually selfish decisions and efforts to bear fruit, then things are fine.... [About] the moral implications... the Hong Kong people hardly care (Thomas W. P. Wong 1993: 21–2).

As illustrations, Wong refers to the Hong Kong people's attitudes towards emigration, work, and political authority, which consistently reflect a pragmatic adaptation to the exigencies and requirements of the situation rather than a moral concern or commitment. Thus, emigration is perceived as a personal strategy to cope with exigencies and is not judged as a moral right or wrong; work is undertaken for money and not imbued with moral sentiments; and the authority of the colonial government is accepted for its role in bestowing a better livelihood rather than on the basis of a moral endorsement. The Hong Kong person in Wong's portrait is a pragmatic, amoral individual immersed in the task of making a living and perhaps achieving an even better living. How does this finding bear on our earlier thesis of 'situational morality'? Is situational morality no more than just an euphemism for amorality?

We observed earlier that one essential characteristic of the Hong Kong people's situational morality is that acts which buttress the social order are deemed as moral. This observation seems to suggest that Hong Kong people do care for the collective interest and that the thesis of situational morality is at odds with Wong's thesis of amoral individualism. The contradiction disappears, however, when we consider the value of social order to the Hong Kong people. Order is the basis of Hong Kong's prosperity and is treasured primarily for its role in facilitating the individual's pursuit of wealth. Agber Abbas makes a similar point when he observes:

The only form of political idealism that has a chance [in Hong Kong] is that which can go together with economic self-interest (Abbas 1992: 5).

The apparent paradox here, as in the aforementioned example of contradictory attitudes towards *laissez-faire* policies, can be seen as a reflection of a fundamental Hong Kong ethos. In the present case this ethos takes the form of the utilitarian upholding of social order for the pursuit of individual materialist interests. In the final analysis, if the Hong Kong brand of utilitarian individualism is devoid of moral commitment, we have to conclude, so is the Hong Kong people's support for social order. What then is the moral element in situational morality? The answer lies perhaps in Wong's observation about amorality, which seems also to describe situational morality:

> Amorality does not necessarily betoken a lack of moral reserves. The Hong Kong Man perhaps fits Bernard Williams' description [in his 1976 work, *Morality*] of the amoralist: one who has intermittent and capricious engagement in moral considerations (Thomas W. P. Wong 1993: 25–6).

The Hong Kong People's Attitudes Towards Social Mobility and Social Inequality: Implications for Social Stability

The amoral, utilitarian, and individualist Hong Kong ethos suggests that the Hong Kong people believe that the society affords abundant opportunities for upward social mobility; for it is only in the context of such a belief that they would so whole-heartedly pursue economic and social advancement through individual efforts. One may add that this belief reduces social discontents and buttresses social stability, as it casts success and failure as a reflection of individual abilities and efforts rather than as a matter of social injustice. It is in this belief—this aspect of the Hong Kong ethos—that we can find an explanation for the society's renowned stability, in addition to support for theses describing a passive refugee mentality and utilitarianistic familism.

The prevalence of the belief among the Hong Kong population in the value of individual efforts is attested to by both past and recent empirical studies. Robert Mitchell's 1967 study, for instance, found that 50 per cent of the respondents believed that the chances for a working-class boy to become a medical doctor were good or excellent. His findings from the Form 5 students in his sample revealed similar optimistic attitudes: only 12 per cent thought that the opportunity for them to be a success in their career was little or none (Mitchell 1969: vol. 1, p. 82). David Chaney and David Podmore's study in 1969 discovered that as many as 62.7 per cent of the young adults in their sample agreed with the statement, 'Hong Kong is truly a land of opportunity and people get pretty much what they deserve here' (Chaney and Podmore 1973: 60).

Subsequent survey studies show a similarly high percentage of people who held the view that upward mobility chances in Hong Kong were plentiful: 60 per cent in the case of the young workers in Lau's 1978 study (Lau 1982: 89), an overwhelming 87.6 per cent for the respondents in Lau and Kuan's 1985 survey (Lau and Kuan 1988: 63–4), and 83 per cent in respect of the respondents in Wong and Lui's social mobility study of the late 1980s (Thomas W. P. Wong 1991: 159). It is noteworthy that there has been a significant rise since the 1980s in the proportion of people who subscribed to the various measures of the 'abundant opportunities' belief—a change which corresponds with Hong Kong's industrial restructuring in the period.

A concomitant feature of the change has been the decline in the Hong

Kong people's dissatisfaction with life, suggesting that the perceived increase in upward mobility chances has had the effect of lowering frustrations and discontents. The percentage drop in dissatisfaction has been impressive, from 40 per cent of the respondents in Mitchell's 1967 study (Mitchell 1969) to 15 per cent and 3 per cent, respectively, in the 1986 (Lau and Wan 1987) and 1990 (Thomas W. P. Wong 1992a: 245, table 10.1) social indicators studies. That the people of Hong Kong have moved far from the trials and tribulations of the 1950s and 1960s is evident from Wong Siu-lun and Shirley Yue's statement of their survey findings:

There is a pervasive sense of well-being among the adult population in Hong Kong, as represented by the respondents in this survey. They have few immediate worries, and they are generally free of economic want. They are quite satisfied with various aspects of their life (Wong and Yue 1991: 1).

The above findings on the belief in abundant opportunities and on life satisfaction would lead one to think that, in recent years at least, people in Hong Kong have held an optimistic view about their own chances of moving up the social ladder. Other research findings, however, tell a different story. A 1987 study of clerical workers (Lui and Chan 1987) revealed that nearly 40 per cent of the respondents saw little or no prospect for promotion in their current job. Seventy-six per cent of the respondents in the 1990 social indicators survey (Lau et al. 1992) reported that they perceived little or no chance of finding a better job than the one they were holding. Wong and Lui's social mobility study (Wong 1991) arrived at a similar conclusion: some 75 per cent of their respondents saw the likelihood of changing to a better job as either none or very little. Furthermore, only 7 per cent and 12 per cent, respectively, of the respondents in the 1988 and 1990 social indicators studies saw their chances of career development as great (Thomas W. P. Wong 1992a: 248, table 10.4).

Put another way, Hong Kong people are optimistic about the opportunity structure of the society but pessimistic about their own opportunities within it. There is a disjunction between the social ideology of abundant opportunities and the personal experience and assessment of social advancement. An important question arises from this paradox: What is the implication of this disjunction for Hong Kong's social stability? While the 'optimistic' social ideology can be expected to lower dissatisfaction and enhance stability, the 'pessimistic' personal expectation may be a source of discontents and hence a destabilizing factor. We have a preliminary answer from Wong's research findings (Thomas W. P. Wong 1992b).

In beginning his study, Wong was interested in finding out how the 'strain' in the respondents' personal experience would correlate with their perception of social inequality and conflict, and with their sense of life satisfaction. The strain in question is measured in part[2] by the respondent's view of his or her chances of changing to a better job; the more pessimistic response denotes greater strain. The research findings indicate, first, that greater strain does not lead to the view that social inequality inevitably generates social conflict, and, second, that greater strain is not significantly associated with lower life satisfaction. Wong's research data suggest that a pessimistic personal expectation regarding social-mobility opportunities does not generate discontents with social inequality or with personal well-being and, by implication, does not constitute a destabilizing factor for the society at large.

Such puzzling findings led Wong to the hypothesis that the personal expectations and experiences in question are overshadowed by, and subsumed under, the social ideology of abundant opportunities. His empirical findings indeed show that holding pessimistic personal expectations does not dispose the respondent to a negative view of the society's opportunity structure. Further, the belief in abundant opportunities is positively associated with life satisfaction. From these findings, Wong derives two important conclusions. In enhancing life satisfaction and overshadowing the strain of pessimistic personal expectations, the social ideology of abundant opportunities contributes to social stability. The widespread subscription to this ideology has had the effect of leading the people of Hong Kong to see their lesser achievements and failures as a consequence of personal inadequacies rather than a matter of social injustice. Moreover, in the grip of such an ideology—the Hong Kong Dream, as Wong calls it—personal strain becomes a powerful motivating force compelling the individual to strive harder, as opportunities for social and economic advancement are believed to be abundant. It is here, in the Hong Kong people's untiring effort to fulfill the Hong Kong Dream, that Wong finds an explanation for the society's economic dynamism and prosperity:

The general effect of the social ideology and of the chasm between it and personal strain is that the society could be driven to higher levels of economic dynamism and prosperity while still being spared the danger of personal strain and discontent... developing and reinforcing more divisive and conflictual imageries of the social order (Thomas W. P. Wong 1992b: 233).

Wong's statement carries the implicit postulate that the people of Hong Kong see work primarily as a means for personal socio-economic advancement and would put up with deprivations and frustrations at work as the necessary cost of realizing the Hong Kong Dream. The following discussion examines the empirical evidence in this connection.

Work Attitudes: Instrumentalism and the Hong Kong Dream

The supposition that Hong Kong's working people would tolerate frustrating work environments in order to reap the benefits of the vibrant economy finds some preliminary support in recent history. Hong Kong has had a remarkable record of industrial peace in spite of the severe work deprivations which the majority of the workers have experienced since the start of the territory's industrialization.[3] The extent to which this postulate is in agreement with empirical findings on the work attitudes of the Hong Kong people remains to be investigated in detail.

Studies of the Hong Kong people's work attitudes were pioneered by Mitchell's 1960s survey research, which showed that in comparison with other Asian cities such as Bangkok, Singapore, and Taipei, the Hong

Kong worker placed a higher value on the income-gaining aspect of work (Mitchell 1969). Later research arrived at similar findings. David Chaney's study of Kowloon shop workers in the late 1960s (Chaney 1971) found that their overall job satisfaction was strongly associated with their level of satisfaction with their pay, but it was not related to other working conditions such as monthly holidays and hours of work. Neil Carr's case-study of workers at the Hong Kong Oxygen and Acetylene Company led him to conclude that 'their first concern was to obtain a better wage for the job, and they would put up with any conditions to earn that wage' (Carr 1973: 108). A 1978 study of workers in the garment and electronics industries (Ting Chau and Ng 1983) showed that level of pay was the most important factor in the workers' consideration for job changes. More significantly, Turner and his associates' large-scale survey study based on a representative sample of 1,000 employees (Turner et al. 1980) found that the respondents most often chose 'good pay' to be the most important aspect of a person's job.[4]

On the basis of these findings, Joe England and John Rear postulated that instrumentalism—an orientation which regards work as a means of acquiring the income necessary to support a valued way of life of which the work itself is not an integral part—was one dominant feature of the work attitudes of the Hong Kong people (England and Rear 1975; England 1989). They proposed that this instrumental orientation towards work, in conjunction with other elements in Chinese culture and the 'don't rock the boat' refugee mentality, were the main attitudinal factors contributing to industrial quiescence. England summarizes the impact of traditional Chinese culture on industrial relations:

Familial traditions of obedience and loyalty to autocratic authority, a shared belief in hard work and economic gain ... the habit of giving face and avoiding confrontation whenever possible, have all played a part in mitigating conflict between capital and labour in Hong Kong (England 1989: 42).

The typical Hong Kong worker, in England and Rear's portrait, is thus one who attaches exceptionally high importance to pay over other conditions of employment, including working conditions and relations with co-workers, and who is highly tolerant of authoritarian management. In other words, the 'personal strain' experienced at work is submerged under the individualist quest for economic rewards and does not translate into an impetus for collective confrontation against management. In descriptive terms, although not in analytic discourse, this image of the Hong Kong worker is consonant with that suggested by our supposition concerning the workers' tolerance of onerous work environments. One may be inclined at this juncture to forge ahead with the thesis and to find the pertinent supporting evidence that cultural predispositions have been reinforced by the ideology of abundant opportunities in shaping the work attitudes of the Hong Kong people. But a caveat is in order before we proceed further, for some of the research findings arrived at by Turner and his associates (Turner et al. 1980) reflect a collectivist orientation and group solidarity among Hong Kong workers.

Some 95 per cent of the respondents in the study by Turner et al. concurred with the view that 'when a fellow worker is in trouble, a man should help him as much as he can', and 76 per cent agreed with the statement that 'a group of men can always succeed better than one man working on his own because they can help each other out'. The data also reveal that most workers preferred to collectively confront management when they were dissatisfied rather than quitting their job. On the basis of such empirical evidence, Turner questioned the validity of England and Rear's depiction of the Hong Kong worker as predominantly instrumental in orientation.

But Turner's critique, as Lui Tai-lok aptly argues (Lui 1992a, 1992b), glosses over the point that a collectivist orientation may well be one aspect of instrumentalism. Workers may see collective action as instrumental in realizing their pragmatic, pecuniary goals. Instead of engaging in the debate on instrumentalism, Lui considers it far more important and fruitful to embark on a fresh examination of the meaning which workers attach to work in the context of Hong Kong's socio-economic development in recent years:

Work values are constituted in a specific socio-economic context—the formation of the economy, the structuring of economic opportunities, inequalities in life chances and family strategies are active forces in shaping the value of work (Lui 1992b: 124).

With these considerations in mind, Lui undertook a programme of research on work attitudes.[5] We should note that Lui's survey data (Lui 1992b) concur with the findings in previous studies that most Hong Kong workers see their work in economic or instrumental terms. Lui's main interest in his study is to explore how this instrumental orientation bears on the worker's commitment to work and why a worker might adopt an instrumental orientation towards work. On the first issue, Lui's findings indicate that Hong Kong workers are far less morally committed to their work than are workers in Britain; in other words, Hong Kong workers are more inclined to work for money than to work as a 'calling' or as a duty to society. Thus, only 24 per cent of the respondents in Lui's study, in contrast to 61 per cent in a similar British study (Mann 1986), agreed with the statement, 'I do the best work I can, regardless of pay'. This finding, however, should not be taken to mean that Hong Kong people are not conscientious about their work, for as many as 90 per cent of Lui's respondents agreed that 'employees should be expected to think up better ways to do their jobs'. Lui's research data further show that a significant portion (31 per cent) of the respondents was pursuing further studies after work, most of whom (65 per cent) did so with the expressed purpose of obtaining the required qualifications to advance their careers. More significantly, some 80 per cent were interested in engaging in economic activities even when there was no financial need to work.

Such findings are puzzling in view of the fact that the people of Hong Kong are said to attach little moral importance to work and not to treasure work for its intrinsic value. What explains their strong commitment to work, especially when financial need is not the motivating factor? Lui derives an answer from the evidence that a sizeable proportion (40 per cent) of the respondents expressed a desire to start their own business. This suggests that Hong Kong people are dedicated to work because they are motivated by the strong desire for socio-economic advancement, because they believe that hard work and investing time and efforts in work through further studies will one day bring rewards in this land of abundant opportunities. In other words, they believe in the 'rags-to-riches' Hong Kong Dream. The relentless pursuit of this dream, which is Hong Kong's brand of instrumentalism, generates and sustains a strong motivation to work hard and to bear the attendant sacrifices and deprivations. Lui's concluding statements indeed bring us full circle to the postulate which launched our discussion of work attitudes:

They [the Hong Kong people] work for themselves (and one can argue, for their families). Their strong desire for entrepreneurship and the motivation to pursue further studies after work are not articulated in moral tones, but are perceived as mundane, practical and related to family and self-interest. In short, the Hong Kong brand of instrumentalism goes hand-in-hand with a strong economic drive (Lui 1992b: 123).

Political Attitudes

The general conclusion that Hong Kong people adopt an instrumental orientation towards work leads us to inquire, in our discussion of political attitudes, whether a similar orientation prevails in this area. We will use this question as the guiding thread in our exploration of the political attitudes of the Hong Kong people.

Studies of political attitudes before the 1980s do not show that the Hong Kong people were instrumentally oriented towards politics in the sense of seeing politics as the means to realize their personal material interests. Rather, these studies (Hoadley 1970; Shively 1972; King 1981a; Lau 1981) reflect a strong tendency to avoid politics, a high degree of political apathy, and a pervasive sense of political powerlessness among the Hong Kong people. Given the exclusive, élitist, and non-interventionist character of the Hong Kong Government, the tradition of paternalism in Chinese politics, and the refugee experience, the Hong Kong Chinese at the time could not but perceive politics as dangerous and beyond their comprehension and control. It is interesting therefore to see to what extent, and in what direction, these attitudes have changed since the early 1980s, when the Government's increasing intervention into society, and the gradual opening up of the political system, prepared the ground for the emergence of a new political culture. A series of studies by Lau Siu-kai and his associates furnish us with valuable information in this regard.

Lau and Kuan's 1982 large-scale survey research in four districts in Hong Kong was the first major attempt made in the territory to gauge the magnitude and nature of changes in the political culture consequent upon reforms in the political system (Lau and Kuan 1986). The data reveal a dramatic change in the people's conception of the role of government. A significant proportion of the respondents (varying between 23 and 40 per cent in the four districts) held the Government responsible for solving their personal and family problems, and an even a larger proportion (varying between 42 and 63 per cent in the four districts) held the Government responsible for solving community problems (Lau and Kuan 1986: 32–3, tables 1.2 and 1.4). The findings also suggest that the Hong Kong people had become more politicized: the respondents showed interest in discussing community problems with friends and neighbours, and some even considered unconventional political tactics (such as petitioning the Governor and undertaking publicity campaigns) as effective means of getting concessions from the Government.[6]

Yet the people's sense of political powerlessness remained, for Lau and Kuan's data indicate that as many as 75 per cent of the respondents thought they could exert little influence on the Government's local policies. Further, in examining the data concerning the respondents' major forms of social and political participation,[7] Lau and Kuan found a low degree of correlation among them; that is, participation in one type of social or political activity did not imply an equally participatory tendency towards other activities. To the authors, this finding reflects a situation in which Hong Kong people would resort only to certain preferred types of participation to solve their individual problems but did not see political participation as either a duty or a right of the citizen:

Individuals tend to concentrate on a few selected types of participation in order to cope with their own idiosyncratic needs. Participation is primarily *instrumental*, hence it is not intrinsically valuable (Lau and Kuan 1986: 43; emphasis mine).[8]

To Lau and Kuan, the increasing politicization of the populace, coupled with a persistent pervasive sense of political powerlessness and an instrumental orientation towards political participation, 'testify to an early "modern", and hence "immature", form of participatory political culture' (Lau and Kuan 1986: 50). They follow the development of this political culture in several of their subsequent studies.

Findings from their 1985 and 1986 joint survey studies show little change in Hong Kong's political culture in the intervening years. The feeling of political inefficacy remained pervasive (some 88 per cent of the respondents in the 1986 research reported this feeling; Lau and Kuan 1989), more so in fact than was revealed in the 1982 findings—a phenomenon which Lau and Kuan believed to be associated with the 1997 issue. Nor had Hong Kong's development towards a representative government succeeded in inculcating a correct understanding of democracy among the people. Thus, while a significant proportion of the respondents saw in democracy the promise of a better government—some 49 per cent of the respondents in the 1985 survey believed that elected leaders could rule Hong Kong better than could the existing Government—most understood democracy in idiosyncratic terms: for instance, as government willing to consult public opinion (44 per cent), or as government which could lead the people (16 per cent). Only 23 per cent of the respondents correctly understood democracy to be a government elected by the people (Lau and Kuan 1988: 75).

Lau and Kuan's data, supported by other research findings,[9] further led the authors to the view that a pragmatic emphasis on social stability and an instrumental concern for self-interest, rather than support for the principle of democracy, continued to characterize the Hong Kong people's approach to politics and government. The statement 'Whichever kind of government is immaterial, provided a minimum standard of living can be safeguarded for myself' was supported by as many as 61 per cent of the 1985 research respondents (Lau and Kuan 1989: 97). In this light, it is not surprising that the Hong Kong people saw democratization in instrumental terms, as a political development which would bring them increased material satisfaction. The respondents in the 1985 survey almost unanimously (93 per cent) charged government with the responsibility for providing housing for all citizens:

Political participation will continue to be influenced by the instrumental consideration of the people. Issues of immediate relevance which can be pursued by tactics that require little sacrifice of personal resources will have a better chance to induce political action than remote causes or ideological goals which may entail heavy burdens in terms of time and effort (Lau and Kuan 1989: 111).

Evidence suggests that at the end of the 1980s, the concern for stability and prosperity, the sense of political inefficacy, the idiocyncratic understanding of democracy, and the demand on government to increase social service provisions remained dominant features of Hong Kong's political culture. Lau's findings from the Social Indicators Project of 1988 (Lau et al. 1991) show that the majority of the respondents (59 per cent) still considered social stability and prosperity more important than democracy; only a meagre 17 per cent thought otherwise. The data also show that the proportion of respondents who believed they had no influence on government policies had increased to 93 per cent. The percentage of people who properly understood democracy to be an elective government remained low: 15 per cent and 28 per cent, respectively, in the 1988 and 1990 Social Indicators Projects (Lau et al. 1991; Lau 1992). A majority of the respondents (72 per cent) agreed or strongly agreed with the statement 'The Hong Kong government should provide more social services even at the expense of economic growth' (Lau et al. 1991).

There are, however, also signs of change towards a more modern and liberal conception of government and politics. Some 39 per cent of the respondents in the 1990 project called for political reform, suggesting that 'public demand for political reform has slightly increased' (Lau 1992: 133). In addition, the proportion of respondents favouring the formation of political parties in Hong Kong increased substantially from 25 per cent in the 1988 survey to 52 per cent in 1990 survey, although the caveat must be added that a significant 44 per cent of the 1990 respondents held the view that parties would bring about social instability. Popular preference for the liberal tendency is also evidenced by the finding that 34 per cent of the respondents claimed they would support the democratic politicians, in contrast to the 1 per cent who would support the conservatives. Yet this finding is confounded by the fact most respondents (74 per cent) favoured a gradualist rather than a rapid pace of democratization in Hong Kong (Lau 1992). The incongruity of the findings on political attitudes from the 1988 and 1990 Social Indicators Projects, and the absence of a conclusion in Lau and his associates' pertinent writings, render it difficult for us to depict Hong Kong's recent political culture in an unambiguous summary form. One statement by Lau and his associates, however, does seem to provide a reasonable assessment of the extent to which the instrumental strain and other remnants of past political attitudes survived in the political culture of the early 1990s:

Despite the preference for a democratic form of government, the response of the Hong Kong people to the democratic appeals propagated in recent years has been neither active nor enthusiastic. This incongruity may plausibly be accounted for by Hong Kong people's usual apathetic attitude towards political matters, their preoccupation with social stability and prosperity, and their particular conception of democracy (Lau et al. 1991: 183).

Popular Culture

Our discussion thus far has been an examination of the ethos of the Hong Kong people through reference to their views on the society's opportunity structure, their orientation towards work, and their approach to politics. For a comprehensive reflection of the ethos of a people, however, there is probably no better domain to explore than that of popular culture. This section examines the evolution of major aspects of popular culture in Hong Kong against the background of the society's socio-economic and political development. Our guiding questions as we undertake this exploration are the following: In what way has popular culture mirrored the Hong Kong experience? Do we find in Hong Kong's popular culture similar values and orientations as those depicted earlier in this chapter? In pursuing these questions, we are implicitly taking popular culture to be a representation of the collective experience and ethos. We do not claim that our approach is methodologically rigorous. Given the paucity of academic research in this area, our discussion is inevitably often informed by writings of a journalistic nature.

Chinese Tradition and Its Encounter with Westernization: The 1950s and 1960s[10]

Popular culture in Hong Kong in the decade or so after the end of the Second World War bore the characteristics of the traditions preserved by the refugees from China who then made up a substantial portion of the territory's population. Coming mostly from rural, pre-modern parts of the mainland, these refugees were disposed to resort to their traditional rural values in coping with urban life in Westernized Hong Kong. In addition, there was also a minority of refugees who came from Shanghai, then China's industrial and cultural centre, and they brought with them, apart from capital and entrepreneurship, a taste for that city's popular culture. Throughout the 1950s, Hong Kong's popular culture was very much the continuation of the cultural heritage of these two groups of new arrivals. The phenomenon was indicative of the lack of a strong cultural tradition and identity among the territory's indigenous Chinese population and of their proclivity to identify with the mainland cultural tradition.

It is, therefore, little wonder that Cantonese movies of the time so often cast their heros and heroines as personifications of traditional Chinese values. The exalted female characters, epitomized in the cinematic roles of actresses Ng Kwan Lai and Yu Lai Chun, despite adverse and oppressive conditions, unswervingly embodied the traditional virtues of chastity, loyalty to the family, and dedication to the husband. The male characters also played traditional roles, as is evidenced in the popular comedies of actors Sun Ma Chai and Tang Kei Chan. Their films were portrayals of how the little man survived and triumphed over the trials and tribulations of modern city life through adherence to the traditional rural values of uprightness, thrift, and mutual help. These values were also given a subtle divine blessing, for the benevolent helping hand of Fate always rescued the hero in the nick of time from what appeared to be insurmountable odds. The adversaries faced by the heroes were personifications of what were then perceived by the struggling masses as the unpleasant, unjust, and oppressive elements of the city: the corrupt police, the stringent landlord, and the arrogant and extravagant rich.

In celebrating the triumph of traditional virtues over the vices of the modern city, the cinema was in effect serving out to the masses an antidote to cope with the trauma of having been uprooted from their homeland and having to struggle to make a new life in an alien environment. A similar effect was achieved in Kwan Tak Hing's renowned cinematic portrayal of the legendary kung fu master Wong Fei Hung, which arguably remains the best embodiment of Confucian virtues in a single character. The astounding popularity of the Wong Fei Hung movies, which invariably depicted the master's victory over his adversary (played usually by Shek Kin, who has now become the comic representation of the bad guy) testifies to the pervasive psychological need among the masses to seek moral support and reassurance from traditional Chinese ethical values in an otherwise anomic socio-cultural setting.

If the Cantonese films of the 1950s mirrored a reliance on traditional ethics in a situation of moral ambiguity, popular music of the time reflected the dominance of incoming virtuosity in a society of undistinguished artistic accomplishment. In musical composition and singing, the Hong Kong artists paled in comparison to their immigrant Shanghai counterparts. This discrepancy gave rise to a situation in which songs in Mandarin Chinese composed and sung by immigrant artists from Shanghai (composer Leung Ngok Yum and singers Chow Suen, Lee Heung Lan, and Pa Kwong were among the best known of these artists) became the popular music of a predominantly Cantonese-speaking population. Songwriter Wong Jim, captured the state and mood of this period of

Hong Kong's popular music with an epithet aptly derived from the title of a popular Mandarin song of the time: 'Shanghai by Night' (Wong Jim 1995).

Indeed, this Mandarin influence also had a substantial impact on the local cinema. Here, the ascendance of the Mandarin movies, especially those produced by the Shaw Brothers Company, was helped by a combination of artistic virtuosity and lavish budgets. By the 1960s, the films of the Mandarin cinema had superceded their Cantonese competitors in popularity.

The legacy of the past, however, did not survive long in a rapidly modernizing Hong Kong. Like many other Asian countries of the time, Hong Kong was modernizing by copying the culture and lifestyle of the Western capitalist countries, particularly the United States and Britain. As the population became attuned to the hybrid, cosmopolitan cultural environment and the fast pace of the city, they also grew increasingly receptive to entertainments imported from the West. At the same time, traditional rural values and Confucian ethics soon proved to be anachronistic and inappropriate behavioural guides in a highly competitive and capitalist Hong Kong, where success was gauged not by moral worth but by the ability to out-compete others to gain material wealth.

The change in the popular ethos was evidenced in the 1960s in the demise of the Cantonese cinema and the concurrent ascendance of the Hollywood movies. The most popular screen heros of the day, in contrast with the virtuous little men of the 1950s, were the individualistic, hedonistic, and womanizing secret agent James Bond, and later the unscrupulous, pecuniary, and manipulative bounty-hunter in Clint Eastwood's 'spaghetti westerns' (two of which carried the tell-tale titles *A Fistful of Dollars* and *For a Few Dollars More*). The phenomenal commercial success of these amoral, action-packed, and violence-prone Hollywood movies not only heralded the end of the era of tradition-oriented Cantonese cinema and contributed to the passing of the Mandarin variant, but also paved the way for the emergence and consolidation of a new genre in local cinema productions of later years.

Popular music suffered a fate similar to that of the motion pictures. Mandarin songs were eventually eclipsed in the 1960s by the popular music of the United States and Britain, and Hong Kong's youth, like their counterparts in the West, were swept away by the vibrant rock and roll music of Elvis Presley, Pat Boone, Paul Anka, and the Beatles. In musical style, lyrics, performance, and personality, these singers represented the quintessential nonconformist youth culture. Their popularity in Hong Kong signified the coming to age of a Westernized, local-born generation whose values and views of the world had moved far from those of their parents. Meanwhile, local composers and singers attempted to meet the Western challenge by modernizing their music; the Mandarin popular songs of the 1960s, as evidenced in the repertoires of singers Ching Ting, Koo May, and Kwok Lan, were highly Westernized in musical style and subject-matter. By the end of the decade, traditional Chinese values and artistry in popular culture had by and large succumbed to the impact of Westernization.

The Indigenization of Popular Culture in Hong Kong[11]

The localization of popular culture in Hong Kong and the concomitant waning of external cultural domination (English as well as Mandarin) began in the early 1970s. The background of this change was the founding in 1967 of the Television Broadcasts Company (TVB) and with this the introduction of free wireless television in Hong Kong. Within a few years TVB's viewership had expanded far beyond that of the existing cable television network (introduced in 1957), which charged a rental fee and remained largely an élite medium. In fact, since the 1970s TVB's Cantonese-language Jade channel has had a near monopoly of viewership, consistently winning over at least 80 per cent of prime-time viewers (Lilley 1993: 265). At the start, Cantonese-language programming on TVB remained much the same as that of its predecessor, consisting mainly of shows imported from the West and Japan dubbed into the Cantonese dialect for local consumption. In the early 1970s, Jade made an innovative move and pioneered the production of domestically produced Cantonese-language programmes. The share of domestically produced programmes on the channel increased substantially from under 29 per cent in 1972 to 62 per cent a decade later, while in the same period the proportion of programmes imported from the West dropped from 41 to 11 per cent (Choi 1990: 540, table 2). Among these domestically produced programmes, the genre of drama serial often using the local lifestyle as its subject-matter turned out to be the most successful, and so it must be accorded the leading role in the indigenization of Hong Kong's popular culture.

In popular music, the turning point was the theme song for Jade's drama serial *Laughs and Tears of Lovers*, sung in Cantonese but in a Westernized musical style and having thus the combined appeal of being indigenous and modern. A whole crop of similarly styled Cantonese theme songs followed, owing their popularity very much to the large captive audience for the drama serial. But if familiarity attained through television broadcasting laid the groundwork for the popularization of Cantonese songs, the shedding of their previous image of inferiority was contingent on the cumulative effort of a new generation of songwriters and singers who injected into Cantonese popular songs an element of sophistication and respectability. A pioneer in this respect is composer-singer Samuel Hui, a graduate from the University of Hong Kong, whose songs go beyond the petty themes of boy–girl romance and address, in the language and philosophy of the person in the street, the joys, disillusionments, and vicissitudes of life in Hong Kong. Witness the lyrics of some of his most popular songs: 'Life is like gambling; winning or losing is a matter of luck'; 'Life is like a dream; in dreams we have no sense of direction'; 'Hong Kong has everything we need; why emigrate?'. Similar examples can be found in the works of his contemporaries: 'Our fortunes are ever-changing, for change is the principle of eternity'; 'Below the Lion Rock we sail on the same vessel, so let us ... strive together to write a glorious script in the history of our territory'.

If lyrics such as the above find easy rapport from a people living in 'borrowed place, borrowed time', the cosmopolitan style of the accompanying music[12] readily strikes a resonance in the international city's residents. It was in such a context that Cantonese songs came to overshadow 'foreign' songs in popular appeal. Since the early 1980s, they have indeed attained a hegemonic position in the domain of popular music.[13]

The indigenization of cinematic films began similarly in the early 1970s, pioneered by Bruce Lee's commercially highly successful kung fu movies, which were in essence localized versions of Hollywood's violent, action-packed movie genre. But here, as in popular music, the television drama serial was primarily responsible for popularizing the Cantonese cinema. Subjects, screen characters, and actors and actresses that captured a large audience on television were transported to the cinema. This approach to film-making was perhaps best exemplified in the Hui brothers' comedies, filmed versions of their popular television serial. The practice of interchange between the two media was then so common that one popular culture critic aptly calls local film-making in the 1970s the period of 'the television-based cinema' (Yiu 1983).

Having attained popularity, Hong Kong-produced films were gradually able to free themselves from dependence on television. Moreover, since the early 1980s there has been a reverse development towards the so-called 'cinema-based television' (Yiu 1983), in part because the public's viewing tastes had been so shaped by the local cinema that television drama serials had to imitate its style and subject-matter, and partly because the clichéd story-lines in the television drama serials could no longer satisfy a more educated and demanding audience. Meanwhile, the Mandarin film industry virtually ceased to operate, and even the most popular Hollywood productions paled in comparison with the local ones as box-office successes. In 1989, for instance, only one foreign film, *Indiana Jones and the Last Crusade*, could make its way (coming fourth in box-office returns) into the list of the year's top ten grossing films; Hong Kong-produced Cantonese films made up the rest of the list.[14]

Popular Culture as an Articulation of the Hong Kong Identity

That the indigenization of popular culture should occur at a time when Hong Kong's first generation of local-borns were coming of age has prompted some popular culture critics to claim that the process mirrored the emergence of a Hong Kong identity among the population. This claim indeed seemed consonant with empirical findings from Lau and Kuan's survey research on the ethos of the Hong Kong Chinese. They observe:

It might not be unreasonable to characterize the basic identity of the Hong Kong Chinese before the 1960s as 'Chinese'.... Gradually, this 'Chinese identity' has undergone slow and subtle changes. In our 1985 survey, an astonishingly large proportion of respondents (59.5 per cent) identified themselves as 'Hongkongese' when they were asked to choose between it and 'Chinese' (Lau and Kuan 1988: 2).

Within the domain of popular culture, its indigenization has been described as a process of cultural decolonization (Choi 1990; Chan Kai-cheung 1991). This description, taken together with the above quotation from Lau and Kuan, suggests that while the Hong Kong people have been shedding their colonial cultural baggage, they are also increasingly disposed to regard themselves as distinct from the mainland Chinese. In other words, the rise of the Hong Kong identity is a dual process of dissociation from colonial cultural domination as well as from the social and political life of the mainland. Seen in this light, the articulation of the Hong Kong identity is a cultural and perhaps subconsciously political project—a project which has acquired added significance with the approach of 1997.

This dual process is evident in the frequent use of Chinese historical figures and tales as the subject-matter in local films and television drama serials. Some notable examples of subjects include the life and times of Cixi, the Empress Dowager, intrigues within the Qing palace, Han insurrections against the Qing regime, kung fu heroes combating injustice, and the Judge Pao saga. These costume presentations restore a sense of cultural and national identity and yet absolve the audience from identification with the Chinese Communist regime. Given Hong Kong's peculiar political circumstances, in which there is both official and self-censorship against references in popular culture to contemporary Chinese history and politics, the popular culture industry has to resort to this apolitical approach to reinstate Chinese culture in its productions. The ensuing cultural products reflect and reinforce ambivalence in the identity of the Hong Kong Chinese: They wish to retain their Chineseness, and yet they perceive themselves as socially and politically distinct from their brethren on the mainland.

In the anachronistic presentation of Chineseness in popular culture, national identity is articulated through Han rebellions against the 'alien' Qing regime, politics is confined to struggles and conspiracies within the Qing palace, and national pride is invoked through the dramatic celebration of Chinese martial arts. Inherent in the Hong Kong identity is an identification with China's past which enables the Hong Kong people to recognize themselves as Chinese in the cultural sense but, perhaps, not in the social and political sense. Political realities aside, their claim to be 'Hongkongese' rather than Chinese is based also on their sense of superiority over their compatriots across the border. The 'Ah Charn' syndrome —a popular topic in local films and television programmes of the 1980s— testifies to this sense of superiority.

'Ah Charn' is a pejorative epithet deployed by the Hong Kong Chinese to identify what they consider to be a country hick from the mainland who is trying to accomodate himself or herself to life in modern and glamorous Hong Kong. There are several versions of Ah Charn as portrayed in local films and television dramas, each reflecting a different dimension of the Hong Kong people's perception of the mainland Chinese. A derogative yet fond version stereotypes Ah Charn as an ignorant but benign person blundering through life in the big city. This Ah Charn is very much the product of China's open-door policy, which has afforded the Hong Kong people increased contact with the countryfolk across the border. The Ah Charn as the subject of ridicule and laughter, yet someone to be educated and enlightened, bespeaks on the one hand the self-congratulating sense of superiority of the Hong Kong people, and on the other their readiness to lend a helping hand to their less fortunate compatriots on the mainland. The Hong Kong identity is demarcated in a humorous, basically good-natured manner, with the blundering mainlander constituting the subject of comical entertainment in popular culture.

Another presentation of Ah Charn in popular culture, however, depicts him or her as disruptive of Hong Kong's peace and order. In this version, exemplified in Johnny Mak's *Long Arm of the Law* series of films (released in 1984, 1987, and 1989), the mainland Chinese appear as psychopathic criminals ruthlessly attempting to make a fortune in this land of wealth and prosperity. This Ah Charn, as one popular culture critic has observed (N. Leung 1990), mirrors the Hong Kong people's perception of threats from the mainland to their way of life. In this case, the contrast between 'we' and 'they' is brought out through dramatizing the ominous presence of the outsider.

Still another version of Ah Charn realistically treats the theme of reunification with the motherland. Ah Charn in this case is not someone the people of Hong Kong can simply look down upon and make fun of, or fear as a ruthless criminal, but a partner with whom they have to cooperate. The epitome of this approach in film-making is Cheung Kin-ting's *Her Fatal Ways* I and II and *His Fatal Ways*, in which mainland and Hong Kong police officers work hand in hand, albeit amidst much misunderstanding and initial distrust, to bring criminals to justice. Yim Ho's box-office success, with the tell-tale title *Homecoming*, takes the message even further. The film tells the story of a Hong Kong businesswoman's visit to her native village in Guangdong province, during which she becomes aware of the cutthroat competition and impersonality of life in the modern capitalist city in contrast to the harmony and warmth of village life in the motherland. The film presents symbolically the bright side of reunification and subtly critiques the Hong Kong way of life.

The Ah Charn syndrome in popular culture seems to represent a Hong Kong identity at the crossroads. With the approach of 1997, the Hong Kong identity that rests on a dissociation from mainland China appears increasingly unrealistic and untenable. In this regard, it is worth noting that at least in some local films, the sense of superiority, the fear of impending doom, seem to be gradually giving way to the wish for harmonious cooperation. It is highly probable that after 1997 this theme of 'cooperation' will become more common and more accentuated in the local cinema.

Popular Culture as a Reflection of the Hong Kong Ethos

We noted in an earlier section that the people of Hong Kong subscribe to an ideology of abundant opportunities despite the fact that in reality many have been frustrated in their endeavour to advance their positions.

This belief in the openness of the society and in the equality of opportunities, we further observed, has had the effect of dampening social discontents, of shelving the issue of social injustice attendant on social inequality, and of reducing the possibility of social conflict. On the other hand, the disjuncture between belief and personal experience constitutes the motivating force to strive harder to fulfill the 'rags-to-riches' Hong Kong Dream. The extent to which Hong Kong's popular culture embodies this ideology and its effects is the subject of the following discussion.

We may first consider Chan Hoi-man's characterization of Hong Kong's popular culture as constituted by what he terms the three contradistinctive cultural discourses of affluence, survival, and deliverance (Chan Hoi-man 1993, 1995). His argument, couched in somewhat abstract language, is that 'the juxtaposition of these general spheres of cultural discourses together defines the dynamic fabric of cultural mentality in present-day Hong Kong' (Chan Hoi-man 1993: 355). The Hong Kong ethos, Chan points out, comprises the contrasting cultures of affluence, survival, and deliverance, and popular culture is an embodiment of this ethos. He defines the culture of affluence as 'the sense of material abundance that has become pervasive in Hong Kong from the mid-1970s onward' (Chan Hoi-man 1993: 355). The culture of survival pertains to the 'quest of individuals for self-actualization through the course of social life', as well as the sustenance of 'collective survival against overwhelming historical odds' (Chan Hoi-man 1993: 356). The culture of deliverance focuses on the search for relaxation, for relief from the tension and the frustrations of life in the modern city. It is this culture of deliverance, Chan adds, which provides the foundation whereby the cultures of affluence and survival can attain a delicate balance. In other words, it has a therapeutic function, a soothing effect, and is instrumental in maintaining the coherence of the Hong Kong ethos. This, he says, is the most crucial aspect of Hong Kong's popular culture.

In Chan's view, the culture of affluence is manifest in the thriving popular culture industries and in the proliferation of their products since the mid-1970s. It is regrettable that he offers no illustration through recourse to the contents of popular culture. For this point we can turn to Rozanna Lilley's observations (1993) for illumination. Commenting on local television programming, she writes:

Many dramas feature secular story lines: fortuitous happenings, ... sudden reversals of fortune in the rags-to-riches vein. ... What these programmes share is a celebration of individualism and wealth (Lilley 1993: 267).

Shows are replete with late capitalist images of prosperity: the manic compulsion to consume, economics as a game of chance, floating visual pleasures and impossible dreams of stardom. In Hong Kong, ideologies of affluence, of glamour and 'style', have had very real effects on much of the population. Consumption is consistently represented as a source of power and pleasure (Lilley 1993: 268).

However, the ideals of wealth and conspicuous consumption are beyond the realization of the majority of the population, for whom securing a decent living is the real concern. It is for this reason, Chan maintains, that cultural products have to embrace the culture of survival. In popular novels and television dramas, for instance, the hero is portrayed as one who stoically meets and survives the challenges of life. Chan cites as a concrete example the popular novelist Yeh Su's more than 120 volumes of fiction and non-fiction prose which depict with great sensitivity the trials and tribulations of individual survival in the city–jungle of Hong Kong.

One may note at this juncture that Chan's culture of affluence is reminiscent of the ideology of abundant opportunities, and that his culture of survival addresses the realistic, often frustrating experiences of the masses striving for success. His remarks attest to this connection:

The city... is rightly seen as an arena of resources, of possibilities and hopes. Yet these may not be readily realized even after dire struggles.... Hence ... beyond the culture of affluence and fulfilment, the popular culture world also epitomizes a more realistic cultural discourse of survivalism (Chan Hoi-man 1993: 356).

As we have noted in an earlier section, the discrepancy between belief (ideology) and personal experiences generates a strain which is psychologically distressing for the individual and potentially disruptive for society. The relief of this strain or 'the tension between fulfilment and survival' (Chan Hoi-man 1993: 357) is the task of the culture of deliverance, manifest in the unmatched popularity in Hong Kong's popular culture market of comedies and mix-genre movies with a clear comical bent. In enabling the audience to derive fun and entertainment from even the toughest obstacles and the noblest ideals, the deliverance element in popular culture renders, if but temporarily, the incompatibility between belief and reality more tolerable and acceptable. Seen in this light, the comic, cynical, and even nonsensical (as in the so-called *mo lei tau*) elements so prevalent in the local popular culture in recent years are indeed an essential, perhaps indispensable, component of the Hong Kong ethos.

The ideology of abundant opportunities and the associated belief in the equality of opportunity have also left their marks on Hong Kong's popular culture in other ways. Here we can consider what Choi Po-king, in her 1990 article, identifies as the two distinct features of the local popular culture: the conspicuous absence of the element of social protest and criticism, and the homogeneity and convergence in the production and consumption of cultural products. For the first feature, as Choi has offered no empirical substantiation, we can use the findings in Wong Chi-wah's study of popular songs (1995) as illustration. Through a meticulous content analysis of the most popular 537 Chinese songs in the period 1979 to the first half of 1991, Wong finds that only about 3 per cent qualify as songs of protest or social critique, while in contrast love songs make up some 67 per cent of the total.[15] We can also find support for Choi's contention in popular culture critic Sze Man-hung's comment (Sze 1994: 53) on local television programmes. Sze observes that when the local television stations introduced political themes in some of their programmes towards the end of the 1980s and the beginning of the 1990s, the change met with poor audience response. As a consequence, present-day television remains depoliticized and geared overwhelmingly to mass entertainment.

The homogenizing tendency in popular culture, in Choi's view, is evidenced in the similarity in the musical and lyrical styles of Cantonese popular songs. The same tendency is discernible in the cinema, as is witnessed in C. T. Lee's finding (1990) that some 70 per cent of the most popular local movies of the 1980s were comedies of a farcical or absurd nature. In a similar vein, Sze (1994) laments the standardization and mediocrity of the local cinema and television drama, in both of which gangster and comedy genres predominate.

If the paucity of the 'protest' element in popular culture denotes a satisfied and quiescent population, its homogenizing tendency bespeaks a people with a homogeneous lifestyle and outlook. Apparently, belief in the openness of the society and in the equality of opportunity has had the effect of obliterating class differences and class inequality in Hong Kong. Popular culture bears the imprint of this effect, reflecting a salient feature of the Hong Kong ethos and social structure.

Cultural consumption speaks much of the absence of class subcultures in Hong Kong. Not that objective class differences are absent, but that, with the lack of well-entrenched social classes and a perceived opportunity for social mobility, subjective feelings of class identities and differences, not to mention enmity, are very weak. This goes a long way towards explaining why the element of social protest and criticism so common in many popular cultures of other countries is conspicuously absent in Hong Kong (Choi 1990: 538–9).

Conclusion

In this chapter we have examined how a uniquely Hong Kong culture has evolved as a product of the interaction between the Chinese culture and the Hong Kong experience. We noted on the basis of empirical studies that the Hong Kong culture is characterized predominantly by an amoral, utilitarian ethos. This ethos is reflected in the Hong Kong people's attitudes towards work, politics, and the relationship between the individual and society. We also pointed out that another prominent feature of the Hong Kong culture is the widespread belief that the society affords abundant opportunities for social and economic advancement. We maintained that the territory's stability and prosperity can be in part attributed to this belief—the so-called Hong Kong Dream—which renders the people willing to bear with the trials and tribulations of life in anticipation of a better tommorow.

The evolution of Hong Kong's popular culture similarly reflects the interaction between traditional Chinese culture and the Hong Kong experience. The emergence and consolidation of an indigenous Hong Kong popular culture took place against the background of the coming to age of a generation of local-borns, whose values and preferences mirrored their life experiences in Hong Kong. Hence the themes of survival, affluence, and deliverance have become the dominant motifs in the society's popular culture. On the other hand, the non-salience of class consciousness and class conflict in Hong Kong has been reflected in the paucity of treatments of social protest and critique in popular culture products. As Hong Kong prepares for its reunification with China, its people are going through a new experience and a new challenge. The Hong Kong people's relationship with their compatriots in the motherland and with their future sovereign political master have been a new subject-matter in the territory's popular culture in recent years.

Notes

1. For a more detailed discussion of traditional Chinese culture, see Lau and Kuan (1988: 1–18).
2. There are two additional measures of strain in Wong's research, centred on questions of 'confidence in the future of Hong Kong' and 'whether it is meaningful to make long-term plans'. For parsimony and the thematic continuity of our discussion, we focus on only one of the three measures.
3. Referring to comments by several industrial relations specialists on working conditions in Hong Kong, David Levin observes: 'For these critics, the lot of many Hong Kong workers is one of misery, oppression, degradation, exploitation and alienation' (Levin 1990: 85). For evidence of the low level of industrial conflict in Hong Kong in comparison with other industrial countries, see J. P. Lee (1988, p. 69, table 1).
4. Turner et al. also claimed that their findings revealed job security and friendly workmates, in addition to good pay, to be their respondents' work priorities. While this finding suggests that the Hong Kong worker has other important work considerations besides pay, it does not refute the assertion that pay is a major concern. See Levin (1990: 99), for a discussion of the ambiguities in, and the possible interpretations of, the data presented by Turner et al.
5. Despite the considerations mentioned, Lui's study falls short of explicitly relating his empirical findings and discussion to Hong Kong's socio-economic context. The following exposition of Lui's study inevitably shares these inadequacies.
6. The proportion of respondents who discussed community problems with friends and neighbours varied between 24 and 46 per cent in the four districts. Lau comments: 'the level of concern for the community and the amount of discussion of local affairs reported by the respondents were not particularly high. However, this is already a far cry from the political apathy and social aloofness so rampant in the past' (Lau and Kuan 1986: 36). Lau's remark applies also to the respondents' support for unconventional political tactics; respondents who considered unconventional political tactics to be the most effective means to change Government policies ranged from 2 per cent to 9 per cent in the districts. For details, see Lau and Kuan (1986: 36, 39, table 1.7).
7. Lau obtained data on participation in eleven types of social and political activities, such as discussing community affairs with others, talking to Government officials, using unconventional tactics to influence the Government, participating in activities to improve one's community, participating in the activities of the Mutual Aid Committees, and registering as a voter in District Board elections.
8. Lau argues that if people see political participation as instrinsically valuable, they should be consistently active in different types of participation. The people of Hong Kong, however, apparently participated in a calculated, ad hoc manner when events threatened their personal interests. For this reason, Lau concluded that they adopted an instrumental orientation to political participation.

9. Among other works, Lau and Kuan referred to an unpublished monograph by Elaine Chan and Joseph Chan, 'Pragmatism in a Changing Political Era: The Ambivalence of Hong Kong College Students' (date not given). On the basis of their empirical data, Chan and Chan conclude that Hong Kong college students were attracted to democracy for pragmatic rather than ideological reasons.

10. The discussion in this section is based on Yiu (1983), Wong Jim (1995), and Luk (1995).

11. The discussion in this section is based on Choi (1990), Wong Jim (1995), Chan Kai-cheung (1995), Yiu (1983), and Lilley (1993).

12. Choi observes that a large number of Cantonese popular songs in recent years are cover versions of Japanese, Taiwanese, and English songs (Choi 1990: 546).

13. The evidence, based on statistics cited in Choi (1990; especially pp. 541–5) attests to this hegemonic position. Towards the end of the 1980s, the domestic-to-foreign ratio in the Hong Kong record market was about 6:4 (notwithstanding the heavy demand for foreign records from tourists), whereas the corresponding ratio for other non-socialist Asian countries with the exception of Japan is 1:9. Cantonese songs also had a virtual monopoly of the annual Top Ten Chinese Gold Songs awards since the late 1970s, with only 5 Mandarin songs, in contrast to 115 Cantonese songs, winning the award in the period 1978–89. Popular concerts held in the 12,500-seat Hong Kong Coliseum have similarly been skewed in favour of Cantonese songs: the ratio of annual attendance at 'local' and 'foreign' concerts from 1983 to 1989 was about 9:1. Evidence such as the above led Choi to conclude: 'Hong Kong has indeed come a long way from the 1960s and 1970s, when Mandarin songs, apart from English ones, dominated the market' (Choi 1990: 542).

14. For a detailed account of the box-office returns of the top ten grossing local and foreign films in Hong Kong in 1989, see Choi (1990: 551–2, especially tables 8 and 9).

15. Apart from attributing this phenomenon to the Hong Kong people's lack of interest in politics, Wong observes that the Chinese people have not been traditionally disposed to use music as a medium of protest or social criticism. He further maintains that there is a general belief among the Chinese that serious subjects, such as social criticism, should be conveyed in the Mandarin literary style rather than in a dialect. In Wong's view, the above conventions impose constraints on the lyrical contents of Cantonese popular songs.

4. The Family and Society

THE family is perhaps the most important social institution mediating between the individual and society. As the primary agency of socialization, it inculcates in its members fundamental values and orientations that bear significantly on the ways they relate to other people and to society. Much of what happens in the society at large can be illuminated through an examination of processes within the family, but the family itself is in turn subject to influences from society. Its structure, functioning, internal relationships, and its impact on individual members are contingent on the character of the social environment. This relationship between the family and society is the main subject of our discussion in this chapter. In the following pages, we attempt to advance our understanding of Hong Kong society and of the Hong Kong family through an investigation of their reciprocal influences.

The Family and Social Change in Hong Kong: The Structural-functionalist Analysis

In regard to the family, structural-functionalists maintain that the family's form, size, and functions are related to other aspects of society, and that these attributes change in adaptation to transformations in the social structure. F. M. Wong adopted this paradigm for his studies of the impact of social change on the family in Hong Kong (F. M. Wong 1972, 1975, 1979, 1981). His arguments, which have been challenged subsequently by a number of scholars, delineate three main stages in the evolution of the Hong Kong family, each corresponding to periods marked by major structural changes in the society.

Early Hong Kong society, which covers the period from the beginnings of the Colony to the 1940s, had a transient population consisting largely of immigrants from China who had come for work and would leave after making enough money for a comfortable life in their homeland. The typical immigrant family at the time consisted of a few relatives, mostly males in their productive age, together sharing an abode or living with a kin-related married couple. Severed temporarily from their kinsfolk and often also from their own family members back home, these immigrants nevertheless maintained close ties with relatives on the mainland. Wong calls the ensuing family 'the temporary, broken extended family', in the double sense that it was a temporary break-off from the extended family in the homeland and that it comprised kinsfolk beyond the nucleus of a married couple and its children. In keeping with the traditional values and practices of the family back home, it remained a patriarchal unit in which power remained with the senior male.

The second stage in the evolution of the family began after the Second World War with the influx of refugees from China who, unhappy with Communist rule, regarded Hong Kong as their permanent home. A new form emerged, as family members were reunited and immigrant families settled in the Colony. According to Wong, the typical Hong Kong family was now organized around the main trunk of a married couple, with the addition of their unmarried children and one or both parents of the husband. Wong calls this the 'settled stem family'. It maintained frequent contacts and exchanges of gifts and assistance with extended kinsfolk in Hong Kong, as these activities were vital for survival in an otherwise unfamiliar social environment, and it retained most of the values and practices of the traditional Chinese family.

Hong Kong's industrialization in the 1950s and after, Wong argues, gradually eroded the stem family and precipitated the rise and prevalence of another form. This is the 'small nuclear family', composed of a married couple with or without unmarried children. This nuclear family, with its reliance on industrial employment, was the main focus of Wong's studies of the Hong Kong family. In analysis of this form, he most directly and explicitly resorts to the structural-functionalist paradigm. Basing his arguments primarily on Talcott Parsons' isolated nuclear family thesis (Parsons 1943; Parsons and Bales 1955), Wong maintains that functional specialization and increased social and geographical mobility in industrial societies have contributed to a loss of most of the functions of the traditional family and to the spatial separation of extended kinsfolk from the family unit. The ensuing nuclear family is hence smaller in size and more isolated from its kinsfolk than was its predecessor, the extended family.

Wong's research (1972, 1975) dwells mainly on the form and size of the family as well as its internal relationships in industrial Hong Kong. His data, based on census reports (Barnett 1961, 1969; Census and Statistics Department, Pilot Census 1960), show that in the early 1960s the majority (some 62 per cent) of Hong Kong families were nuclear families consisting of a couple with unmarried children, and that the overall average family size was 5.81 persons. In his view, the evidence attests to the predominance of the small nuclear family in industrial Hong Kong. He believed that a trend toward nuclear families would become more accentuated in the process of industrialization.

Hong Kong's industrialization, Wong maintains, has substantially increased employment opportunities for women and, as a result, has significantly advanced their position within the family. He observes, on the basis of his research findings (F. M. Wong 1979, 1981) that the wife's paid employment has contributed to much greater equality between the spouses, in the sharing of household duties and in decision-making:

With the participation of women in the occupational world, the traditional husband-dominant family has rapidly decreased in importance and practice, and the conventional home-making role of the mother has greatly diminished and is increasingly shared by other members of the family, particularly the husband (F. M. Wong 1981: 229–30).

Wong further finds support for the isolated nuclear family thesis in indications of a heightened interdependence among family members. He notes that the nuclear families 'became structurally isolated from external social systems, and tended to evolve into an independent, closely knitted system of their own' (F. M. Wong 1979: 109). His data indicate, for instance, that children continued active involvement in household duties and other family matters, as well as frequent exchange of support and assistance between parents and children, even after the latter have married and set up their own separate households. In industrializing Hong Kong, members of the nuclear family had to rely for support primarily on themselves and each other, as extended kin were no longer a readily available source. Wong's portrait of the contemporary Hong Kong family and the role of industrialization in its development, however, have been thrown into doubt by subsequent studies.

The Family and Social Change in Hong Kong: Myth and Reality

Wong's thesis on the family in industrial Hong Kong has been challenged on both empirical and theoretical grounds. Empirically, a host of census and research data argue against the supposition that industrialization has contributed to the increasing prevalence of the small nuclear family in the territory. Lee Ming-kwan (1987a) was one of the first critics to systematically debunk on the basis of statistical information what he castigates as the 'myth of the nuclear family'. Citing census reports, Lee observes that while in 1976 nuclear families made up 60 per cent of all families in Hong Kong, by 1981 the figure had dropped to 54 per cent. In the same period, the stem family increased from 9 to 13 per cent of all Hong Kong families. Although subsequent census statistics (Census and Statistics Department 1987b: 8; 1993: 5) reflect an increase in the proportion of nuclear families (to 59 per cent in 1986, 61 per cent in 1991), the overall picture indicates that the nuclear family has not in the process of industrialization attained the prevalence predicted by Wong.

In place of Wong's thesis, Lee (1987a, 1987b) looks for an explanation to the Government's public housing policies, which carried different specifications for family size and membership of public housing tenants at different times.[1] The impact of these policies on the family has been great, as over 40 per cent of Hong Kong's residents have lived in public housing since 1981. This is Lee's explanation for the fluctuating trend in the percentages of nuclear families over the years. His central message is that factors other than industrialization are more pertinent in accounting for the size and form of the Hong Kong family.

Wong's view on the family's relationships with kin and other social groups has also been subjected to criticisms, although in this case some seem to be unjustified. Lee (1987a), for instance, attacks Wong for allegedly glossing over the family's frequent interaction and exchange of assistance with kinsfolk. Lee's 1977 research (Lee 1987a) shows that the people with whom the families in his study most often spent their leisure time were close relatives, followed by colleagues, friends, distant relatives, and lastly neighbours. His more recent findings from the large-scale Social Indicators Project (Lee Ming-kwan 1991) further reflect the importance of kin, friends, and neighbours as a source of assistance and support for the family.[2] These findings led Lee to the conclusion that 'the families are far from being structurally isolated' (Lee Ming-kwan 1991: 46).

In a similar vein, Ng Chung-hung (1989) launched a scathing attack on Wong with reference to empirical studies. In respect of family values, Bartlett Stoodley's study (1967) of students at the Chinese University of Hong Kong shows that they believed their parents had the right to intervene in their choice of marital partner; the students also subscribed to the view that children should follow their parents' instructions. David Podmore and David Chaney's research (1974) similarly testifies to the persistence of traditional family values, such as filial piety, mutual help, and respect within the family, among the young respondents in their sample. Sherry Rosen's intensive study (1976) of twenty middle-class families reveals close interaction and mutual help between parents and children even after the latter's marriage. Janet Salaff's study (1981) of twenty-eight working daughters demonstrates in detail how they made sacrifices in their education, career, and marriage for the collective interests of the family. Studies such as the above fuelled Ng's criticism that Wong had grossly underestimated the viability of traditional family values and practices in urban industrial Hong Kong.

Many of Ng's criticisms, however, as well as a number of Lee's, are misdirected, for one of Wong's central arguments is that the nuclear family compensates for the breakdown of its wider social networks through strengthening the ties between parents and children and among siblings (F. M. Wong 1979: 109–11).[3] In this light, the studies Ng used to refute Wong—all of which are about the strength of the parent-child relationship—turn out to be supporting testimonies. Lee's criticism, in so far as it addresses the continuing importance of the wider kin and social networks to the family, is much closer to the mark. In particular, his use of the term 'modified extended family' to describe the contemporary Hong Kong family (Lee Ming-kwan 1987a) rectifies some of the misrepresentations in Wong's portrait.

It is in the area of marital relationships that Wong's observations have proven to be least able to stand the test of subsequent empirical studies. Data from the Social Indicators Project (Lau and Wan 1987: 36) indicate that in the majority of cases (over 60 per cent of the respondents), the female household head was primarily responsible for household duties such as cooking, cleaning, washing and ironing clothes, and managing daily expenses. Only slightly over 10 per cent of the respondents reported having the male household head in primary charge of these duties. Lee's more recent study (1992: 13) on gender issues similarly finds the wife to be the person in charge of household chores in the majority (72 per cent) of the cases; the husband was responsible for such duties among only 4 per cent of the respondents. A study of married women in Tuen Mun (Tuen Mun District Board 1991: 18–19) shows a still more uneven division of household tasks between spouses. Household duties and child care were the main responsibilities of the wife among some 80 per cent of the respondents; the husband was responsible for these tasks in less than 1 per cent of the homes surveyed.

However, the wife's much greater role in household duties has not given her a corresponding share of power within the family. In fact, it is often the husband rather than the wife who makes the important decisions on family matters. Findings from the Social Indicators Project (Lau and Wan 1987: 36) show that some 26 per cent of the respondents reported having such decisions made by the husband; in only 12 per cent of the cases were they made by the wife. In Lee's study (1992: 13), the corresponding figures are 32 per cent for the husband and 14 per cent for the wife. The above studies on division of labour and decision-making within the family prove beyond doubt that the husband–wife relationship is far less egalitarian than Wong would have us believe.[4]

It is evident that in applying the structural-functionalist paradigm uncritically to the local context, Wong has exaggerated and misconstrued the impact of industrialization on the Hong Kong family. Part of the problem with his analysis lies in the structural-functionalist assumption that the extended family is the prevalent form in pre-industrial societies and that the predominance of the small nuclear family in industrial societies therefore testifies to a 'revolution in family patterns' consequent upon industrialization.[5] Research on the pre-industrial family has found this assumption to be an erroneous one. Historian Peter Laslett's research (1972, 1977), for instance, found that only about 10 per cent of households in pre-industrial England contained kin beyond the nuclear family. The percentage remained the same for England in 1966. He similarly demonstrated that the nuclear family was the prevalent type of family in America and many European countries in the pre-industrial era.[6] The situation in pre-industrial China was probably no different. C. K. Yang's study (1959) of a village in China in the late 1940s found the average size of the family there to be about 4.8 persons. Olga Lang (1946) cited statistics from a survey conducted by the Chinese government in 1934–5 in twenty-two provinces which showed that the average family size was 5.5 persons. Evidence such as the above discredits the thesis that the small nuclear family is the by-product of industrialization.

Despite the refutation that industrialization has itself prompted a change from an extended to a nuclear family unit, sociologists do agree generally that industrialization has affected the family in a number of ways. Wong's work fails in that he has not taken sufficient account of the special circumstances of Hong Kong's industrialization when he has analysed its impact on the family. A different picture of the contemporary Hong Kong family emerges when this shortfall is rectified, as is witnessed in the following studies.

Ramifications of Traditional Familism in Industrial Hong Kong: The Utilitarianistic Familism Thesis

Lau Siu-kai (1981) was the first scholar to advance the thesis that familistic values and practices were valuable assets in the individual's struggle for survival and socio-economic advancement in the early phase of Hong

Kong's industrialization. At a time when refugees were flooding in from China and trying to adapt to life in a new social environment, the colonial government adhered to its *laissez-faire* policies and was both unwilling and unable to look after the needs of a quickly expanding population. To cope with the exigencies of the situation, the Hong Kong Chinese turned to the family and familial groups for assistance, as they traditionally had been disposed to do in times of difficulties. This was the context for the reinforcement of traditional familism.

It was a modified form of Chinese familism which eventually emerged in Hong Kong. If traditional Chinese familism was functional, integrating the individual into the social-political system through its close linkages with wider social and political networks, the Hong Kong brand of familism had the effect of creating a gulf between the individual and the larger society. This distancing, in Lau's view, was the consequence of Hong Kong's special political and economic circumstances. The territory's undemocratic political system, coupled with a rapidly growing industrial economy, meant that opportunities for social advancement were abundant in the economic realm but non-existent in the political sphere. The family was therefore important to the individual only for the pursuit of economic and material interests, for in the Hong Kong context it was wealth rather than engagement in social and political affairs that conferred status and influence. Lau termed the resulting familial ethos 'utilitarianistic familism':

Utilitarianistic familism can be defined as a normative and behavioural tendency of an individual to place his familial interests above the interests of society or any of its component individuals and groups, and to structure his relationships with other individuals and groups in such a fashion that the furtherance of his familial interests is the primary consideration. Moreover, among the familial interests material interests take priority over all other interests (Lau 1981: 201).

Relationships within the family and between the family and the larger society, in Lau's view, can be understood from the perspective of utilitarianistic familism. Thus, intra-familial relationships tended to be predicated on mutual exchange of material assistance rather than on status hierarchy. The boundary of the family could also be pragmatically extended to include distant relatives and even friends if they were important in advancing the family's material interests. It was this 'familial network', rather than social welfare organizations and government departments, which the individual turned to for material support in times of need. The above contentions, Lau noted, were supported by his research data. A significant percentage (slightly above 50 per cent) of the respondents, for instance, reported having recently exchanged financial or other assistance with family members. In addition, the prevalence of family-owned and operated business firms in Hong Kong was evidence of the proclivity of family members to cooperate as an economic unit to advance their collective material interests.

This cooperative activity was undertaken often at the cost of compartmentalizing and alienating the family from other social groups. Lau's view on the utilitarianistic family is deprecatory: 'society is considered to be largely insignificant, and the family is to "exploit" society for its own utilitarian purposes' (Lau 1981: 202). His research findings show that only a minority (13.5 per cent) of the respondents considered society to be more important than the family, and that the proportion of respondents who had joined voluntary associations of any kind was as low as 19.6 per cent. Evidence such as the above led Lau to the conclusion that the people of Hong Kong would shun involvement with other social groups so long as it did not serve the private interests of the individual and the family. It would appear from Lau's perspective that if the Hong Kong family was socially isolated, it was because of its utilitarian ethos rather than the effect of functional specialization in industrial societies as Wong alleged.

Despite its close look at the dynamics of family involvement in the territory, Lau's study of the family was guided by a still larger objective: the explanation of political stability in Hong Kong. In this investigation we have an exemplary illustration of the bearing of family values and practices on the functioning of the whole society. Castigating the clichéd 'traditional political apathy' explanation (King 1981a)[7] as devoid of institutional grounding, and the 'élite support' theory (King 1981b)[8] as deficient in failing to address the mobilization potential of the masses, Lau sought to fill in the lacunae through recourse to his utilitarianistic familism thesis. The family, he contends, was the institution which nurtured and sustained political apathy. Furthermore, the family's role in catering to the material needs of the individual had the unintended consequence of absorbing social discontents which otherwise would be a potent source of social disruption. Finally, the utilitarianistic ethos of the family in severing the ties between its members and other social groups rendered mass mobilization for collective action extremely difficult. In Lau's view, it was such 'familial absorption of politics' that contributed to Hong Kong's political stability.

Lau's utilitarianistic familism thesis carried a foreboding for the future. The Government's vast expansion in social service and welfare provisions since the mid-1970s has substantially relieved the family of its welfare role. Familism has declined, Lau maintains, but the utilitarian ethos persists. The outcome has been the rise of a new ethos which Lau terms 'utilitarian' or 'egotistical individualism' (Lau 1983). Deprived of the depoliticizing buffer of the family, the Government and emergent political leaders have now to gear their policies and political platforms to the self-interested, utilitarian demands of the masses.[9]

Ramifications of Traditional Familism in Industrial Hong Kong: The Modified Centripetal Family Thesis

The term 'centripetal family' was introduced by Bernard Farber (1975) to denote the type of family which gathers the resources and contributions of its members for the furtherance of their collective interests as a familial group. It prevails in social-political systems in which particularistic interests and connections, including those of the family and the kin group, play a legitimate and crucial role in the attainment of wealth and power. In such societies, the family can command the loyalty of its members because their well-being often depends on that of the family. The family in traditional Chinese society is of the centripetal type, and Salaff's research (1981, 1995)[10] has led her to the view that the centripetal family still prevails in a modified form in contemporary Hong Kong. On this conceptual basis she conducted an analysis of gender inequality in Hong Kong families and society. To argue for the survival of the traditional Chinese family, albeit in a modified form, in modern industrial Hong Kong implies a rejection of the thesis (Inkeles 1960; Kerr et al. 1960; Miller 1976) that across all cultures, industrialization has uprooted and transformed traditional social institutions.[11] This convergence thesis, Salaff points out, overlooks the continued relevance, and hence resilience, of traditional values and practices in particular socio-cultural settings. The Hong Kong family is a good illustration of this resilience.

In Salaff's view, the harsh conditions of Hong Kong's first phase of industrialization—low wages combined with the lack of welfare provisions from the Government—rendered it necessary for the majority of the population to rely on family and kin for economic assistance. The family thus became the centre of the individual's concern and allegiance, but as its control over individual members was by no means as pervasive as that of its traditional counterpart, Salaff refers to it as the 'modified centripetal family'. The modified centripetal family was able to gather, allocate, and use its members' contributions for the purpose of economic survival and betterment. This form of domestic cooperation and management of resources is called the family wage economy. The way of its operation had a significant impact on the lives of its individual members. To expound on this point, Salaff focuses on the patriarchal nature of the centripetal family.

The centripetal family in traditional China was a patriarchy in that it was a male-dominated institution in which power resided ultimately with the male household head. The survival of patriarchal values and practices depends much on the family's sway over its members. Consequently, in reinforcing the individual's reliance on the family, industrialization in Hong Kong also sustained the patriarchal tradition. The family wage economy operated under the shadow of the patriarchal family. In vivid details, Salaff (1995) describes how the twenty-eight working daughters in her study made sacrifices in their education and career, and contributed a substantial part of their income, for the well-being of their family and their brothers. In times of economic hardship, they were usually the ones to quit school, working to supplement the family's income and thus to enable their brothers to continue with their education. It was also usually they, rather than their brothers, who assisted in household duties and shouldered the responsibility of looking after younger siblings. Despite their contributions, however, they were barred from important family decision-making. In short, the prerogatives of the patriarchal family circumscribed their major choices and endeavours in life. It is from this perspective that Salaff moved from a study of the predicament of working daughters within the family to an analysis of the social foundation of gender inequality in Hong Kong.

The Family and Society

Underlying Salaff's analysis is the thesis that the modified centripetal family, with its patriarchal values, contributed to and sustained a vicious cycle of gender discrimination in Hong Kong. The patriarchal family substantially detracted from women's achievement in the occupational world, both because it instilled in them the view that a woman's priority was the home and because it made disproportionately heavy demands on their time, energy, and resources. The outcome was women's generally poorer educational attainment, lower occupational position, and lower pay, compared to those of their male counterparts.

Women's subordination to the demands of the patriarchal family also rendered them the easy target of exploitation by employers, as the following remark from the factory managers in Salaff's study reflects: 'The girls are willing to work hard for long hours at piecework occupations in order to boost their take-home pay.... [This] raises our productivity and profits' (Salaff 1995: 22). On the other hand, the family's patriarchal practices fuelled the belief common among government and private employers that women's main concerns and commitments in life were to the family rather than to their career. The result was a lack of job training for women workers and a further depression of their pay and career prospects. Women's inferior status and lower pay in the occupational domain in turn fed back into the family and reinforced its patriarchal practice of investing in the son's rather than the daughter's education and career for the long-term benefit of the family wage economy. Gender discrimination was recycled through the family to the larger society and back again to the family.

In this light, the patriarchal values and practices characterisitic of the modified centripetal family may be seen as a main culprit in the perpetuation of gender inequality in Hong Kong. For this reason, the battle against gender discrimination had to launch a frontal attack on the modified centripetal family. The only solution, in the final analysis, was a rectification of the social foundation that nurtured this type of family in Hong Kong:

Change in the centripetal family form presupposes the establishment of a central political structure with institutions that will reward the populace for expending its energies toward fulfilment of societal goals. A social security system with guaranteed assistance in old age and other times of need and a universal education system to recruit members into wider societal institutions are preconditions to an alternative family form (Salaff 1995: 44).

The alternative family form which Salaff deems to be conducive to greater gender equality within the family and in the larger society is the centrifugal family, in which the members' well-being and advancement depend far more on their roles and performances in extra-familial institutions than within the family itself. One may note in this connection that Hong Kong's socio-economic and political changes in the past two decades—the opening up of the society's opportunity structure, the Government's vastly expanded role in welfare and social service provisions, the institutionalization of nine years of free, compulsory, and universal education, and the development towards a more representative form of government—have had the effect of reducing the population's dependence on the family and shifting their commitment and concern to societal goals and issues. Yet in Salaff's view (1995: Preface to the Morningside Edition), most Hong Kong people still rely heavily on the family for support and services:

> Today, as was the case in the 1970s, the colonial government's social policy is referred to as 'minimum support'.... The development of the economy and technical infrastructure have taken place without a welfare state program.... The underfunding of support services places a particular burden on women and on their family members to help each other (Salaff 1995: xxvii–xxviii).

As notable examples of the inadequacy of Government-funded social services, Salaff refers to the lack of low-cost public child care and of low-cost homes for the elderly. The latter is creating an increasing burden for families, as Hong Kong since the mid-1980s has witnessed a rising proportion of elderly people in its population, and as the Hong Kong Chinese value support of the elderly (Salaff 1995: xxviii–xxix). To the extent that the care for the young and the elderly still falls largely on the family, the modified centripetal family is sustained in present-day Hong Kong. Indeed, there is ample evidence that patriarchal values and practices linger on, both within the family and in society at large. Ng's writings on the family (1991, 1993, 1994, 1995) testify to the veracity of this observation.

The Modern Domestic Ideal and Household Strategies in Industrial Hong Kong

The modern domestic ideal upholds the home as the primary domain for the realization of values among the most cherished in advanced industrial societies. According to some writers (Hall 1982; Hareven 1991), this ideal is the product of advanced industrialization and is widely held among the middle class in such societies. In relocating economic production from the home to other specialized social units, industrialization has concomitantly made it possible for the home to be regarded as the place for recuperation from the toil of work, as well as for the pursuit of comfort, tastes, and a lifestyle that distinguishes its incumbents from the less fortunate members of society. The middle class is particularly well equipped, socio-economically, to use the home as the signifier of material and cultural accomplishments. The movement towards the ideal of the small nuclear family, with the attendant exclusion of extended kin and non-familial members from the home, mirrors the quest of members of the middle class for domestic privacy, another integral feature of the modern domestic ideal. At the same time, the child becomes the centre of the family's concerns. Ng (1993, 1994, 1995) contends that with the rapid expansion of the middle class in recent years, the Hong Kong family has been developing towards this modern domestic ideal.[12]

Ng advances the thesis that industrialization, in inculcating the modern domestic ideal, has accentuated the importance and independence of the family, at least among the middle class, in modern industrial Hong Kong. The family has become the zealously guarded domain of private choices and actions, and it conveniently falls back on time-honoured familial roles in fulfilment of the modern domestic ideal. The traditional 'breadwinner' role of the father–husband and the homemaking and child-caring role of the mother–wife have been revived in contemporary Hong Kong. The so-called double burden of the modern woman can be understood in this light, for her paid employment outside the home has by no means liberated her from the yoke of household chores and child care. But this burden is often submerged under the romance and glory of the modern home. Empirical findings, Ng observes, bear testimony to the camouflaged and suppressed discontents of the modern Hong Kong woman:[13]

Most [female respondents] said they were satisfied with their family life, and thought sex discrimination to be not a major social problem.... Yet on deeper and more unstructured probes, many expressed frustrations with various aspects of housework and generally felt discontented with the housewife role, be it a full-time or a 'dual-career' one. They also resented the fact that their career plan and economic activities had been involuntarily interrupted by childcare and household responsibilities (Ng Chung-hung 1994: 106).

The modern domestic ideal is the product of an advanced, affluent industrial society, and it is widely practised only among the economically better-off middle class. Throughout much of the history of Hong Kong's industrialization, and among a substantial portion of the population, the more down-to-earth concerns of survival and economic betterment have remained the imperatives of the family. Lee Ming-kwan and Ng Chung-hung's study (1991) of the life histories of twenty-two families in Hong Kong since the early 1950s throws light on the strategies these families adopted in response to the challenges and promises of industrialization. The findings lend further support to the thesis that Hong Kong's families relied primarily on their internal resources to survive economic hardships, and in doing so, absorbed the harsh impact of the early phase of industrialization and contributed to the society's smooth transition to an advanced industrial economy.

The strategies deployed by the families—or household strategies as they are called in the pertinent literature—were geared to the attainment of a variety of family objectives which differed in relation to each family's socio-economic situation. In Lee and Ng's account (Lee and Ng 1991; Ng 1991), these objectives ranged from the modest goals of survival, piecemeal aggrandizement, or professional advance, to the ambitious ones of entrepreneurship and corporate business advance.[14] The families in their study, having mostly a working-class origin, seldom reached beyond the objective of piecemeal aggrandizement. Survival remained their highest priority during the 1950s and 1960s, when the meagre income of the male household head had to be supplemented by financial contributions from his wife and grown children. Indeed, everyone of the grown females in Lee and Ng's study had had some sort of employment experience—a fact which suggests that the traditional Chinese ideal of the full-time housewife does not apply to the family in financial difficulty. It was only when the family's fortunes improved that the mother–wife gave up her job, often at the dictate of family prerogatives, to attend to household chores and child care. Nor were the sons given privileged treatment in education and career in times of hardship; many had to interrupt their education to work in order to contribute to the family budget. Their sacrifice in this respect was no different from that of the working daughters in Salaff's study. Economic hardship, Ng observes (1991), demands resource mobilization from all able family members, obviating in effect the family's gender-based considerations.

In the course of their struggle for survival, these families seldom relied on the Government or voluntary welfare agencies for assistance. Ng (1991) notes that only in three cases was the church mentioned as a source of major help in times of crisis, and assistance from the Government was conspicuously absent. Yet despite their strife and endeavour, most of these working-class families did not succeed in uplifting themselves to the ranks of the affluent. Towards the end of the 1980s the children had moved ahead of their parents socio-economically, but still none had more than a secondary education, and none were in a position to advance themselves further through financial investments. As Ng remarks, 'one can hardly term their mobility as long-ranged or spectacular' (Ng Chung-hung 1994: 100). Lee and Ng's study reflects a central truth of Hong Kong's recent history: that the birth pangs of the territory's industrialization were borne stoically by working-class families, and that behind the miracle of the territory's economic success lie such hidden injuries of class.

There were exceptions to the general picture presented above. There were also other, better-off families whose household strategies were targeted at the objectives of entrepreneurship and corporate advance. Their success is further testimony to the continual relevance of traditional Chinese family values and practices in Hong Kong's industrial economy.

The Family and the Hong Kong Economy

Economic sociologists generally subscribe to the view that the modern capitalist economy operates on principles antipathetic to those of the family. The former seeks to maximize efficiency through following the impersonal principle of meritocracy. The latter treats its members as equally deserving of its care and benevolence irrespective of their individual capabilities. From this perspective, the development towards modern capitalism is impeded in societies where family values and practices spill over into the economy. The Hong Kong experience, however, tells a different story.

A salient feature of Hong Kong's economy is the prevalence within it of family-owned and operated business enterprises. Wong Siu-lun remarks, on the basis of empirical evidence, 'there is little doubt that family firms have been prevalent in Chinese commerce and industry operating on capitalistic principles' (Wong Siu-lun 1985: 59). As illustrations, he cites the case of the cotton-spinning industry, in which at least half of the enterprises in 1978 had the majority of their stock held by single families. Family ownership similarly prevails in the area of finance, as Wong's citation from a Hong Kong-based banker shows: 'all overseas Chinese banks [are] run by banking families' (Wong Siu-lun 1985: 59). Familism also characterizes the managerial style of many of these Hong Kong Chinese enterprises. A leading Hong Kong businessman observes:

The principles of family organization were applied in the business unit. There were those who governed and there were those who were governed, each according to his ability but all having an equal interest in the success of the operation. ... Decision-making was patriarchal and autocratic, control was centralized and delegation minimal.[15]

In a similar vein, industrial relations specialist Joe England describes the Hong Kong worker's attitude as heavily moulded by the Chinese 'familial traditions of obedience and loyalty to autocratic authority' (England 1989: 42). Nepotism, the preferential recruitment and promotion of one's relatives, has also significantly infiltrated into the business operations of the local Chinese. Wong (1988b) estimates this to have been practised by about half of the Hong Kong Chinese firms. It is evident that familism in the forms of family ownership, paternalistic management, and nepotism has been a widespread practice among the territory's business enterprises. Yet Hong Kong's capitalist economy has been phenomenally successful. This anomaly requires an explanation.

We can first explain the prevalence of family firms through recourse to the household strategies discussed in the previous section. Wong (1988b) coins the term 'entrepreneurial familism' to refer to the household strategy that uses the family's resources for the inauguration and operation of business enterprises. This familial economic ethos permeates the whole society, and a combination of factors accounts for this commonality. In the first place, traditional Chinese familism predisposes the individual to view the family as the primary basis for socio-economic advancement. This predisposition, coupled with the abundant business opportunities created by Hong Kong's rapidly expanding economy, motivates the less well-off family to seek advancement through launching a business on the basis of pooled familial resources.

Better-off families, on the other hand, have rather different business considerations. Trust is an important element in business operations, and in Chinese communities personal trust has been an essential ingredient of business trust (Wong Siu-lun 1991; Redding 1991).[16] Given the special circumstances of Hong Kong's industrial take-off, in particular the disruption of the refugee population's social networks and their unfamiliarity with the new environment, family members and extended kin afforded a readily available—and the most reliable—form of personal trust. Family ownership and control of business was deployed as the strategy to cope with the problem of risk in an uncertain economic environment. In addition, one's own trustworthiness in business could be greatly enhanced with the backing of the family, especially in the case of the emigrant entrepreneurs from Shanghai, many of whom had substantial capital assets and a renowned business reputation.[17]

The family firm's paternalistic style of management, on the other hand, often turns out to be a strength rather than a drawback in Hong Kong's socio-cultural setting. In the first place, it is congruent with employees' expectations. Herbert A. Turner's large-scale study of work attitudes in Hong Kong reveals that the majority of workers (63 per cent of a sample of 1,000 respondents) believed that 'the employer of a firm should look after the interests of his workers like the head of a large family' (Turner 1980: 198). Benevolent paternalism, with its ensuing personalized relations between employers and employees, also helps to promote loyalty to the firm and to strengthen organizational solidarity. The paternalism of the Chinese family firm, in other words, has the effect of sapping the strength of trade unionism and minimizing industrial conflict in Hong Kong. England observes:

It is consistent with such a value system that employers should decide wages and benefits unilaterally and should be opposed to trade unionism, while workers expect employers to be paternal and are themselves little interested in unions (England 1989: 42).

In this light, familistic values and practices have not only buttressed the firm's organizational strength, but also contributed to Hong Kong's peaceful transition to industrial capitalism.

Nepotism, however, the third form of familism, can substantially detract from a firm's viability in a competitive capitalist economy. The Hong Kong Chinese firm overcomes this problem, and in fact turns it into a competitive advantage, by practising a qualified form of nepotism. It is worth noting that Chinese employers are nepotistic mainly with regard to immediate family members and are reluctant to appoint extended kin to their enterprises. For this reason, as Wong (1988a) discovered, nepotism usually accounts for only a small fraction of the firm's staff and is unlikely to handicap the firm's operation. Wong points out further that passive nepotism—the employment of relatives out of a sense of kinship obligation—is typically confined to positions of little importance within the firm.

Chinese employers, on the other hand, practise active nepotism through choosing to appoint family members for the sake of business interests. This strategy helps to ensure loyalty to the firm and to prevent the dissipation of family property and profits to outsiders. To minimize inefficiency in adopting this practice, family members to be appointed to top positions are meticulously prepared for the attendant responsibilities. Active nepotism is also resorted to, especially in small enterprises, to reduce operational costs and to cope with the problem of fluctuating demands in an export-oriented economy. A study by Sit and his associates (Sit et al. 1979) found that only 67 per cent of small Hong Kong factories gave as much pay to their kin employees as to non-kin workers. Moreover, family members can be relied on to provide flexible labour, to be expanded or contracted as market demands require. The resilience and success of the Hong Kong family firm are more often buttressed than hampered by its qualified nepotistic practices.

Familism not only impinges on the firm's daily operations but also defines the main contours of the family firm's long-term development. In this respect, Wong (1985, 1988a), on the basis of his empirical studies, has constructed a developmental model of the Hong Kong Chinese family firm. In the first, *emergent* phase, the family head, the so-called pater–entrepreneur, uses family savings to launch a business enterprise, often in partnership with non-kin members. When the pater–entrepreneur has amassed sufficient capital from this initial venture to set up his own business, the family enterprise enters the phase of *centralization*, during which business decisions are highly centralized in the hands of the pater–entreprenuer. The third phase, *segmentation*, begins with the pater–entrepreneur's retirement or death, when the family business goes to his male heirs. Sibling rivalry is contained in this phase usually through a formal agreement among the brothers on the division of responsibilities and company profits. The family enterprise thus remains intact until the sons of the brothers succeed the business. The number of members in the family economy has now so greatly multiplied that the family firm is constantly plagued by internal discords and conflicts of interests. This final *disintegration* phase is characterized by break-offs from the family business, many of which will in turn re-emerge as new family enterprises and go through the above cycle of development. As these off-shoots seek out economic opportunities and build their own business empires, they help to keep alive that spirit of entrepreneurial familism which has proved to be such a vital invigorating force in Hong Kong's economy.

Conclusion

Family studies in Hong Kong began with the attempt to demonstrate the alleged effects of industrialization on the family and its social networks. F. M. Wong's writings in this respect argue that under the impact of industrialization, the small isolated nuclear family emerged as the predominant family form in Hong Kong. His thesis has been subjected to a barrage of criticisms from other writers. In the first place, it has been pointed out that in following the structural-functionalist paradigm, Wong glossed over the fact that the nuclear family has been the prevalent form of family in both industrial and pre-industrial societies. A number of studies have also found that in the course of industrialization, the Hong Kong family has undergone no significant change in form and size. These studies argue further that the contemporary Hong Kong family is by no means socially isolated, as it still maintains fairly frequent contacts and exchanges of assistance with kin and other social networks. Lee Ming-kwan (1987a), in particular, suggests that the Hong Kong family of today can be viewed as a 'modified extended family': while the family is nucleated in form, its close ties with extended kin give it the resemblance of an extended family.

Wong has also been criticized for failing to couch his analysis in the specific context of Hong Kong's industrialization. This shortcoming was rectified in part by the studies of Lau Siu-kai (1981, 1982) and Salaff (1995), whose respective utilitarianistic familism thesis and modified centripetal family thesis converge in attributing the continuing centrality of the family to the individual's heavy reliance on the family to survive the hardship of Hong Kong's industrial take-off. But while the main objective of Lau's thesis is an explanation of Hong Kong's political stability in terms of the familial absorption of politics, that of Salaff's is to articulate a conceptual framework to account for the persistence of patriarchy and gender inequality in modern Hong Kong. Salaff's work, in addition, provides detailed ethnographic data to substantiate the numerous survey studies which show that gender relations within the family are far from the egalitarian pattern portrayed in Wong's studies.

It is worth pointing out that while crediting the family for bearing the burden of catering to the individual's welfare needs during the harsh years of Hong Kong's industrialization, Lau (1981) nevertheless depicts it as a fountain of egoistic and predative sentiments. In his view, family members relate to each other and to outsiders on a utilitarian basis. Other studies, however, present a far more positive image of the Hong Kong family. Salaff's working daughters (1995) made sacrifices in their education and career, and contributed a substantial part of their income, for the well-being of the family. Lee and Ng's (1991) study describes how, through household strategies, family members unselfishly shared family responsibilities and stoically bore the brunt of Hong Kong's economic transformation. It cannot be overlooked that even in these studies the family remains the individual's stronghold against the outside world, but this is a far cry from Lau's assertion that the Hong Kong family exploits society for its self-interests. Indeed, Salaff's study and Lee and Ng's study give us good reasons to believe that Hong Kong's success has been built by the self-reliant and self-sacrificing efforts of the family. It seems that in harping on the material support which the family affords its members, Lau has overstated the negative, utilitarian dimension of the Hong Kong family.[18]

Wong Siu-lun's entrepreneurial familism (1988a, 1988b) is a variation on utilitarianistic familism shorn of its predecessor's pejorative connotations. Wong's thesis is consistent with the notions of household strategies and family economy which inform Salaff's work and Lee and Ng's study. In his view, traditional Chinese familism is not necessarity a stumbling block to economic development. In a 'refugee' context of uncertainty, it in fact constitutes a solidary basis of trust and cooperation for the pursuit of economic interests. Economically aspiring families in Hong Kong have capitalized on this facet of traditional familism. The prevalence, resilience, and success of family enterprises in Hong Kong—an anomaly in modern capitalist economies—are in Wong's account explicable in terms of the population's familistic ethos. This ethos fuels the entrepreneurial spirit essential to modern capitalist development and inculcates a work ethic which disposes the worker to view the workplace as a familistic setting of collective cooperation and benefits. This work ethic, in turn, has reduced the incidence of industrial conflict in Hong Kong.

This last point brings us back to the objective of the chapter as stated in our opening remarks. Our primary concern has not been to provide a full account of family life in Hong Kong—the existing literature in any case does not warrant such an endeavour—but to advance our understanding of Hong Kong society through an investigation of the reciprocal relationship between the family and society. We hope to have established a view that much insight about Hong Kong's politics, gender relations, and economy can be distilled from studies of the Hong Kong family.

Notes

1. For instance, Lee pointed out that in the 1970s a married couple with one child would be eligible for public housing. Small nuclear families thus predominated in public housing units. In later years, in an attempt to encourage married children to live with their parents, the Housing Authority allowed public housing tenants to add to the household their married children and the children's family. This policy had the effect of increasing the size, and altering the composition, of families living in public housing units.

2. The proportion of respondents who had given financial and other forms of assistance to their parents in the previous six months were 71 per cent and 61 per cent, respectively. On the other hand, some 27 per cent and 46 per cent of the respondents had received financial and other kinds of assistance, respectively, from their parents in that same period. With regard to offering financial and other assistance to siblings, the figures were 41 per cent and 46 per cent. The corresponding figures for assistance among relatives were 30 per cent and 38 per cent, among neighbours 7 per cent and 38 per cent, and among friends 48 per cent and 60 per cent (Lee Ming-kwan 1991: 45, table 3.3).

3. Wong comments on the nuclear family's effort to cope with social isolation in this manner: [The families'] members were interdependent among one another not only for economic support and protection, but also for emotional sustenance. Hence in most cases, the relations between the parents and their children were strong.... [T]he parents' expectation of their children's responsibility, i.e. financial support of the parents in old age, tended to come true in both the views and conduct of their children. An overwhelming majority of the children, especially the first child, deemed it their duty to give money to their parents when they were gainfully employed. This was considered so even when they were married and had to support their own families or even if they happened to live away from their parents' (F. M. Wong 1979: 109, 111).

4. Wong's conclusions in this respect were that 'with the participation of women in the occupational world, the traditional husband-dominant family has rapidly decreased in importance and practice, and the conventional home-making role of the mother has greatly diminished.... [T]he working mother is seen to have moved out of her past institutional role and into a new role which allows her to ... collaborate with her husband in routine household tasks' (F. M. Wong 1981: 229–30). The studies just examined do not support this portrait.

5. Talcott Parsons and William Goode are two of the best known structural-functionalists who have advanced this thesis. See Parsons and Bales (1955) and Goode (1963).

6. In contrast, Michael Anderson (1980) pointed out on the basis of his empirical research that extended families were very common in pre-industrial Sweden, and that in pre-industrial Britain the gentry and yeoman farmers tended to have

large families. Still, one can say that on balance there is no substantial evidence to support the assertion that the large extended family was the prevalent form in most pre-industrial societies.

7. King's argument is that the Hong Kong Chinese continued to subscribe to the Chinese tradition of avoiding politics and of regarding politics to be the affairs of government officials. He considered the influence of these traditions to be a primary explanation for the territory's political stability.

8. The 'élite support' theory here refers to King's thesis of the 'administrative absorption of politics'. King maintains that the colonial government of Hong Kong depoliticized the Hong Kong Chinese through the strategy of absorbing members of the Chinese élites into the Government's administrative structure. For a more detailed discussion of this point, see Chapter 8.

9. See the section of Chapter 1 devoted to Lau Siu-kai's theoretical perspective for a more detailed discussion of this point.

10. Salaff's study was first published in 1981 and republished in 1995 with the addition of the 'Preface to the Morningside Edition'. The contents (and pagination) of the two editions in all other respects remain the same. The reader should bear in mind that the 1995 book—except for the new preface, in which she briefly updates her analysis on the basis of other scholars' research findings—refers to Hong Kong in the 1970s. I refer to the 1995 edition in my discussion as the first edition is now out of print.

11. For a detailed and critical analysis of the impact of industrialization on women in Hong Kong, see Benjamin K. P. Leung (1995).

12. As evidence for his argument, Ng cites the younger generation's preference for the neolocal, nuclear family; the blossoming of consumer goods such as toys, clothes, and educational packages that cater to the needs of children; the portrayal in the mass media of women as the contented moral guardians of juniors in the modern home; and the assumption in Government policies of the father–husband as the principal income-earner and the mother–wife as the dependent in the family (Ng Chung-hung 1993).

13. Here, Ng refers to the research findings reported in *The Hong Kong Women File* (Association for the Advancement of Feminism 1993: 76–8), rather than to specific individual empirical studies. The pertinent studies mentioned include Lau and Wan (1987), Lau et al. (1991), Tuen Mun District Board (1991), and Hong Kong Young Women's Association (1984).

14. 'Piecemeal aggrandizement' refers to modest improvements in the family's standard of living, such as a better-equipped household, increased purchasing powers, and better education for the children. 'Professional advance' refers to improvement in the family's socio-economic status consequent upon a member or members' entry into a professional or semi-professional occupation. 'Entrepreneurship' and 'corporate business advance' refer, respectively, to the family's setting up of a business enterprise and expanding the scale of the enterprise.

15. These remarks were made by Sir Chau Sik-nin, the first Chairman of the Hong Kong Management Association, in his paper, 'Family Management in Hong Kong', *The Hong Kong Manager*, 6(2) (March/April 1970); cited in England (1989: 40).

16. Wong writes: 'The ethic of trust is central to the business success of Chinese entrepreneurs in Hong Kong and in overseas communities. The importance of this value has been underlined by numerous empirical studies' (Wong Siu-lun 1991: 13). He further maintains that personal trust is an important component of this business trust; empirical evidence shows that Chinese entrepreneurs and business executives in Hong Kong stress the significance of friendship and interpersonal relations in establishing business networks. Redding makes a similar point,

specifying in addition that 'family coalitions handle the problem of mistrust by extensive networking to cement crucial specific relationships' (Redding 1991: 38).

17. In *Emigrant Entreprenuers*, Wong observes that 'in profit-making organizations where entrepreneurs feel that their interests or positions are threatened, kinsmen or others who can be relied on will be rallied' and that these entrepreneurs prefer to employ relatives because 'trust and loyalty are primary' (Wong Siu-lun 1988a: 145). Chapter 3 of that work provides detailed information on the background of the Shanghai-born entrepreneurs.

18. See Lee (1987: 165–72) for a convincing critique of Lau's utilitarianistic familism thesis. Among other weaknesses, Lee points out that Lau based his thesis on research findings that financial and material aid constituted the primary item of exchange among family members and relatives. In doing so, Lau discounted the importance of financial and material support as an expression of concern and affection, especially in times of economic hardship. In this light, one can justifiably describe the Hong Kong family as affectively oriented rather than utilitarianistic.

5. Deviance, Crime, and Social Control

DEVIANCE is generally defined as behaviour that does not conform to the norms and expectations of a society. Social control, on the other hand, refers to collective efforts to ensure conformity to social norms and expectations. These definitions suggest that what counts as deviance, and the amount of deviance, in a society depends on the degree of stringency of its social control. From this perspective, the study of deviance and social control informs us about the cherished values and interests of a society, as well as the social mechanisms and practices that have been instituted to protect these values and interests. This is the guiding thread of our discussion in this chapter.

Some further clarification is necessary, however, before we proceed with our investigation of these issues. Sociologists distinguish two types of social control: informal and formal. Informal social control includes the inculcation of conformity in an individual through socialization and the bond of conventional social relationships. The primary agencies of informal social control are the family and the school. Formal social control is the enforcement of conformity through well-defined regulations and specialized institutions, of which law and the police, respectively, are the most salient examples. We shall discuss deviance in Hong Kong with reference to both informal and formal social control. We focus our attention on crime or law-breaking behaviour as the primary type of deviance, although we also touch on certain types of juvenile delinquency not legally defined as criminal.

A Historical Profile: Crime Trends and Socio-economic Development

Societies undergoing industrialization and urbanization experience vast changes in social structure and social values, and it is commonly held among criminologists[1] that such changes impact on the incidence of crime. One dominant thesis in this connection maintains that industrialization and urbanization have the effect of weakening the forces of informal social control, a situation which in turn contributes to a rising level of crime in the developing society. Harold Traver's studies of crime trends (1980, 1984, 1991) investigate to what extent this has happened in the case of the two major categories of crime—property crimes and violent crimes—in Hong Kong.[2] It should be noted that the crime trends which Traver analysed were based on official (that is, police) crime statistics which may not accurately reflect the level and categories of crime in the society. In a later section, we shall look at the problems and biases in Hong Kong's official crime statistics and propose an explanation of the crime trends different from that suggested by Traver. Table 5.1 provides the relevant crime statistics which informed Traver's studies.

Figures 5.1 and 5.2 below, constructed on the basis of the above table, show that except for the period after 1980, the two crime trends move in different directions. Traver attributes this divergence to what he considers to be the different effects of Hong Kong's socio-economic development on the two crimes in question.

With respect to property crimes, it is worth noting, as Traver points out (1980, 1984), that the crime trend does not seem to support the thesis that urbanization and industrialization generate a higher level of crime. Population size and density, two accepted indices of urbanization, increased rapidly between the mid-1950s and the mid-1970s.[3] At the same time, Hong Kong's industrialization was proceeding at a fast pace.[4] These conditions, in turn, are believed to heighten the social isolation, anonymity, and heterogeneity of city life, and to weaken the control of the family and kin group on the individual, producing a higher level of crime as a result. Yet, Hong Kong's property crime rates were declining in this period. This anomaly is further confounded by two other features of the property crime trend. First, the property crime rate stood at a high level in 1956 and, we may assume, was at the same high level in the first half of the 1950s,[5] when the social impact of urbanization and industrialization was arguably at least as pronounced as in the following two decades. Second, the property crime rate climbed from the mid-1970s and reached an unprecedented high level in the early 1980s, when Hong Kong had already passed through the most intense years of its urbanization and industrialization. In short, the effect of Hong Kong's socio-economic development on crime is by no means straightforward or consistent.

Traver (1980, 1984) attempts an explanation of this bewildering trend regarding property crimes as follows. He attributes the pre-1957 high crime rate to the economic hardship of Hong Kong's early industrialization; in other words, material deprivation forced more people to commit property crimes. When economic conditions improved in the following two decades, the crime rate dropped. The rise in property crime since the mid-1970s, in Traver's view, can be explained by the theory of *relative deprivation*. The people of Hong Kong were generally better-off than before, but the rising expectations generated by the society's growing affluence made them feel that they were still not getting enough. It was also such relative deprivation that accounts for the high property crime rates since the early 1980s. In explaining Hong Kong's property crime trend, Traver by and large dismisses the alleged negative impact of socio-economic development on social control. He explains the crime trend before the mid-1970s in terms of need, after the mid-1970s in terms of greed.

With a slight twist, Traver applies the same explanation to the violent crime trend. He holds the view that the economic hardship of the 1950s

Table 5.1 Hong Kong's Crime Rates for Property Crimes and Violent Crimes, 1956/7 to 1989/90 (incidents per 100,000 population)

Year	Property Crimes	Violent Crimes
1956/57	617.5	24.8
1957/58	454.7	22.1
1958/59	381.3	24.9
1959/60	335.6	22.4
1960/61	342.6	26.8
1961/62	343.7	31.4
1962/63	306.2	29.8
1963/64	286.6	28.0
1964/65	313.3	41.5
1965/66	365.7	38.1
1966/67	364.0	52.5
1967/68	352.6	81.1
1968/69	307.2	76.2
1969/70	341.9	107.4
1970/71	367.2	134.9
1971/72	391.4	184.1
1972/73	350.1	262.5
1973/74	480.6	307.9
1974/75	540.2	418.9
1975/76	506.3	361.2
1976/77	530.6	307.3
1977/78	530.2	271.1
1978/79	622.1	249.8
1979/80	696.3	311.2
1980/81	812.0	316.6
1981/82	841.4	288.7
1982/83	897.3	314.7
1983/84	897.2	313.3
1984/85	846.2	282.5
1985/86	892.9	276.6
1986/87	819.9	259.3
1987/88	796.7	260.9
1988/89	701.5	266.6
1989/90	737.1	307.7

Sources: Commissioner of Police (Hong Kong Government), 1956/7–1974/5, *Annual Reports*, Hong Kong: Government Printer; Census and Statistics Department (Hong Kong Government), 1976–90, *Monthly Digest of Statistics*, Hong Kong: Government Printer; cited in Harold Traver (1991: 13, 16). Note: Property crimes include burglary, theft from person, and miscellaneous theft. Violent crimes include murder/manslaughter, rape/indecent assault, robbery, armed robbery, and serious assault.

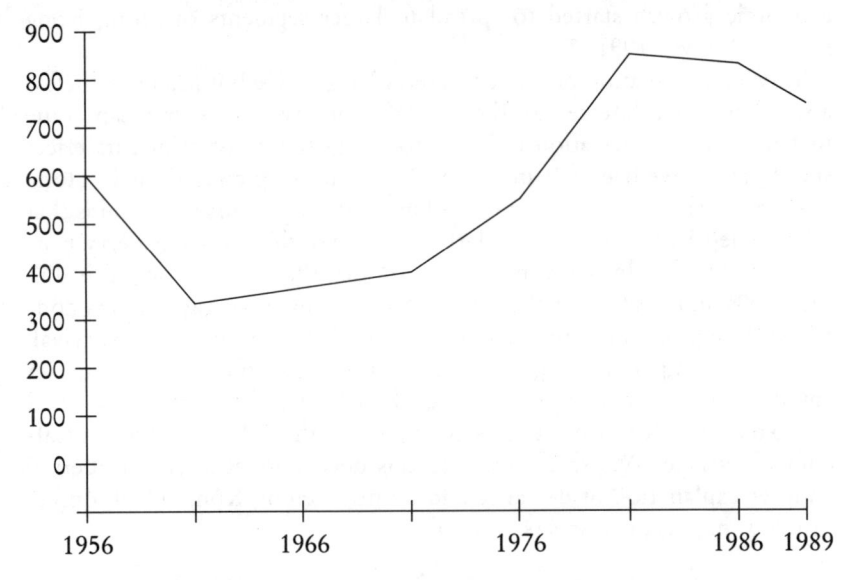

Figure 5.1 Hong Kong Crime Rates per 100,000 Population for Property Crimes, 1956–1989

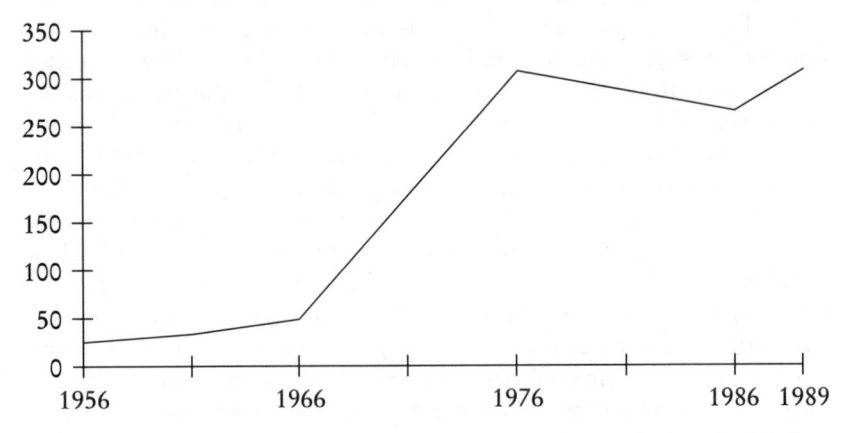

Figure 5.2 Hong Kong Crime Rates per 100,000 Population for Violent Crimes, 1956–1989

and 1960s had the effect of diverting the individual's propensity for violence to the quest for material sustenance: 'Frustrations of poverty are deflected into the problems of physical survival rather than into overt forms of aggression' (Traver 1980: 551). This supposition would seem to explain the low violent crime rates but high property crime rates in the period. The rising trend in violent crimes since the 1970s is accounted for through recourse to the theory of relative deprivation. Traver supports this contention with the empirically substantiated observation (Gurr 1970; Berkowitz 1962) that rising expectations rather than absolute deprivation precipitate collective violence. Finally, he contends that both the property and violent crime trends levelled off in the 1980s because 'the benefits of economic growth started to spread to larger segments of Hong Kong society' (Traver 1991: 23).

Traver's explanation of crime trends is imaginative but has nevertheless a number of weaknesses. In the case of property crimes, one can argue that if relative deprivation did lead to a higher rate of crime, its effect should also have been felt in the 1960s, when living conditions in Hong Kong were significantly improving. Ian Scott, for instance, maintains that relative deprivation was the underlying cause of the 1966 Star Ferry riots (Scott 1989a: 84). Further, the contention that the struggle for survival in the 1950s and 1960s had the effect of absorbing aggression seems contrived. It appears more reasonable to argue that the struggle for survival, and the accompanying high number of property crimes, would in fact entail a higher level of violent crimes. In a 1991 article, Traver modified his explanation of crime trends to highlight the role of formal social-control agencies. We shall return to this development after considering another explanation of deviance and crime in Hong Kong which differs in many important respects from Traver's.

Juvenile Delinquency and Socio-economic Development

The steady rise in the crime rate for juveniles (in the 7–15 years age group) and young persons (in the 16–20 years group) since the early 1970s[6] has prompted a number of important investigations into the relationship between socio-economic development and juvenile delinquency (which refers to both juvenile and young offenders in the present discussion). This series of inquiries began with Agnes Ng's research in the 1970s (Agnes Ng 1975, 1980). Ng's pioneering 1975 study established family relationships as the most important variable in the genesis of violent crime among young offenders in Hong Kong. Her findings show that the offenders, in comparison with a control group of non-offenders, were more likely to have a broken or disrupted family background, characterized by the separation of parents or serious disharmony between them. Unsatisfactory family life paved the way to juvenile delinquency in that it detracted from the child's commitment to school, and disposed him or her to seek entertainment and recreation away from home. Ng observes in conclusion:

Family condition, living environment and school system are the long-term causative factors of delinquency while school drop-out and triad involvement are ... immediate factors contributory to crime and delinquency (Agnes Ng 1975: 148).

This finding led Ng to follow up with a study on family relationships and delinquent behaviour (Agnes Ng 1980), which demonstrated that inadequate maternal supervision, in addition to an unsatisfactory parental relationship, was one of the major conducive factors to juvenile offence. The findings of these two studies testified to the importance of informal social-control agencies, in particular the family and the school, in the genesis and control of juvenile delinquency.[7] It is primarily from this social-control perspective that later studies undertook the investigation of the relationship between socio-economic development and juvenile delinquency in Hong Kong.

One such study is the large-scale survey research (Working Group on Juvenile Crime 1981) commissioned by the Government in response to the sudden and steep rise in the juvenile crime rate at the end of the 1970s. This study also located the root of juvenile offence in poor family relationships, which it attributed to the change in family structure from the extended or stem family to the small nuclear family,[8] the increase in the proportion of mothers employed outside the home, and the growing generation gap between young people and their parents—conditions which are generally held to be by-products of industrialization and modernization. These conditions had long existed in industrial Hong Kong, however, and the working group recognized that they alone could not therefore satisfactorily explain the sudden upsurge in juvenile crime. In response, the research team searched for historically specific contributing factors, including the introduction of three years of compulsory junior secondary education in 1978 and the more stringent enforcement of the minimum-age requirement for employment around the end of the 1970s.[9]

To understand the effect of these developments on juvenile crime, we begin with the following comment from the then Director of Education, Mr K. W. J. Topley, on the new education policy: 'We have, with our eyes open, taken problems from our streets and transferred them to the classroom.'[10] When combined with the minimum-age requirement for employment, the change had the consequence of aggravating problems both in the classroom and the streets. In the first place, compulsory junior secondary education substantially increased the number of unqualified, unmotivated, and problematic students. They exerted a bad influence on fellow students, which impacted negatively on commitment to school. The effect was to drastically raise the number of school drop-outs, who were then highly susceptible to inducement to delinquent pursuits. In addition, the minimum-age requirement for employment had the unintended effect of depriving many young people of an alternative conventional channel of commitment. Such conditions produced a large pool of juveniles 'at risk', and the risk was accentuated, in the research team's view, through association with delinquent gangs and frequent exposure to violence on television.

Risk and temptation also came, perhaps rather unexpectedly, as a result of the phenomenal growth in the number of supermarkets open for business in the territory, from 94 in 1977 to nearly 300 at the end of 1980 (Working Group on Juvenile Crime 1981: 205). The ensuing increased opportunity for shoplifting and the readiness of supermarkets to report such an offence to the police had the effect of inflating the juvenile crime rate, as is evidenced by the fact that petty theft made up the largest single category of juvenile offence in both of the last two years of the decade.

The working group's study not only confirmed the validity of the social-control perspective in explaining the upsurge of juvenile crime at a specific historical juncture; its discussion of the impact of policy changes on juvenile crime also prompted later studies to highlight this dimension in the interpretation of crime in Hong Kong. One such example is Agnes Ng's (1994) examination of the effect of the Government's New Towns Policy on juvenile delinquency.

The New Towns Policy was officially introduced by the Government in the early 1970s to divert population from the congested urban areas to the less populated New Territories, where new towns with a high proportion of public housing were to be developed to accomodate the new arrivals. An undesirable outcome of this policy, according to Ng, has been the loosening of informal social control in the new towns:

> It breaks up neighbourhood networks... residents have to adjust to a new community. Naturally their friendship ties become loosened. Some of them even have to commute every day to the city for work. This further reduces their time to spend with their families (Agnes Ng 1994: 9).

In Ng's view, this weakening of informal social control is the primary factor contributing to the generally much higher juvenile crime rates in the new towns (varying between 0.4 and 0.6 per cent) in comparison with those in the old urban districts (0.2 per cent or less in most cases).[11] It is worth noting in this connection that there has been a massive internal migration of population to the new towns since the early 1970s, resulting in a disproportionately high rate of population growth in these areas. The combined population in the three new towns with very high juvenile crime rates—Tsuen Wan, Tuen Mun, and Yuen Long—for instance, increased from 446,783 (11 per cent of Hong Kong's total population) in 1971 to 950,000 (19 per cent of total population) in 1980, to 1,322,790 (23 per cent of total population) in 1991.[12] In this light, we can attribute part of the rise in the juvenile crime rate since the early 1970s to Hong Kong's new towns development and the attendant expansion of public housing.

These studies suggest that the loosening of informal social control in the course of Hong Kong's socio-economic development is the main contributing factor to the rising level of juvenile delinquency. Yet, while the pertinent evidence shows poor family relationships, lack of commitment to school, and the disruption of conventional social ties to be related to juvenile offence, it does not empirically demonstrate in what way these factors lead to such behaviour. Cheung Yuet-wah and Agnes Ng's analysis of the path to juvenile delinquency (Cheung and Ng 1988), to which we now turn, fills the gap in our knowledge in this respect.

The Path to Delinquency

Cheung and Ng's study (1988) is an attempt to test the validity of their 'path model' on the basis of a sample of 1,139 secondary school students. Simplified slightly for the sake of our discussion, the model begins with the *family* variable of attachment to parents, but the findings show that this variable has no direct effect on deviant behaviour. The path then leads to the *school* variable of attachment to school, which is also found to have no direct effect on deviant behaviour. In other words, the evidence considered so far does not seem to support the social-control perspective. The data, however, do show a positive relationship between attachment to parents and attachment to school, implying that a close relationship with parents would enhance the child's commitment to school, and a poor relationship would detract from such commitment.

Attachment to school, in turn, is found to be negatively related to association with deviant friends, which is the next variable in the path model. This finding substantiates the argument mentioned in the previous section that unmotivated and uncommitted students are particularly susceptible to the influence of delinquent associates. Cheung and Ng's data do show that association with deviant friends is the direct and major contributing factor to delinquent behaviour. Their analysis further establishes that deviant values acquired through delinquent association play only a minor part in disposing the individual to deviant behaviour. Most of the delinquent youths in their sample misbehave either in imitation of their deviant associates' misconduct or under their group pressure.

Cheung and Ng's study seems to show that inadequate social control, reflected in this case by low attachment to the family and the school, contributes to juvenile delinquency only indirectly. Low attachment to the family tends to lead to low attachment to the school, which is in turn conducive to association with deviant friends, and such association is the direct and primary cause of delinquent behaviour. This, it seems, is the path to delinquency for Hong Kong's youth. Cheung and Ng's path analysis suggests that the explanation of juvenile delinquency and its rising trend has to be couched mainly in the context of the youths' exposure to deviant associates. In this light, the effect of compulsory junior secondary education on delinquency, discussed earlier, warrants the vigilant attention of the concerned authorities. For the same reason, the impact of the New Towns Policy and public housing development on juvenile delinquency should be examined in terms of the possibly greater opportunities such areas afford for association with delinquent friends and criminals, rather than solely from the perspective of the weakening of family and kinship ties. In this respect, the easy access to communal amenities—playgrounds and recreational centres, in particular—in the new towns and public housing estates may have had the consequence of creating a social environment conducive to deviance and crime.

On a more general societal level, one can similarly attribute the rise in juvenile offence to the proliferation in the past two decades of commercial billiard rooms, video-game and karaoke centres, cafés, and fast-food restaurants, all of which are favourite hang-outs of youths and thus must substantially increase their chance of falling into bad company. Studies by the Young Women's Christian Association (1986) and the Young Men's Christian Association (1986), for instance, reported that a significant percentage of the youths in their samples visited video-game centres and billiard rooms regularly. The studies also discovered that many of them had been invited by the new friends they met in these places to join criminal associations.[13]

Our discussion so far has focused on interpretations of overall crime trends and of juvenile offence in terms of socio-economic conditions conducive to deviance and crime. We have by-passed the consideration that the level of crime in a society could be an artefact of the law enforcement agencies and of societal attitudes towards deviant behaviour. Clearly, the police crime statistics which we have used to indicate the level of crime in Hong Kong were constructed on the basis of the number of reported crimes or of criminal prosecutions. Both of these figures in turn depend on the readiness of the public to report crime, as well as on the scope and effectiveness of law enforcement. A critical analysis and a judicious interpretation of official crime statistics, therefore, not only affords us a less biased picture of the actual extent of crime in the society, but also throws light on the way law enforcement agencies discharge their public responsibilities. Ian Dobinson points the direction of inquiry when he says: '[Police crime statistics] are beset with technical problems and numerous potential distortions arising from political and public relations pressures' (Dobinson 1994: 27).

Crime Trends in the Light of Changes in Social-control Policies

As a law enforcement agency, the Hong Kong police force is charged not only with the responsibility of controlling crime but also of reinforcing the political stability of a colonial regime. This 'political pressure' on the Hong Kong police was particularly heavy before the 1970s, when rivalries between pro-Communist and pro-Guomindang factions (as in the 1956 riots), and occasional hostile outbursts of nationalist, anti-colonial sentiments (best exemplified in the 1967 riots), signalled ominously that Chinese politics could be catastrophically disruptive of the colonial order.[14] In discharging what some writers (Lethbridge 1980; Traver and Gaylord 1991) have called a paramilitary function, the Hong Kong police acquired massive power—and power corrupts. In the view of some writers (Vagg 1991; Lethbridge 1980; Traver 1991, 1994), official crime statistics for the territory from before the 1970s should be interpreted against the background of the political role of the police as well as the pervasive police corruption of the time. Henry Lethbridge, for example, explains the low crime rates before the 1970s as follows:

In the 1950s and 1960s . . . the police, then largely a paramilitary, colonial-style security force, were mainly concerned with public order, keeping the peace, and not so much with the suppression of conventional crime. The criminal statistics for these decades reflect the priorities chosen by the police. Much crime, low-level crime in particular, was allowed to flourish (Lethbridge 1980: 582).

Lethbridge's study of sexual violence in Hong Kong (Lethbridge 1980), which reveals a very low rate of reported sexual offence before the 1970s—in particular, the incredibly low rate of only one reported case of rape in 1965 for a population of 3.7 million—demonstrates poignantly the possibly gross under-reporting of crime due to the lack of police concern about conventional offences.

Jon Vagg (1991), on the other hand, attributes the low rates of reported crimes and the high detection rates before the early 1970s[15] to an alliance between the police and the triads. He maintains that in return for the enormous amount of graft received from the triads, the police connived at their criminal operations. The triads, on their part, controlled petty crime in their areas so as to ensure the smooth running of their business and, when necessary, acted as police informers. Vagg argues further that the police were likely to have omitted a certain number of reported crimes from their records, as well as persuading persons already in custody to admit to offences which they did not commit. The overall consequences of the above practices were artificially low reported crime rates and artificially high detection rates.

The Government's social-control policies changed, beginning in the 1970s, concomitant with improvements in relations between China and the West. With the fading of political threats from China, the colonial government shifted the priority of social control from the containment of political opposition to the suppression of crime. The change was evidenced by the launching of the Government-sponsored Fight Violent Crime campaign in 1973, and the setting up of the Independent Commission Against Corruption (ICAC) in 1974 to combat corruption in all branches of Hong Kong society, including the police. To meet its goal of controlling crime through the cooperative efforts of police and the public, the anti-crime campaign established new neighbourhood police units and crime-reporting centres in populous residential areas. The campaign ended in 1975, but its by-product, neighbourhood organizations named Mutual Aid Committees, carried on its mission of combating crime through community participation. An important outcome of this development was a greater willingness to report crime, contributing to much higher official (reported) crime rates since the mid-1970s (Lethbridge 1980; Traver 1991, 1994).

On the other hand, the campaign against corruption, especially that directed at the police, had the effect of eradicating to a significant extent the protection and cover which the triads used to enjoy through their illicit liasion with the police. The demise of the police-triad alliance also ended the triads' 'informal policing', ironically leading to an increase in street crimes such as theft, robbery, and serious assault (Traver 1994). Crime detection rates, however, dropped as the police, severing their ties with the triads, lost an important source of information on criminal activities. Reforms within the police further reduced substantially its past practice of artificially deflating the number of reported crimes and inflating detection figures. The consequence was a rise in reported crime rates and a drop in detection rates (Vagg 1991).

The Police and its Organizational Interests: Implications for Crime and Social Control

In the preceding section we attributed changes in police practices to improvements in international relations between China and the West, and to the attendant adjustment in Hong Kong's social-control policy. Political scientist Michael Ng-Quinn (1991), however, interprets such changes as a part of the police force's attempts to safeguard its organizational interests in the course of Hong Kong's political development. He contends that crime and its control has been the force's principal bargaining leverage against the threat of external encroachment on its power and resources. His study adds a new perspective to our discussion, carrying as it does the implication that crime trends in Hong Kong bear the imprint of the changing power relationship between the police and the larger society.

Ng-Quinn's thesis is premised on the argument that the Hong Kong government's attitude towards the police has long been one of ambivalence. It has endowed the police with extensive powers to safeguard colonial rule, and yet it has to monitor and curb such powers to ensure that police operations remain subordinate to the prerogatives of governmental administration.[16] This balance had to be re-established in the early 1970s, when the police force had acquired additional power after its suppression of the 1967 riots and police corruption had so outraged the public that police powers became more a liability than an asset in colonial governance. It is from this perspective that Ng-Quinn views the significance of the establishment of the ICAC, whose prime target of attack in the 1970s was police corruption. The campaign against police corruption, Ng-Quinn argues, was also a strategy of the Government to mobilize public support in its move to curb police powers: 'In order to maintain and restore its own bureaucratic control over the police, the government needs the public to report cases of police corruption...' (Ng-Quinn 1991: 19). This effort put the police force on the defensive, a condition aggravated by Hong Kong's democratization in the 1980s.

A concomitant feature of this democratization was increased public control over governmental institutions, including the police. To the extent that police operations and resources were increasingly subject to public scrutiny and the censure of politicians, the police faced the prospect of a further set-back in power and autonomy. To defend and advance its organizational interests, the force now had to negotiate with both the Government and the public for power and resources. Its bargaining leverage was crime and its control:

While politicians criticized the police's excessive powers and possible dysfunction, the police responded by appealing to the public's fear of crime in order to rally public support for even greater police authority (Ng-Quinn 1991: 26).

One can derive from Ng-Quinn's thesis the argument that Hong Kong's high crime rates since the mid-1970s have partly been the outcome of the police's dramatization of crime.[17] The ensuing heightened public awareness of crime precipitated the perception that the community was experiencing a 'crime wave', which in turn enhanced the role and importance of the police in the maintenance of order and security. This perception also facilitated the police's efforts to mobilize public support through community relations strategies.[18] All of these factors had the effect of boosting the public's confidence in the police, resulting in a greater readiness to report crime. Higher crime rates, in turn, furnished the police with a strong justification for expansion.

Crime Trends: A Re-examination

We return now, after this long detour, to the interpretation of crime trends in terms of Hong Kong's socio-economic development. We have now good reason to believe that the generally low and declining *property* crime rates in the 1950s and 1960s could be accounted for in large part by the then current policy and practice of social control, which led to substantial camouflaging and under-reporting of crime. The gradually rising *violent* crime rates in the same period may be due to the fact such crimes caused serious injuries to people and hence were more often reported than were property crimes. We are suggesting, in effect, that the crime trend before the 1970s is in all probability more accurately reflected by the violent crime rates than by the property crime rates. On the other hand, much of the steep rise in crime trends in the 1970s, and the high crime rates since then, can reasonably be attributed to reforms and re-adjustments of policies within the police. Intriguing questions remain: To what extent do Hong Kong's rising crime trends reflect an actual increase in the incidence of crime? Or are these trends little more than the artefact of changes in social-control policies? We can derive preliminary answers to these questions from the Government's victimization surveys (Census and Statistics Department 1979, 1982, 1987a, 1990).

These surveys were conducted through interviews with a large sample of the population[19] concerning the particulars of criminal acts. The surveys' objective was to provide information, not otherwise available from official records, on the nature and extent of crime and on reasons for not reporting crime. The resulting crime statistics were constructed from the data on victimization, defined as 'a specific criminal act which affects a single victim, whether a person or a household' (Census and Statistics Department 1990: 147). We can obtain from these surveys information on the incidence of crime which is more accurate than are the figures given as official statistics, as well as indications of the extent of crime reporting in the period of study.

The findings show that the victimization rate, indicating the number of victimizations per 1,000 members of the population aged 12 years and older, increased substantially between 1978 and 1986, and then declined in 1989 (Census and Statistics Department 1990: 112, table 69).[20] On the other hand, the findings also show that the percentages of victimizations reported to the police were rising continually, from 18.2 per 1,000 in 1978 to 34.0 in 1989 (Census and Statistics Department 1990: 121, table 80). The evidence indicates that the level of crime was on the increase at least for the period 1978 to 1986, and possibly also for the two decades before that, although the magnitude of such increase had been inflated by the rise in crime reporting. Since 1986, however, the level of crime has been dropping moderately. In other words, we argue that the level of crime was most likely on a continual rise until the mid-1980s, when it started to level off and even decline slightly.

We can find an explanation for this pattern in the criminological development theories of William Clifford (1973, 1974) and Marshall Clinard and David Abbott (1973). According to these theories, rapidly developing societies would experience a rising level of crime as a result of the loosening of the traditional mechanisms of informal social control and the increased opportunities for crime attendant on growing affluence. The theory also points out that when the pace of economic development has slowed, and when a large portion of the population begins to benefit from the fruits of development, the crime rate levels off and even declines. Hong Kong's crime trend has apparently displayed such a pattern.

Crimes of the Affluent and Powerful: Commercial Crime and Corruption

Our discussion so far has focused on street crimes, consisting of violent offences and property offences which are mostly committed by the poorer members of society. In terms of the economic cost to the community, however, these offences pale in comparison with the crimes of the affluent and powerful. Yet, Hong Kong's style of governance and economic policy, some writers argue, have necessitated a social-control policy which treats the crimes of the rich and powerful with tolerance and leniency. Mark S. Gaylord, for instance, in attributing the territory's commercial crime problem[21] to the Government's policy of positive non-interventionism, observes: 'Hong Kong has been, historically, unwilling to regard as criminal or even illegal many sharp business practices outlawed elsewhere' (Gaylord 1991: 71). In a similar vein, Vagg (1994) argues that commercial crime flourished in Hong Kong because the territory's ambition to become a world financial centre inhibited the development of restrictive financial laws. Both the government and the businsess sector, he points out, considered such laws as detracting from Hong Kong's attractiveness to overseas investors.

Such arguments suggest that the coincidence of perspectives and interests between the Government and the business community circumscribes the territory's handling of the crimes of the rich and powerful. T. Wing Lo (1993) analyses such a coincidence and its implications for Hong Kong's social-control policy from the perspective of the neo-Marxist theory of the modern capitalist state.

The central concept in Lo's study is 'hegemony', a term used early in this century by the Marxist theoretician Antonio Gramsci (1971) to analyse the modern capitalist state's maneuvers to attain and preserve political and moral leadership. To maintain its hegemonic position, Gramsci argues, the capitalist state cannot simply rely on coercion and the support of the capitalist class; it has also to win the consent of the dominated classes by presenting itself as the guardian of common interests in society. The capitalist state, therefore, has constantly to adjust its policies with reference to class interests and to the power relationship between the dominant capitalist class and the subordinate classes. Its ultimate objective, however, is to safeguard the interests of the capitalist class, for the state's survival and well-being are contingent on the perpetuation of the capitalist system. This is the perspective which informs Lo's analysis of the Hong Kong capitalist state's approach to crime, in particular the crimes of the rich and powerful. His focus is on corruption within the civil service and the business sector.

The Hong Kong government's campaign against corruption began in 1974 with the establishment of the ICAC. To Lo, this change in the Government's policy on corruption was an attempt to resolve the crisis of hegemony generated by the mounting opposition from the subordinate classes to the colonial capitalist order. Before the crisis, the imperative of legitimizing colonial rule ordained that the Government must not expose to the public the rampant corruption within the civil service. As Lethbridge remarks:

The one limited justification for imposing alien rule over indigenous peoples has always been the notion of 'good government', the establishment of an efficient and incorrupt administration.... To insist loudly in public that the Hong Kong civil service was ripely corrupt had, therefore, dangerous implications (Lethbridge 1985: 78).

This danger, Lo contends, was the reason for the Government's half-heartedness in its attempts to deal with the problem of corruption in the 1950s and 1960s. This policy, he continues, was no longer practicable in the quickly changing political circumstances of the late 1960s and early 1970s. The 1967 riots had sown the seeds of anti-colonial and anti-capitalist sentiments, which a few years later were to resurge in the form of widespread student and public attacks on corruption as part and parcel of the colonial capitalist order. To restore its hegemony, the Government had to put its own house in order and, indeed, to present itself as the vanguard in the fight against corruption. It had, however, to present itself as such in a way that did not run counter to the interests of the capitalist class or threaten the security of the colonial order. This was evidenced, Lo argues, in two events of the late 1970s: the Government's compromise with the Chinese business community on the issue of 'illegal commissions', and Governor Murray MacLehose's granting of a partial amnesty to corrupt police officers to avert an impending police mutiny.[22]

Lo maintains further that the Government's campaign against corruption was a calculated move to deflect the discontent of the dominated classes onto a few scapegoats, particularly white expatriates, within the civil service. In demonstrating to the public its determination to punish its own decadent staff, the Government presented itself as the impartial and unswerving champion for the cause of a clean and just society, and so re-established its hegemonic position. The rampant corruption within the business sector, meanwhile, receded into the background. In having their grievances directed at certain delinquent individuals within the civil service, the subordinate classes lost sight of the fact that the root of the problem lay in the capitalist system. The censure of corruption, in other words, had the effect of obviating class exploitation and class conflict through the mobilization of collective efforts against a common enemy. Lo sums up his argument thus:

[The censure of corruption] helped transcend class conflict and unite capital and labour on the same front.... It facilitated the dominant class bloc to dominate its subordinate and re-establish domestic order for capitalist production (Lo 1993: 107–8).

The covert illicit practices among members of the capitalist class were increasingly exposed to public scrutiny during Hong Kong's democratization in the 1980s. To maintain its hegemony, the capitalist state could no longer shy away from the problem of corruption in the business sector. The ICAC's re-deployment of resources in the 1980s to target business corruption, according to Lo, has to be viewed in this light. To appease the subordinate classes, and yet to preserve its cooperative relationship with the capitalist class, the Government resorted to the strategy of punishing, in a highly publicized and dramatized manner, only certain black sheep of the business community.[23] In doing so, the state safeguarded the interests and hegemony of the capitalist class as a whole through purging it of its most wayward elements. The overall effect was similar to that achieved in the campaign against civil service corruption: the censure of corruption contributes to the perpetuation of colonial capitalism by reducing its most disruptive consequences.

The Class Perspective on Crime and Social Control

It is on the basis of his study of corruption that Lo proposes a re-examination of crime and social control in Hong Kong through the perspective of class power and class relations. To the extent that the state is the site of class power and the arena of class conflict, its social-control policies, and hence its control of crime, are contingent on the balance of class power in society. In the 1950s and 1960s, the massive influx of refugees from mainland China and the prevalence of the materialist ethos culminated in the disorganization and political acquiescence of the dominated classes. At the same time, the imperative of capital accumulation in this early phase of Hong Kong's industrial capitalist development enhanced the political clout of the capitalist class. In this socio-economic context, the state became the instrument of capitalist class domination. Social-control policies were accordingly geared to the disciplining of the dominated classes, and hence the control of working-class crime, so as to secure a peaceful environment for capital accumulation. The crimes of the rich and powerful, as exemplified in the case of corruption, were seldom the target of law enforcement activities.

The resurgence of class consciousness among the dominated and the restructuring of class power in the 1970s—a consequence of the upsurge of anti-colonial and anti-capitalist sentiments in the aftermath of the 1967 riots—were reflected in a reorientation in social-control policy, from the enforcement of capitalist class domination to the management of class conflict. The most conspicuous delinquents of the dominant power bloc, the corrupt state officials, were publicly censured and punished in an attempt to contain the opposition of the dominated classes. But it was only when the political clout of the capitalist class suffered a further setback, concomitant with the rising power of the dominated classes in the 1980s, that the state attained the 'relative autonomy'[24] to grapple with, reluctantly and selectively, the crimes of the capitalists.

The validity of Lo's class analysis of crime and social control in Hong Kong obviously depends to a large extent on the plausibility of his interpretation of the fight against corruption. In this connection, it is important to note that several other studies (Rance P. L. Lee 1981; Kuan 1981; Lau and Lee 1981; King 1980) have interpreted the issue of corruption in Hong Kong in a manner different from that adopted by Lo. Rance P. L. Lee (1981), for instance, observes that gift-giving, many forms of which would be construed as illegal and corrupt practices in colonial Hong Kong, had long been accepted by the Chinese people as a convenient way to cultivate personal connections and, even, as a requirement for achieving certain goals. Lee's 1971 survey research found that only 29 per cent of the respondents considered corruption to be a serious social problem, demonstrating the persistence of the pertinent traditional orientation in modern Hong Kong. This incongruence between Chinese folk norms and the Colony's legal code has meant that the feasibility and success of any anti-corruption campaign hinges on a change in the attitudes of the Hong Kong Chinese towards corruption.

The social and political climate of the early 1970s was opportune for the Government to launch a campaign against corruption by way of bringing about a 'quiet revolution' in society.[25] It is in this sense that Lee writes: 'Being a major factor in the change of social perception, the ICAC can be conceived of as a "cause" of the problem of corruption' (Rance P. L. Lee 1981: 6). His interpretation carries the implication that a major reason behind the Government's reluctance before the 1970s to launch a large-scale attack on corruption was the inappropriateness of the current social climate. This supposition contrasts with Lo's interpretation drawn from the perspective of class domination.

Ambrose Y. C. King's study (1980) lends further support to Lee's view that public attitudes circumscribed the Government's anti-corruption measures. In this respect, it is particularly worth noting the differences between the interpretations put forth by King and Lo regarding the significance of two issues, the movement against illegal commissions and the avoiding of a police mutiny, in the fight against corruption. The Government's attack on illegal commissions, King observes, was constrained by the public's worry that such an action would endanger the prosperity of the society. A territory-wide survey in 1977[26] found that 39 per cent of the respondents considered the ICAC's activities to have adversely affected Hong Kong's business.

On the issue of the police mutiny avoided by Governor MacLehose, King cites reactions from the mass media and the public. These statements apparently convinced the Government that the granting of a partial amnesty would be consistent with the public's much greater concern for law and order than for rooting out corruption.[27] Public expectation, as revealed in the 1977 survey findings,[28] similarly disposed the Government to set its own house in order before turning to corruption in the private sector. King comments: 'This is the basic structure of the public mood, beyond which no governmental action, including the ICAC's, can have a chance of success' (King 1980: 130).

The studies of Lee and King suggest that the Government's policies regarding corruption might have been guided by considerations other than those of class power and class relations. They should not, however, be taken as a refutation of Lo's thesis. After all, the 'social climate' or 'public mood' in question could well be construed to be the ideological product of capitalist class domination.[29] One must also bear in mind that as factors circumscribing the Government's approach to corruption, public opinion and class power need not be mutually exclusive. Lo's class analysis is possibly one-sided, but it fills a lacuna in the conception and interpretation of the issue of corruption and of crime and social control in Hong Kong.

Conclusion

In pursuing the objective of articulating a panoramic perspective on the territory's society, we have in this chapter dwelt on the socio-economic and political dimensions of deviance and social control in Hong Kong. We started with the study of crime trends in order to assess the bearing of the society's socio-economic development on the incidence of crime. We were puzzled to find that, contrary to what most theories of crime would predict, Hong Kong's property crime rates were low and declining during the early phase of industrialization but climbed to a high level after the society had gone through the most challenging and disruptive period of its economic development.

The study of juvenile delinquency, which established that the weakening of social control and an increased association with delinquent peers during urban-industrial development were major factors contributing to juvenile offence, reinforced our suspicion that the actual level of crime in the 1950s and 1960s was substantially higher than that indicated in the official statistics. We subsequently examined the social-control policies and practices that impinged on the making of crime statistics in order to uncover reasons for a misrepresentation in official statistics of the actual number of incidents of crime.

The pertinent studies suggest that the interpretation of Hong Kong's crime trends has to be informed by changes, since the early 1970s, in the Government's social-control policies and in the relationship of the police force to the larger community. But the broader message is that the control of crime in Hong Kong has been closely bound up with the political considerations and strategies of the Government and its principal law enforcement agency, the police. Before the 1970s, the Government's preoccupation with controlling political opposition and the police's connection with the triads had the effect of masking, and hence artificially deflating, the extent of criminal activity in society. Since that time, both the Government and the police have had to adopt more stringent measures against criminal activities in order to boost their image and enhance their legitimacy in a context of mounting public discontent with civil service corruption. The public's confidence in the police subsequently increased, and crime reporting increased with it. The higher crime rates since the mid-1970s are to a significant extent a reflection of the public's greater willingness to report crime.

If crime control is circumscribed by political considerations, then we can expect the crimes of the rich and powerful to be treated by the social-control agencies with more tolerance and leniency than the crimes of the underprivileged. The class perspective on crime argues in this vein through demonstrating the subservience of social-control policy to the imperative of safeguarding the hegemonic position of the capitalist power bloc. Although the analysis appears to be one-sided, it is nevertheless a powerful reminder that crime and its control in Hong Kong, as in other capitalist societies, are subject to the state's manipulation to buttress the power configuration of capitalism.

Notes

1. See, for instance, Marshall Clinard (1964), Oliver R. Galle et al. (1972), Clinard and David Abbott (1973), and William Clifford (1973) for further discussion of this point.
2. Property crimes and violent crimes accounted for 55 per cent and 19 per cent, respectively, of the total number of crimes in Hong Kong between 1980 and 1989 (Traver 1991: 12, 15).
3. Hong Kong's population increased by 57.5 per cent between 1951 and 1961, and by 26 per cent in the following decade. Its population density was 2,365.6 persons per square kilometer in 1957; it increased to 4,236.2 persons per square kilometer by 1977 (Traver 1980: 534).
4. This point is evidenced by the fact that in 1957 only 5.3 per cent of Hong Kong's population were employed in manufacturing, whereas by 1978 the figure had increased to 17.4 per cent (Traver 1980: 537).
5. Statistics on property crimes before 1957 are not available. We must therefore make inferences, as does Traver (1980), on the basis of the 1957 crime statistics.
6. The prosecution rate for juveniles and young persons (obtained through dividing the number of juvenile and young persons prosecuted by the number of people in the 7–20 years age group) was 0.41 in 1972. It rose steadily to 0.46 in 1975, 0.71 in 1980, 0.83 in 1985, and 0.99 in 1990. In other words, as indicated by the prosecution rate, the crime rate for juveniles and young persons more than doubled between 1972 and 1990. For details of this progression, see Agnes Ng (1994: 392–4).
7. A number of studies in the 1980s lend support to Ng's thesis. B. H. Mok's survey research on the problem behaviour of adolescents in Hong Kong (1985) found that in comparison with the 'promising' students, the problem students more often had poor relationships with their parents and were more likely to perceive relationships within their family as disharmonious. M. K. Cheung's path analysis (1985) of Mok's survey data showed that unsatisfactory family relationships contributed indirectly to adolescent misbehaviour. The studies of Chow et al. (1985, 1987) found that delinquent youths were more likely than non-delinquent youths to come from families where the mother was working full-time outside the home, and where the parents showed little concern for their children's schoolwork and leisure activities. Their studies also discovered that many of the delinquents were often absent from school and claimed that they attended school only because they were forced to do so.
8. The argument put forth here is that the change weakens the 'social control' role of the kin network. As was stated in Chapter 4, this is a dubious assertion: There is no unambiguous evidence that the Hong Kong family has seen a development from the extended to the nuclear form, and empirical studies have shown that many families maintained regular social contacts with extended kin.
9. The minimum age of 14 years for employment in the industrial sector was extended to the non-industrial sector beginning in September 1979. A year later, the minimum age for all types of employment was raised to 15 years. Government statistics show a decline in the number of prosecutions for the illegal employment of children in industry towards the end of the 1970s, reflecting a higher degree of conformity with the law (Working Group on Juvenile Crime 1981: 197).
10. From a speech in the Legislative Council, November 1980.
11. Ng makes brief reference to the findings of the Government's Working Group on Juvenile Crime (1981), which show a generally high juvenile crime rate in the new towns of Shatin, Tuen Mun, Yuen Long, and Kwun Tong. The juvenile

crime rates by districts for 1991, which Ng (1994: 398) worked out on the basis of arrest statistics provided by the police, indicate a broadly similar picture. These rates are expressed as the number of juvenile offenders (7–16 years old) as a percentage of the total number of juveniles in the 7–16 age group. The 1991 juvenile crime rates for selected new towns are: Yuen Long, 0.6 per cent; Tsuen Wan, 0.5 per cent; Kwun Tong and Tuen Mun, each 0.4 per cent.

12. Population statistics for the new towns in 1971 and 1980 are based on Leung Chi-keung 1980: 296, table 1. Other statistics are based on *Hong Kong 1991 Population Census: Main Report*, 1991: 32, table 2.1; 47, table 2.25.

13. The Y. W. C. A. study (1986) found that some 40 per cent of the schoolchildren in their sample visited video-game centres frequently, and that about 62 per cent of the sample reported meeting their new friends in these centres. Of the latter group, around 28 per cent claimed that these new friends invited them to join the triads. The Y. M. C. A. study (1986), on the other hand, discovered that 42 per cent of the youths visited billiard rooms regularly.

14. See Chapter 7 for a detailed analysis of the rivalry between the pro-Guomindang and pro-Communist factions, and of opposition movements against the Hong Kong government. The chapter also contains a description and analysis of the 1956 and 1967 riots.

15. The crime rate (indicated by crimes reported per 100,000 population) in the years before 1974 was generally well below 1,000. It rose to 1,200 and above in subsequent years. On the other hand, the detection rate (number of convicted criminal offences as a percentage of the number of reported crimes) was around 76 per cent in the period 1968–71. It dropped to below 60 per cent in the remaining part of the 1970s, and to an average of around 47 per cent in the 1980s. For details, see Vagg (1991: 243, table 2).

16. Both in absolute numbers and in its relation to the size of the population, the Hong Kong police force qualifies as one of the largest in the world (Traver and Gaylord 1991). Regarding the relation of the force to the Government, Vagg writes: '[T]he police are a department of government. There has never been any pretence of a constitutionally independent position. The governmental arrangements for the colony make the commissioner of police accountable to the governor' (Vagg 1991: 239).

17. In this respect, we can take note of Vagg's (1994) comment on the police's approach to the 'triad problem'. He writes: '[T]riads are discussed in terms reminiscent of the dramatization of elemental forces. They are depicted as evil ... [and] anti-triad strategies are repeatedly symbolized as the enactment of the moral drama of good against evil' (Vagg 1994: 364). We can take this as an illustration of the dramatization of crime, in which the police emerges as the moral guardian of the community.

18. In this regard, Traver and Gaylord's (1991) discussion of developments in police-community relations since the mid-1970s is worth noting. A crime prevention bureau was established within the police force in 1977, with the objective of promoting public awareness of crime and collecting public advice on crime prevention strategies. In the 1980s, the police made further appeals for public support in crime control through an extensive neighbourhood watch scheme and a Fight Crime campaign. At the same time, the reformed and enlarged Police Public Relations Branch, with a huge task force of community and school liasion officers, facilitated the exchange of information between the police and the public, in particular via the mass media. Traver and Gaylord comment on the implication of these developments: 'By the end of the 1970s, the police were well on their way to establishing themselves as the legitimate guardians and protectors of society.... As the major source of information about the incidence of crime in

society, the police have considerable power to channel and shape the perceived significance of crime trends' (Traver and Gaylord 1991: 108, 109).

19. In the 1990 survey, for instance, a total of 16,856 households (50,956 persons aged 12 years or older) were interviewed. The four surveys had similar sample sizes and research methods.

20. The victimization rates for personal crimes were 21.9 (1978), 39.2 (1981), 40.2 (1986), and 24.3 (1989). The rates for household crimes were 46.5 (1978), 86.4 (1981), 73.7 (1986), and 61.2 (1989). The survey reports do not provide composite rates for personal and household crimes.

21. Commercial crime, an example of the crimes of the affluent, covers a range of offences, the most typical of which include bank fraud, securities fraud, and the fraudulent use of letters of credit. Gaylord illustrates the commercial crime problem in Hong Kong through several case studies. The Overseas Trust Bank fraud, for instance, apparently started in 1979 but was not investigated by the Government until 1985. Another example is money-laundering (often involving drug money), which despite its wide practice in the territory was not seriously tackled by the Government until 1989. Gaylord uses examples such as the above to illustrate the Hong Kong government's non-interventionist and tolerant attitude towards commercial crime.

22. The offering and receiving of commissions, while illegal, had long been a common business practice in Hong Kong, and so when the Government began to prosecute these illegal commissions in the mid-1970s, the Chinese business community protested strongly. The Government apparently conceded, and the number of prosecutions dropped from 66 in 1976 to 25 in 1979. Lo observes: 'either a compromise between the two parties might have been arrived at, or . . . the Government understood the "limit and scope" of combating corruption in the private sector' (Lo 1993: 98). Commenting on the threatened police mutiny in October 1977 and the subsequent granting of a partial amnesty a few days later, Lo writes: 'the police were the state's "reserve army" which disciplined the working class into a reliable labour force, protected the capitalist mode of production, and maintained the power and ideologies of the colonial state. In this respect, how could the state afford to distance itself from the police?' (Lo 1993: 101). For a detailed description of these two incidents, see Lo (1993: 96–101).

23. Lo substantiates this argument with several case studies, including the public housing scandal of 1985–8, the stock market scandal and the subsequent trial and conviction of Ronald Li in 1990, and the investigation and trial of the directors of Carrian Investment Ltd and Bumiputra Malaysia Finance in the second half of the 1980s. For details, see Lo (1993: 110–35).

24. 'Relative autonomy' is a concept used by some Marxists to refer to the state's bureaucratic power not directly subject to the domination of the capitalist class. The state's autonomy remains relative in the sense that, in the view of these Marxists, the power of the capitalist state in the final analysis is subservient to the interests of capital. For a detailed exposition of this concept, see Miliband (1969).

25. King writes: 'the war against corruption . . . ultimately involves a fundamental change in the value orientations of the Hong Kong people; to use the Governor's words, "a quiet revolution . . . a revolution in public attitude to corruption" had to be made' (King 1980: 120).

26. This survey was conducted by Survey Research Hong Kong in September 1977. A total of 1,974 people within the 15–64 years age range were interviewed on their attitudes towards corruption and other social problems in Hong Kong.

27. In addition to citing evidence from the press, King refers to a mass survey conducted in 1978 which found that of those respondents who knew of the issue, 52.1 per cent supported the Government's granting of the partial amnesty. King

comments: 'It seems clear that on the whole, the people of Hong Kong placed a much higher priority on law and order, the value of which they cherished much more than the value of combating corruption' (King 1980: 130).

28. The findings of the 1977 Survey Research Hong Kong survey showed that the public expected the ICAC to give priority to corruption in Government departments and among high-ranking civil servants.

29. This view is in fact an integral part of much Marxist class analysis, as is evidenced in Marx's famous statement that those who control the process of material production also control the process of mental production. Steven Lukes refers to ideological control as the third dimension of power. For details, see Lukes (1974).

6. Social Policy

SOCIAL policy is a comprehensive term in that it refers to all 'central and local governmental policies [which] affect the lives of individuals and communities' (Jary and Jary 1991: 590). In this chapter we shall examine selectively those social policies in Hong Kong, in particular social welfare policy and public housing policy, which affect a sizeable portion of the population. Our discussion will be guided by the consideration that a number of factors—including the society's economic conditions and power configuration, the values and beliefs of the population, and the objectives, structure, and capacity of government—bear on the making and implementation of social policy.

It is in this light that Ian Scott and Kathleen Cheek-Milby (1986) delineate the social-policy process as involving three stages. The first stage sees the conversion of societal values into government goals. It is followed by the second stage, the allocation of resources for goal attainment. Both these events are circumscribed by the distribution of power in society, and by the government's perception of what best advances its own legitimacy and the interests of society. The final stage is policy implementation, which is primarily contingent on governmental efficiency and capacity, for example its internal co-ordination, the quality of its personnel, and its ability to enlist public cooperation. Most studies of social policy in Hong Kong do not use this procedural framework, but they do address to varying degrees the issues which it covers. This is evident in the perspectives on social policy in Hong Kong articulated in some of the pertinent studies. We shall examine these before turning to a detailed analysis of selected social policies.

Perspectives on Social Policy in Hong Kong

Laissez-Faire and Positive Non-Interventionism

A *laissez-faire* government limits its role to the fundamental duties of protecting members of the society from oppression and injustice, of establishing an administration of justice, and of erecting and maintaining certain public works and institutions which serve the common interests of society but which private individuals do not find it profitable to provide (Smith [1776] 1963). A *laissez-faire* government, in other words, safeguards the operation of the market economy but refrains from interfering with the free play of market forces. Hong Kong's social policy, according to some writers (Friedman 1980; Rabushka 1979), is that of a *laissez-faire* government.

This description of the Hong Kong way of social policy as *laissez-faire*, in the view of the territory's former Financial Secretary Sir Philip Haddon-Cave, was inappropriate and misleading and should be qualified as 'positive non-interventionist'. He explained:

> Attempts to frustrate the operation of market forces will tend to damage the growth rate of the economy, particularly as it is so difficult to predict, let alone control, market forces that impinge on an open economy. But ... the government must play an active role in the provision of those services and facilities essential to life in a civilized community (*Hong Kong Hansard* 1977–8: 813).

Implicit in Haddon-Cave's explanation is the argument that as Hong Kong's open economy has depended largely on the import of raw materials and resources from other countries and the export of products to overseas markets, and as it was beyond the Government's capability to control the international market forces of supply and demand, governmental attempts to intervene in the local economy would be futile. Non-intervention, in addition, would have the effect of sharpening the vigilance and adaptability of private enterprises to international market fluctuations, thus enhancing the efficiency and competitiveness of the local economy. Non-intervention is, in this sense, positive. Moreover, when non-intervention is deemed to have negative consequences, as when private enterprises are losing their competitiveness in the world market or when there are widespread public discontents with those services and facilities which the population consider essential to life in Hong Kong, the Government will see it as its duty to intervene. Seen in this light, positive non-interventionism is a prudent and pragmatic social policy.[1]

Some writers have explained the Government's non-interventionist stance in other ways. Lau Siu-kai (1982), for instance, views it as largely a strategy of the Government to depoliticize society through making economic matters outside the jurisdiction, and hence the responsibility, of the governing body, and through refraining from meddling with the customary values and practices of the Hong Kong Chinese. This strategy, Lau maintains, was complemented by the self-reliance of the local Chinese community and by their political apathy and aversion to interventionist government.[2] In other words, non-interventionist policy was, according to Lau, a combined product of political strategy and social attitudes.

There was at least one section of the Hong Kong Chinese—the industrial capitalists—who, contrary to what Lau argues, did expect active assistance from the Government in the early years of Hong Kong's industrialization. They demanded most of all government assistance in finding and developing sites for the burgeoning manufacturing industries.[3] The Government's response to this demand is the main subject of Stephen Chiu's analysis (1992: chap. 6) of its non-interventionist industrial policy.

Chiu begins his discussion with what he views as an anomaly in the Government's industrial policy: its reluctance to provide assistance to industrialists[4] was at odds with the increasing importance of manufacturing industry and industrial capitalists in Hong Kong's economy. Powerful forces must have been at work which deterred the Government from adopting an interventionist industrial policy. Chiu explores these forces from the theoretical perspective of historical institutionalism. His analysis furnishes an explanation of Hong Kong's non-interventionist social policy in terms of the society's power configuration.

The term 'institutions' in historical institutionalism refers to the established rules and practices within the state, as well as the political linkages between the state and powerful groups in society (Steinmo et al. 1992). According to this perspective, these institutions, which vary in different socio-historical circumstances, shape the making of social policies. In this regard, the linkage between the state and the capitalist class is held to be of particular import in a capitalist society. Chiu argues that during the early phase of Hong Kong's industrialization, the state's policies were constrained on the one hand by its institutionalized practice of financial conservatism, and on the other by its political linkage with certain sections of the capitalist class. He views the practice of financial conservatism as partly the outcome of pressure exerted during the nineteenth and early twentieth centuries by the merchant class on the state to minimize its public expenditure, and partly as a legacy of the British colonial policy of ensuring the financial solvency and self-sufficiency of its colonies. In other words, Hong Kong's non-interventionist social policy is attributable in the first instance to the state's obligation to maintain a balanced or even surplus budget. The state's alliance with the commercial capitalists (that is, the merchants) and the financial capitalists was in Chiu's view the additional factor which contributed to its *laissez-faire* industrial policy of the 1950s and 1960s.

The political linkage between the state and the commercial and financial capitalists was evidenced by the latter groups' predominance in Hong Kong's highest policy-making bodies. Chiu observes that in 1951, for instance, almost all of the unofficial members of the Executive and Legislative councils were businessmen from the territory's commercial and financial sectors; none was an industrial capitalist. This power structure of the state mirrored the power configuration in the society, hitherto an entrepôt economy and just at that time beginning to industrialize. It was in the interests of the established capitalist power bloc to oppose state subsidies to the burgeoning manufacturing industries, for such a policy would mean an increase in state expenditure, which in turn might entail higher taxes on commercial and financial capitalist enterprises. In short, Chiu views the state's non-interventionist industrial policy as the combined product of two institutional factors: its principle of financial stringency and its political linkage with the commercial and financial capitalists.

While Chiu's study is about Hong Kong's industrial policy in the period of initial industrial growth, his historical institutionalist thesis can be applied to an analysis of the territory's social policy in general. It suggests that a change in the institutional factors—the state's linkage with the capitalist class, for instance—will have a significant impact on policy-making. In this light, the state's more interventionist industrial policy since the 1970s would suggest an increasing dominance of industrial capitalists in the local economy as well as within the state's policy-making bodies.[5] On a more general level, the state's expanded role in social service provision in recent years could have been a response to the transformation in the society's power configuration concomitant with the process of democratization.

The Capitalist State and Its Bureaucratic Practices

The studies discussed above are predicated on the assumption that *laissez-faire* approaches and positive non-interventionism characterize the Hong Kong way of social policy. Scott (1986, 1987, 1989b), in contrast, premises his work on a critique of both descriptions as inappropriate to Hong Kong's experience. Hong Kong's social policy, he argues, is far more interventionist than either of these descriptions suggests, as is seen most clearly in the Government's comprehensive public housing scheme, its extensive investment in public works and transport facilities, and its provision of nine years of free education and low-cost medical and health services. He proposes an interpretation of the territory's social policy in the context of a capitalist state (Scott 1989b). The central concept that informs his analysis is the Marxist concept of 'the relative autonomy of the capitalist state'. He observes:

> In the Hong Kong case . . . the state plays an important role in safeguarding the long-term interests of capitalism against parochial short-run considerations and also provides for the authoritative adjudication of disputes arising between capitalists. . . . [I]n order to ensure the reconciliation of different and sometimes conflicting capitalist interests, the state must possess a certain degree of autonomy (Scott 1989b: 190).

In this passage, Scott explains in one broad stroke the nature of the capitalist state in Hong Kong and the reasons for its intervention into the society and economy ('safeguarding the long-term interests of capitalism' and 'adjudication of disputes arising between capitalists'). The concept of relative autonomy is deployed to denote the state's capacity to intervene: The more the state is free from external constraints on its autonomy, the greater its capacity to intervene, and vice versa. This is his paradigm for understanding the nature of Hong Kong's social policy and its variation over time. He proceeds to analyse the territory's social policy in terms of what he considers to be the three principal features of the Hong Kong state's bureaucratic practice: 'value for money', effective line implementation, and the ability to manage crises. Before we examine his analysis, however, we should take note of one fundamental conceptual problem in Scott's study.

Scott's delineation of his 'capitalist state' approach holds the promise of offering an explanation of social policy in terms of the state's attempts to serve the long-term interests of capitalism. Yet his subsequent analysis dwells on the bureaucratic practices of the state and their impact on social policy. It does not explain in what sense these bureaucratic practices can be considered to be unique to a capitalist state, or in what way the ensuing social policy serves the long-term interests of capitalism. The problem is fundamental because it raises the question of whether Scott's study qualifies as a 'capitalist state' analysis. This problem aside, the study remains a valuable contribution to our understanding of social policy in Hong Kong, highlighting the main features which characterize the Hong Kong way of making social policy.

'Value for money', the first feature of bureaucratic practice identified by Scott, resembles Chiu's idea of 'financial conservatism' examined in the last section: 'The Hong Kong Government is extremely cost-conscious.... Operating expenses are pared to a minimum' (Scott 1989b: 192). The consequence of this conservatism is a social policy geared to the minimization of public sector expenditure. The second feature of bureaucratic practice, effective line implementation, refers to line officials'[6] effective implementation of policies formulated by the senior administrative staff of the government bureaucracy. The guiding principle of the Hong Kong civil bureaucracy, Scott argues, is 'getting things done' (hence effective line implementation) rather than careful long-term policy planning. This emphasis, according to Scott (1987), has arisen mainly due to the fact that many of the territory's crises—immigration from China, the arrival of Vietnamese refugees, the 1967 riots—have been externally generated and hence very much beyond the capacity of the Government to anticipate.

The policy orientation of the Government has, then, been typically reactive rather than proactive. 'The government's attention has been concentrated on the immediate critical problem at hand rather than on forecasting future problems or devising long term plans' (Scott 1987: 3). The cumulative effect of this practice is a civil service adept at implementing policies that address immediate, individual problems but ill-equipped to formulate comprehensive and far-sighted policies. As a result, Scott argues, the Government's social policy has on the whole been ad hoc, incremental,[7] and devoid of principled objectives.

In Scott's view (1986), the imbalance between policy formulation and line implementation did not pose a serious problem for government before the 1980s, because the social-political circumstances then did not require radical and pervasive changes in policy. The Government's incremental policy-making and its effective line implementation were on the whole well-suited to the generally stable and depoliticized environment of the time. After all, its policies and practices had apparently brought the territory economic success. 'Its legitimacy ... was based on what were perceived to be its results. So long as the environment remained stable, there was little need for political reform or for further improvements to the policy-making system' (Scott 1986: 459). Thus, while the crisis generated by the 1966 and 1967 riots did force the Government to make drastic policy changes, the stability and prosperity of the subsequent years disposed it to fall back on its previous methods of policy-making.

Hong Kong's social-political environment since the early 1980s, Scott continues, has been fundamentally different from that before that period. The intervention of China and Britain into the territory's affairs, the competition among politicized social groups for resource allocation, and their mobilization into the policy process, have produced what Scott (1986) calls a turbulent environment. The Government's ability to manage the ensuing crises—the third feature of bureaucratic practice in

Scott's account (Scott 1989b)—is now severely handicapped by external constraints on its autonomy: 'Thus at the very moment when its public policy role is, of necessity, increasing, its "relative autonomy"—the ability to enforce new decisions effectively—has substantially decreased' (Scott 1989b: 191). The situation has been aggravated by the Government's continuing reliance on its 'ad hoc, incremental and reactive' mode of policy-making (Scott 1986: 461). As a result, the setback in the Government's relative autonomy, and its entrenched incapacity to make radical and comprehensive policy changes essential for coping with a turbulent environment, has plunged it into crises which are beyond its ability to resolve:

> These are not the sorts of crises that can be easily or wholly solved by making resources available and then using effective line implementation. They require negotiation, bargaining skills and some measure of forward planning, qualities which the Hong Kong Government does not possess in abundance (Scott 1989b: 197).

Scott's studies suggest that the ingrained bureaucratic ethos and practices of the Hong Kong government—in particular its 'value for money' mentality, its emphasis on line implementation rather than on policy planning and formulation, and its ad hoc, incremental approach to problem-solving—have rendered the territory's social policy deficient in vision and principle, and made it incapable of addressing the problems of a turbulent environment. In contrast with Scott's work, the study we examine next holds a more positive view of the territory's social policy.

Social Policy-making as Non-Purposive Adaptation

To describe social policy-making as non-purposive adaptation is to say that social policy is not the outcome of deliberate (or purposive) planning, but rather the product of pragmatic and situational reactions (or adaptations) to environmental changes. This mode of thinking is based on the cybernetic view that decision-making in individual human beings and in organizations is a 'self-steering' and 'automatic' process. The gist of this perspective is admirably captured in Ross Ashby's allegory (Ashby 1952) of a cat sleeping by the fire who moves closer to the fire when it grows dimmer and farther away from it as it grows hotter.[8] Implicit in this illustration is the central thesis in the cybernatic perspective: The self-steering proceeds on the basis of previous experience and knowledge (sensation of heat in the example) and is an automatic response to feedback from the immediate environment (degree of heat). Andrew W. F. Wong (1980) maintains that Hong Kong's social policy and governmental administrative change can best be illuminated from this perspective.

Wong's clarification of the cybernetic perspective will help us comprehend some of the details of his arguments. He points out that the cybernetic perspective views decision-making (or policy-making) in an organization as characterized by the following features. The first feature is attending to, and making decisions on, problems or tasks at the level at which they arise. In the context of government, this means that departments or units in charge of the pertinent tasks are entrusted with the responsibility of making the required decisions and resolving the emergent problems. The central administration monitors the departments' problem-solving performance through established feedback channels. When the performance is deemed to be unsatisfactory, the central administration will seek to introduce policy changes on the basis of its repertoire of existing policies. It is only when this repertoire proves to be inadequate that the administration will try out 'new' policies—policies which to its knowledge have worked successfully in other locations under similar circumstances.

According to the cybernetic perspective, organizations rely on this pattern of decision-making in order to reduce their tasks to a manageable level and to enhance their survival chances by eliminating uncertainties and risks (such as those arising from implementation of untried policies). This implies that policy-making in organizations is typically ad hoc, marginal, and cautious. This depiction of organizational decision-making, incidentally, also shows the organization to be a self-steering and self-modifying mechanism adapting non-purposively to environmental changes. The Hong Kong government's policy-making, according to Wong, is characterized by the cybernetic process described above. His arguments, I think, are as relevant today as at the time of his writing.

Wong takes the view that social policy-making in Hong Kong has been cautious and realistic, as opposed to reactive or impetuous: cautious, in that it is based largely on previous policies, realistic because it is geared to the immediate issues at hand rather than guided by abstract principles. He sees this cybernetic style of policy-making as ensuing from the Government's endeavour to ensure survival in a precarious social-political environment:

With China's ever presence, [the Government] cannot afford to make mistakes, for fear that anti-government and anti-colonial sentiments may flare up, for fear that major policy changes may overstep into Chinese sensitivities, and for fear that major changes might not be acceptable to the population who have been used to continued economic success and social progress without undue government intervention and without having to pay excessively high taxes (A. W. F. Wong 1980: 64).

Hong Kong's social policy is, in Wong's view, circumscribed by the Government's 'politics of survival'. In Hong Kong's context, survival is contingent on the territory's political stability and economic prosperity. The critical variables monitored by the Government in its 'politics of survival' are therefore political stability and economic prosperity, within the parameters of which social policy is made and implemented. And as the two variables are closely bound together—the attainment of one depends on the existence of the other—social policy must not detract substantially from either. In policy-making, the Government is like the allegorical cat, adjusting its positions with reference to these two variables critical to survival. In Wong's view, these are the major constraints on Hong Kong's social policy-making.

Wong sees the Hong Kong government as a cybernetic mechanism reacting and adjusting to changing circumstances with vigilant attention to the twin critical variables of political stability and economic prosperity.

He asserts that the Government's positive non-interventionist policy can best be understood in this light, as is witnessed by the almost cybernetic terms in which the Financial Secretary explained the circumstances for intervention: 'The purposes of intervention must be . . . to facilitate and expedite the adjustment process (*rather than to change the course of the economy*) if it becomes evident that there is a need to do so' (1979 statement by Haddon-Cave, cited in A. W. F. Wong 1980: 70; emphasis added by Wong). Wong also supports his contention with reference to a number of changes in social policies in the 1970s. The expanded public assistance scheme, the introduction of additional free and compulsory education, and the stepping up of labour legislation for the protection of workers had all 'come about naturally and automatically as a result of evolution, of adaptation, and of trial-and-error' (A. W. F. Wong 1980: 70).

More illuminating than the examples given above is his illustration from social welfare policy. Before the 1970s, as the population's welfare needs were catered to by voluntary agencies in the private sector, the Government minimized its expenditure (as the entailed tax increase would detract from economic prosperity) and required tasks by pursuing a largely non-interventionist welfare policy. In the 1970s, however, mounting welfare demands from the public posed threats to the territory's political stability, to which the Government responded by drastically expanding its welfare provisions. In this way, the Government adapted to the environment through a pragmatic monitoring of the two variables critical to its survival. In other words, the Government's social policy, as exemplified in the case of social welfare, is shaped by its survival orientations rather than by any benign or sinister motives:

Hong Kong's . . . policy is best understood in terms of cybernetic ideas, not as 'considered decisions' of the Government machinery for the good of Hong Kong or as exploitative 'crude capitalism' achieving economic success at the expense of the 'human drudgery and suffering' of the working class (A. W. F. Wong 1980: 68).

Judged by its results—the society's renowned stability and prosperity—the Hong Kong way of social policy seems to have been well-suited to the territory's special social-political circumstances. Yet, as these results have come about as a consequence of the Government's non-purposive adaptation, Wong depicts this success (sic) in social policy as a 'muddling through', as 'accidental and not intentional' (A. W. F. Wong 1980: 66, 79). The people of Hong Kong, he notes insightfully in conclusion, understand well the precarious political circumstances of the territory and have learned to be moderate in their expectations and demands on the Government. Wong maintains that the Hong Kong people have been cowed by adversity into being content, and that it is this contentment which underwrites the viability of the territory's way of social policy.

Comments and Critique

Wong's cybernetic analysis suggests that it would be misleading to view Hong Kong's social policy as shaped by the interests and perspectives of a capitalist power bloc.[9] As such, his view differs from Chiu's (1992) as it was expressed in the study examined above. If we subject the two critical variables of political stability and economic prosperity in Wong's discussion to a more searching analysis, however, the way is open for a possible narrowing of the two scholars' different positions. Hong Kong's economic well-being, and by implication its political stability, undoubtedly hinge substantially on capital accumulation. In this sense, to safeguard the territory's prosperity and stability, the Government in making its policies is under the constraint to solicit the good will and cooperation of the capitalists. One does not have to postulate, as Chiu (1992) seems to have done, a collusion between the Government and a capitalist power bloc. The Government's primary task may be as Wong asserts—survival—and survival obviously involves more than simply placating the capitalists. It serves the Government's survival needs to attach a high priority to capitalist interests in policy-making. To omit this consideration is to overlook an important feature of social policy in Hong Kong.

Wong's study also differs from Scott's in its assessment of the Government's policy formulation and implementation. Scott views the Government's ad hoc, incremental policy-making, and its emphasis on effective line implementation, to have seriously detracted from its capacity to adapt to crisis situations. Wong maintains that this style of policy formulation and implementation is typical of a cybernetic mechanism, of which the Hong Kong government is an example. He argues further that this is in fact well-suited to Hong Kong's social-political environment. He sees the Government as possessing the 'cybernetic capacity'—in its feedback channels, its repertoire of experiences and policies, and its propensity to borrow from other countries' policies in times of need—to respond effectively to crises. The Government's drastic policy changes in the wake of the 1966 and 1967 disturbances lend support to his contention.

It might be expected that Wong would agree with Scott, however, that the reduction in the Government's relative autonomy during the transition to 1997—in cybernetic terms, an adverse interference with the organization's self-steering and self-modifying capabilities—contributes to a crisis which the Government lacks the policy-making ability to resolve. Perhaps most noteworthy is the thesis underlying both writers' studies that survival orientations circumscribe policy-making and policy changes in Hong Kong. In this respect, Wong's 'politics of survival' finds a counterpart in Scott's discourse on the Government's crisis management and on legitimacy and policy change.[10] In that light, we now examine to what extent Hong Kong's social welfare policy and public housing policy bear the features identified in the above perspectives.

Case Study One: Social Welfare Policy

In Hong Kong, social welfare in the broadest sense refers to services such as education, medical and health care, public housing, social security, labour services, and services for disabled persons, elderly people, children and youth, and offenders.[11] This section is a general discussion of the development of social welfare policy in Hong Kong. The following section will deal specifically with the case of public housing, which has been of great importance in the territory in recent decades.[12]

Trading Post Policy: 1841–1941

Catherine Jones' description of Hong Kong's social policy before the Second World War as a 'trading post policy' (1990: 115) applies aptly to the Colony's welfare policy at the time, for the Government's very meagre welfare provisions were indeed geared to the territory's status and value as an entrepôt. The interests of the merchants were the overriding concerns of the Government, and these were pursued with little regard for the welfare needs of the Chinese population. In any case, the Chinese were mainly sojourners from the mainland, who had come to earn an income to support their families and to finance their retirement in their homeland. Pressure from the merchants to minimize public expenditure[13] was reinforced by the Government's own feeling that it had little moral obligation to look after a transient population who did not regard Hong Kong as their permanent home (Jones 1990: 121). Generosity from the Government, according to a senior official of the time, would in fact have undesirable consequences for the Colony:

Indiscriminate and lavish aid afforded in Hong Kong to destitutes... would practically add like a magnet attracting from all nooks and corners of the Canton [Guangdong] Province swarms of professional beggars and lepers to a Colony like this where money is more plentiful than anywhere in the province of Canton (Inspector of Schools Eitel, cited in Hodge 1981: 6).[14]

After all, the tradition of self-help among the Chinese enabled the Government to substantially limit its welfare provision without incurring public discontent. Hong Kong's welfare policy before the war—and some would say there was hardly any[15]—was confined to the bare necessity of ensuring the Colony's viability as an entrepôt. Even in this activity, the Government's role was little more than to supplement the work carried out by voluntary agencies. The accounts by Jones (1990, chap. 5) and Nelson Chow (1991, chap. 2) testify to this self-limitation.

In a circumstance in which care and support would not be immediately forthcoming from family and relatives on the mainland, and could not be expected from the Government, the Hong Kong Chinese found a solution by setting up a network of mutual help in the form of the Clansmen Associations. These associations, Chow observes, could afford but short-term and limited welfare assistance on account of their inadequate resources and restrictive membership. It was not until 1870 that the Government saw the need to give the Chinese community material support in founding an institution—the Tung Wah Hospital—to care for, initially, the sick and the dying, and later, the poor and the needy as well. The Government's support was nevertheless meagre, consisting of the provision of the site and some money. The Chinese merchants took up the main financial and managerial responsibility. An offshoot of the Tung Wah Hospital, the Po Leung Kuk, was established in 1883, with the assurance of Government support, to remedy the then growing problem of the kidnapping and sale of women and girls into servitude and prostitution. Apart from the Chinese merchants, missionaries also played a major part in welfare provision, particularly in the care of orphans, children, and the elderly (Chow 1991: 22–3).

The Government's welfare role was confined mainly to the redressing of grievances and anomalies that would detract from the territory's attractiveness as an entrepôt. Thus, Jones notes (1990: 122), it was only in the wake of the 1920s labour unrest that the Government made the first moves to promote general safety at work. Moreover, it was not until the trauma of a bubonic plague outbreak at the turn of the century that the Government was propelled into adopting an interventionist role in medical and health matters, culminating in the provision of free or cut-price medical services to the general public by the end of the 1930s (Jones 1990: 133–5). Jones' assessment of policy-making in this period echoes the views of the writers in our earlier discussion:

This has been a tale of piecemeal social policy contrivance and unforeseen, unintended policy accumulation. No overriding sense of purpose or direction is apparent or to be expected (Jones 1990: 149).

Coping With a Refugee Population: 1945–1967

Despite the massive influx of refugees in the late 1940s and 1950s, the Government's welfare policy in this period remained fundamentally the same as before the immigrants' arrival. The Social Welfare Office, established in 1948, was intended for the purpose of providing short-term emergency relief and of maintaining a liaison with voluntary welfare agencies; its prime objective was not to provide long-term welfare services itself (Jones 1990: 166–167). The Government still adhered strictly to the policy of encouraging the Chinese to help themselves. This policy was evidenced in its declared 'emergency relief' objective:

[The objective was] to help only the most genuine cases of distress amongst women and children and the old and infirm, and to this end careful checks ensured that only 2% of the 3,000 to 4,000 daily clients [in 1947] were adult males, that few if any were professional beggars, and that children formed nearly half the total number (Hong Kong Government 1948: 81).

More long-term welfare services, meanwhile, were expected to come by way of revitalizing traditional Chinese neighourhood organizations—the Kaifong Associations—which the Government helped to launch in 1949. Yet this effort of the Government to inculcate mutual help among the Chinese could generate but token assistance to the quickly expanding refugee population, many of whom, as newcomers, had neither knowledge of nor entitlement to *kaifong* welfare services. Their survival and well-being owed much to the massive aid provided by voluntary agencies funded by international relief and religious organizations.[16] The 1950s and early 1960s were indeed Hong Kong's golden era of voluntary welfare activity (Webb 1977). This involvement enabled the Government to retreat again into playing a supplementary and reactive 'crisis management' role in welfare provision, seen mostly starkly in its public housing policy of the time. Chow observes: 'Welfare services in those days were provided mainly by voluntary agencies. Whether in terms of quantity or variety, the services run by voluntary agencies exceeded those coming from the government' (Chow 1990: 27).

This 'golden era', however, was drawing to an end by the mid-1960s, when Hong Kong's growing affluence rendered it no longer a deserving target for international aid. The Social Welfare Department (reconstituted in 1958 from the Social Welfare Office) had now to shoulder the main responsibility in welfare provision, but its approach was still to limit the Government's role through reinvigorating the tradition of self-reliance among the Chinese population. In keeping with this intention, the Government stated in its first White Paper on welfare policy that 'everything possible must be done to support and strengthen the sense of family responsibility, since the family can deal with needs arising from poverty, delinquency, infirmity and natural disaster' (Hong Kong Government 1965: 11). Its policy, as Jones aptly observes (Jones 1990: 195), was little different from that in its first hundred years, 'piecemeal and incremental', and characterized by a dedication to 'carrying on'.

A policy targeted at a tradition-oriented, acquiescent refugee population soon proved to be inadequate in response to the rising expectations of a rapidly Westernizing society and of a new generation of local-borns. The 1966 and 1967 riots signalled to the Government that a revamping of its welfare policy was vital to the territory's future stability and prosperity.

Building a New Hong Kong: From 1968

The Government's new welfare policy orientation is epitomized in an oft-quoted statement from Governor MacLehose's speech to the Legislative Council: 'people will not care for a society which does not care for them' (speech to the opening session, 6 October 1976). The Government, it seems, had come to recognize that Hong Kong had entered into an era in which a policy of 'caring for the people' was socially and politically more opportune than was one of 'encouraging the people to care for themselves'. It accordingly sought to build a new, better Hong Kong on what it identified as the 'four pillars' of the future society: housing, education, medical and health care, and social welfare.[17]

The Government announced in 1972 its ten-year housing programme with the aim of providing public housing for 1.8 million people by the year 1982. It introduced the policy of six years of universal free and compulsory primary education in 1971, and extended it to cover three years of secondary education in 1978. A public assistance scheme was instituted in 1971 to cater to the financial and material needs of the poor, the elderly, and the disabled. And the Government's 1974 White Paper on 'The Further Development of Medical and Health Services in Hong Kong' paved the way for a shift in emphasis from epidemics prevention and control to the provision of more and better health services for the population.[18] At the same time, the public were mobilized to contribute their efforts to this grand scheme of community-building. The ensuing Community

Chest, a multi-purpose charitable fund-raising vehicle founded in 1968, has arguably been the most noteworthy and long-lasting testimony to the public's commitment to helping their less fortunate fellow citizens. It remains an important source of funding, in addition to that granted by the Government, for the territory's voluntary welfare agencies.

The voluntary welfare agencies also embarked on their programme of community-building, but in a manner which the Government did not deem complementary to its own effort. A new breed of welfare workers, the first crop of professionally trained social work graduates from the territory's universities, imbued with the ideology of justice and equality for all, set themselves the task of organizing and mobilizing at the grass roots to pressure the Government to give more attention to the needs of the society's deprived and underprivileged members (Chow 1994). A host of grass-roots 'protest' organizations were formed in the late 1960s and 1970s, the best-known of which include the Society for Community Development, the People's Association for Public Housing, and the Christian Industrial Committee. For the first time, the Government's welfare policy was subject to organized popular scrutiny and challenge.

Nonetheless, the impact of this scrutiny on welfare policy-making in the 1970s was probably slight, for as Chow (1985: 484) points out, these 'pressure groups' had no mutually agreed goals, displayed no consistent effort or strategy in their action, and seemed unable to carry the masses with them. Nor was the social-political climate ready to accommodate their confrontational approach to social welfare. As yet, 'professional social work and organized "legitimate" social action were notions new to the general run of Hong Kong Chinese' (Jones 1990: 225). This inchoate welfare activism was to exert a much greater impact on welfare policy later, however, for many of these early welfare activists were to become the territory's popular politicians and leaders during its development towards a representative government. Welfare policy-making in Hong Kong since the early 1980s, according to Chow (1985), has evolved into the 'politics of social choice'.

This 'politics of social choice' has ushered in a new phase in Hong Kong's welfare development, as before the 1980s welfare policy-making was almost entirely the business of the civil bureaucracy with no democratic participation from the masses. In contrast, the politicization of the society in the wake of the Sino-British negotiations about Hong Kong's future and the entry of elected members into the Legislative Council in the mid-1980s have increasingly subjected policy-making to the demands and choices of the people. Chow (1985) maintains that the future shape of Hong Kong's welfare system will be contingent on the interplay of political forces in the community, on their relative ability to influence and mould the preferences and choices of the people. It is here that the ideology of 'justice and equality' of the welfare activists of the previous decade bears significantly on contemporary welfare policy-making, for their history of social service to the community and the grass-roots networks they established have greatly facilitated their mobilization for popular support in democratic political competition.

The extent to which this ideology can become the principle of welfare policy-making, Chow points out (1994), depends ultimately on the pace and scope of democratization and on the population's attitudes towards the Government's role in welfare provision. For this reason, many of the welfare activists of the past are today's champions of democracy, who simultaneously take on the task of educating the masses about their rights as citizens and their entitlement to welfare services. The efforts of these activists are generating a substantial impact on welfare policy-making:

There is no doubt that the trend is now set for more and more people in Hong Kong to regard the enjoyment of social welfare as their right. And together with the progress of democracy, people will also ask for a greater share in the making of policies on services to which they think they are entitled (Chow 1994: 333).

This increased popular involvement in policy-making is, unfortunately, no guarantee that social welfare policy will be guided by long-term and principled objectives. Policy development in the recent past, it is clear, did not seem to be moving in that direction. Both Chow (1985) and Scott (1986) register a tendency on the part of the Government to fall back on ad hoc and piecemeal policy-making as a safe way to cope with the 'turbulence' of the current political situation, 'to avoid making major mistakes' (Chow 1985: 448), and not to 'risk another upheaval by overhauling the policy-making system' (Scott 1986: 465). Jones (1990), on the other hand, holds a sceptical view of the current trend of development:

The picture is scarcely one of solidarity, either between people or between people and Government. People forever on the demand, Government forever on the defensive: there is little sense of joint venture, whatever the rhetoric of community building... might have sought to imply (Jones 1990: 258–9).

Nor is Chow (1995) optimistic about the prospects for social welfare development in Hong Kong. Referring to the constraining stipulations in the Basic Law, he cautions against viewing democratization as conducive to any fundamental change in Hong Kong's welfare policy after 1997. In particular, he draws attention to two articles (Chow 1995: 405, 408) of the Basic Law which lay down the parameters for social welfare policy in the Hong Kong Special Administrative Region:

On the basis of the previous social welfare system, the Government of the Hong Kong Special Administrative Region shall, on its own, formulate policies on the development and improvement of this system in the light of the economic conditions and social needs (Basic Law, Article 145).
The Hong Kong Special Administrative Region shall follow the principle of keeping expenditure within the limits of revenues in drawing up its budget, and strive to achieve a fiscal balance, avoid deficits and keep the budget commensurate with the growth rate of its gross domestic product (Basic Law, Article 107).

The pro-democracy political parties and groups, Chow observes further (Chow 1995: 409), despite their growing influence within the legislature, will have little power to initiate new policies or to change policies enacted by the Government. Chow believes that while there is evidence[19] that the 'choice of the people' is changing towards an expectation of expanding welfare provisions from the Government, the pro-democracy political parties will face great difficulties in translating this choice into policies:

One can... predict, in accordance with the stipulations of the Basic Law, that social welfare in Hong Kong will remain largely residual in nature, with the government confining its help to people who, for one reason or the other, cannot have their needs satisfied through the family or the market.... The future for political parties to make an influence on social welfare looks... rather pessimistic (Chow 1995: 408, 409).

Case Study Two: Housing Policy

Coping with Emergencies: 1954–1971

Hong Kong's housing policy began by accident. The background was the presence of a massive squatter population (estimated at around 300,000 persons by the end of the 1950s), most of whom were refugees from China. The circumstance was the fire in 1953 in the Shek Kip Mei squatter area, which rendered some 50,000 people homeless, followed by another the next year in the Tai Hang Tung squatter area resulting in a further 24,000 homeless. Fire victims roaming the streets of Hong Kong posed a menace to public order; emergency relief for them cost money; and squatters were proliferating and occupying land much needed for urban and industrial development. Pragmatic considerations such as the above prompted the Government to introduce in 1954 an emergency housing policy to rehouse squatters in government-built low-cost and high-density resettlement blocks. The Government was candid about its policy objectives:

Squatters are not resettled simply because they need or deserve hygienic and fireproof homes. They are resettled because the community can no longer afford to carry the fire risk, health risk, and threat to public order and prestige which the squatter areas represent and because the community needs the land of which they are in illegal occupation. And the land is needed quickly (Commissioner for Resettlement 1955: 46).

Still another housing problem surfaced in the early 1960s, not only constituting a potential threat to the territory's order and stability but also aggravating the squatter problem. The rents charged for private tenements were then so high that many of their residents were forced to economize either by living in overcrowded and substandard units, or by escaping into squatter areas. Keith Hopkins's 1968 survey study, for instance, revealed that over half the squatters at the time of the study had been living in private tenements before they moved out into squatter huts, and that most of them had become squatters since 1960 (Hopkins 1971: 286). The Government thus deemed it necessary to supplement resettlement housing with an additional form of public housing for existing tenants of substandard tenement buildings. This was low-cost housing, which the Government introduced in 1961.[20] In both cases, however, the main criterion for rehousing the residents was not their relative deprivation, but the economic cost and benefit of the operation (Drakakis-Smith 1979: 44). In this connection, a number of writers have observed that the Government's housing policy was guided by the imperatives of revenue and capitalist industrial development rather than the housing needs of the low-income groups.

John K. Keung (1985) points out that most of the land reclaimed from the squatters was used for purposes other than the provision of public housing—the amount of cleared land allocated for the construction of public housing was in fact far below the 40 per cent originally designated by the Government. Ho Kwok-leung (1989, chap. 4) considers the housing policy to have been targeted at two economic objectives: first, to boost government revenue through the sale of the cleared land, and second, to relocate the affected population to sites close to outlying industrial complexes so as to supply an easily available source of labour for capitalist industrial production. Manuel Castells et al. (1988), on the other hand, view public housing as vital to the stability and success of the local capitalist industrial economy. Public housing, they maintain, lowers the cost of living for workers, thus enabling the capitalist to pay low wages without provoking militant action in return. A cheap and contented labour force reduces substantially the cost of production, and hence enhances the competitiveness of the territory's products in overseas markets. They argue, in addition, that public housing had the effect of curbing rent increases in the private sector, making it possible for the territory's many small and medium-sized industrial enterprises (a sizeable proportion of which operated in rented residential units) to compete successfully in international markets.

On the whole, the housing policy in this period was geared to rehousing the settlers cleared from squatter settlements. By 1972, some 90 per cent of the residents in public housing were former squatters (Rebecca Chiu 1994: 341). As the pertinent housing blocks were constructed very much as an emergency measure and at low cost, they were of poor quality and incurred high maintenance costs. It took the turmoil of the mid-1960s to convince the Government that the emergency measures fell far short of meeting the population's housing needs and had to be replaced by a more long-term and comprehensive housing policy.

The Ten Year Housing Programme and the Home Ownership Scheme: 1972–1986

The 1970s was the era of community-building, and housing was designated as one of the pillars on which a new Hong Kong was to be constructed after the shattering experiences of the 1966 and 1967 riots. It was in this spirit that the Ten Year Housing Programme was launched in 1972, on the initiative of Governor MacLehose:

300,000 people still live in squatter huts or temporary housing. Many units in resettlement estates are badly overcrowded, or have no separate wash places or lavatories.... It is my conclusion that the inadequacy and scarcity of housing and all that this implies, and the harsh situations that result from it, is one of the major and constant sources of friction and unhappiness between the Government and the population. It offends alike our humanity, our civic pride and our political good sense.... It is not a situation which we can accept indefinitely (MacLehose, in speech to the Legislative Council, 18 October 1972).

Specifically, the housing programme aimed at eliminating all squatter areas and providing self-contained accommodation for those living in overcrowded dwellings, both in private tenements and public resettlement estates. The plan was to rehouse, within the ten-year period, some 1.8 million people in public housing estates. But since land was in short supply in the urban areas on Hong Kong Island and in Kowloon, the public housing estates were to be built mainly in the more spacious new towns in the New Territories.[21] These new towns were designed to be self-contained communities with all manner of facilities: private and public housing, industry, shopping and commercial areas, and a wide range of recreational and community services.

The provision of public housing in the period, however, did not live up to the promise of the programme. The housing units subsequently completed provided accommodation to only around one million people (about 56 per cent of the targeted number). The shortfall could not have been induced by financial difficulties, for as Benjamin K. P. Leung (1991a: 85) notes, the decade 1973–82 was on the whole a period of remarkable economic growth and gross government budget surpluses.[22] Leung views the shortage, instead, as reflective of the Government's reversion to a policy of financial stringency in the circumstances of the social and political stability of the decade. Scott (1989b: 155) similarly explains it in terms of the Government's 'traditions of fiscal conservatism' and its 'vulnerability to criticism from business and financial interests on social policy'.

Other debilitating factors, Scott observes, were the Government's lack of a sustained commitment to the programme, and the different policy priorities of departments at the implementation level. For example, the New Territories Administration, which at the time had the overall coordinating responsibility for the building of the new towns, was primarily concerned with maintaining the stability of the New Territories and minimizing the discontent which the new towns policy was generating among the local population. Policy implementation was subordinated to the priority of securing the good will of the local residents, who demanded compensation for the land to be cleared and who were worried that the influx of new residents from the urban areas would disrupt the established power structure of the area (Scott 1987: 13; 1989a: 156). Scott comments:

Implementation implies a willingness to clear obstacles (in the form of other value choices) out of the way to enable projects to be completed on schedule. In the case of housing, other values assumed greater immediate priority and frustrated the achievement of specified targets. Adequate housing for all was never the Hong Kong government's prime objective despite the rhetoric of its leaders (Scott 1987: 14).

It was partly to make up for the shortfall in the housing programme, and partly in response to the rising affluence of the public housing tenants and the general population, that the Government introduced in 1978 the Home Ownership Scheme and the complementary Private Sector Participation Scheme.[23] Many of those residing in public housing were now earning an income which far exceeded the upper limits set for entry into this sector. Yet, eviction on grounds of excessive income or a striking increase in rent levels on the 'disqualified' tenants seemed politically unpractical, as both options were likely to provoke the affected residents to confrontation with the Government. Meanwhile, improved living standards were generating among the public an aspiration for home ownership, at the same time that property prices in the private sector were well beyond the financial capability of the majority. The Government's attempted solution was to offer for sale, to both public housing tenants and the lower-income and middle-income families in the private sector, housing units at below market prices. Demand, however, soon grossly outstripped supply, and by 1987 sales of these government-subsidized properties were fifteen times over-subscribed. It was in this context that the Government launched, in the same year, its Long Term Housing Strategy to extend the range of options available to home buyers.

Catering to the Housing Needs of an Affluent Society

The Long Term Housing Strategy, which provides a framework for Hong Kong's housing policy up to the year 2001, has as its prime objectives the redevelopment of older public housing estates (that is, resettlement housing and former government low-cost housing), and the promotion and accommodation of public demand for home ownership. Both objectives were apparently targeted at easing the territory's problems in the transition to 1997. The overall goal of the strategy, according to an official statement, was 'to promote social stability and sense of belonging to Hong Kong by improving the needy's living conditions and maximizing the opportunity for home purchase'.[24] The strategy also includes a plan to provide permanent public housing to those residing in government-built Temporary Housing Areas, which at the end of 1992 were offering accommodation to some 65,000 people rendered homeless by squatter clearance and disasters (Leung Wai-tung 1993: 269–70).

The emphasis of the strategy, however, is on promoting home purchase. Hence, as a supplement to the Home Ownership Scheme, the Home Purchase Loan Scheme was introduced in 1988. Through this programme, the Government would provide a subsidy, in the form of an interest-free loan for the initial down payment, to eligible families to buy flats in the private sector. In 1991, the Government extended the loan scheme to include the option of a subsidy in the form of a monthly contribution towards mortgage repayment for three years.

The public's response to the Home Purchase Loan Scheme was far from enthusiastic. Property prices in the private sector were soaring, and the Government's subsidy (which was only about 31 per cent of that in the Home Ownership Scheme) proved to be grossly insufficient for home purchase. The loan scheme fell far short of its objective of enhancing home ownership through government subsidy and private sector participation.[25] In any case, the above schemes were intended to cater to the home purchasing needs of the lower and lower-middle income groups. The majority of the middle class were earning an income which rendered them ineligible for the Government's housing subsidies.

Hong Kong has been developing into a middle-class society since the late 1970s. It seemed clear to many obervers by the early 1990s that to ensure the territory's future stability, and to foster a sense of belonging to the community under the shadow of 1997, the Government's housing policy, like its other social policies, had to take into serious account the needs and demands of the middle class.[26] It was in such social-political circumstances that the Government in 1992 launched its Housing Scheme for Middle-income Families.

This housing scheme for the 'sandwich class' is in essence an extension of the Home Ownership Scheme to include better-off middle-class families. For the purpose, six sites have been reserved to produce about 5,000 flats by 1996–7 for sale to eligible families at below market prices. As the first flats would not be available until 1995, the Government adopted the interim measure of offering low-interest loans of 20 per cent of the flat price, up to a loan limit of HK$500,000, to help the beneficiaries to buy domestic units in the private sector. One thousand families benefited from the scheme in 1993, the first year of its operation. The coverage is obviously limited, but the scheme seems to be successful in communicating the message that the Government is attending to the housing needs of the middle class.

Conclusion

We examined in the first half of this chapter a number of perspectives on social policy in Hong Kong, in the light of which we surveyed the development of the territory's social welfare and housing policies. While these perspectives differ in analytic focus, they converge on one underlying theme: promoting political stability and economic prosperity has been the Hong Kong way of social policy.[27] This theme provides us with the guiding thread for summarizing and comparing the contributions of these perspectives to our understanding of the making and development of social policy, in particular social welfare and housing policies, in Hong Kong.

Wong's cybernetic perspective dwells on the organizational goals and dynamics of the Hong Kong civil bureaucracy. The overriding 'goal' is survival, and given the territory's precarious existence, survival requires a vigilant monitoring of the twin variables of economic prosperity and political stability. The 'dynamics' is to adapt to changing circumstances by relying and improving on existing policies; this practice reduces risks and hence enhances survival chances. This description seems to match closely the Government's perception of its policy objectives in social welfare and housing. In the nineteenth century, the Government economized on welfare provision, because generosity would bear negatively on the Colony's stability by attracting a massive influx of 'professional beggars and lepers' from across the border. It found little need to change its welfare policy in the two decades after the Second World War, as it considered the welfare services of the voluntary sector already adequate for a population accustomed to self-reliance.

Moreover, the Government's vastly expanded welfare role since the early 1970s, coming in the aftermath of the crisis of legitimacy of the mid-1960s, was predicated on a pragmatic political calculation: People will not care for a government which does not care for them. In a similar vein, we can perceive the evolving housing policy as a series of ad hoc pragmatic solutions to environmental challenges: resettlement housing to contain the threat to public order posed by the squatters and to clear land for industrial and urban development; the ten-year housing programme motivated by the 'political good sense' of community-building in the wake of traumatic riots; home-ownership schemes to inculcate a sense of belonging to the territory to combat the confidence crisis in the transition to 1997.

This style of ad hoc, short-term policy-making and implementation, with its emphasis on tackling only immediate problems, Scott argues, has very much been the product of the exigencies of Hong Kong's social-political circumstances. The territory was time and again 'invaded' by externally induced crises which the Government could neither anticipate nor forestall. Its policy was to cope with each crisis as it occurred, for its survival was more a matter of immediate crisis management than long-term policy planning. Thus, it handled the post-war influx of refugees and the attendant squatter problem with an emergency resettlement housing programme. It reacted to the 1967 anti-colonial disturbances—a crisis induced by the Cultural Revolution in China—with drastic changes in social policies aimed at restoring the legitimacy of the colonial government. Taking care of individual problems and crises as they arose, it seems, has been the prime motor of policy development in Hong Kong. Jones expresses a similar view in her concluding remark on the Hong Kong way of social policy:

A prolonged 'caretaker' administration, confronted with a sequence of crises and potential crises—environmental, demographic, economic, political in varying combination—is drawn by stages into taking on more and more responsibility for the domestic well-being of the Colony (Jones 1990: 283).

This ad hoc, reactive approach to social policy-making, Scott maintains, has contributed to a trained incapacity among the policy-makers. They lack both the will and the know-how to formulate—and coordinate the implementation of—long-term policies. This deficiency is evidenced starkly in the failure of the Ten Year Housing Programme to achieve its targets, and in the Government's inappropriate reliance on incremental, piecemeal policy-making in the turbulent period of the late 1980s. In this light, one can hardly be optimistic about the fulfilment of the promises of the current Long Term Housing Strategy, especially in view of the fact

Table 6.1 Social Service Expenditure as a Percentage of Public Expenditure: Selected Years

	Hong Kong	Other Countries
1949–50	16.7	Singapore (1993): 37.1
1959–60	36.4	
1969–70	40.7	Taiwan (1992): 37.4
1979–80	43.6	
1989–90	44.7	The United Kingdom (1985–86): 55.1
1993–94	44.9	
1994–95	46.8	
1995–96	47.0 (estimate)	

Source: Data for Hong Kong based on Hong Kong Government, *Annual Budget*, various years. Data for other countries based on Singapore Ministry of Information and the Arts, 1994, *Singapore 1994*, p. 309, appendix 26; Council for Economic Planning and Development, Republic of China, 1993, *Taiwan Statistical Data Book 1993*, p. 158, table 9–3b; Jones (1990: 256, table 7.6). Note: For Hong Kong and the United Kingdom, 'social services' refers to social welfare, housing, medical and health services, and education. For Singapore, the relevant item in *Singapore 1994* Appendix 26 is entitled social and community services; there is no specification as to what such services cover. For Taiwan, the relevant item in *Taiwan Statistical Data Book 1993* covers social security, education, science and culture.

that the Government's Home Purchase Loan Scheme has fallen far short of attaining its objectives.

In the final analysis, however, social policy is shaped by the economic and social-political make-up of the society. Policy development in Hong Kong, indeed, has been contingent on transformations in the territory's economic and political structure, as well as on the changing ethos of the Hong Kong Chinese. A *laissez-faire* policy might have been the Government's only viable option at a time when the Colony was little more than a trading post and when the capitalist class held a hegemonic position in the economy and society. Their continued predominance in industrializing Hong Kong, and their nearly exclusive representation in policy-making institutions, could reasonably be expected to have set the parameters of positive non-interventionism. From this perspective, promoting political stability and economic prosperity also meant securing the good will and prioritizing the interests of the capitalist class.

We also have to take note of the fact that over the past few decades, as Table 6.1 shows, Hong Kong's government has been spending an increasingly large proportion of its total expenditure on social services. While the Government's role in social service provision still falls behind that of a welfare state such as the United Kingdom, it compares favourably with other Asian Chinese societies such as Singapore and Taiwan. In addition, the politicization of the community since the early 1980s, and the subsequent entry of popularly elected politicians into policy-making bodies, have increasingly subjected social policy to the scrutiny and choice of the people.[28] The emerging power configuration holds promise of further changes in the Hong Kong way of social policy-making.

Notes

1. For a fuller clarification of the policy of positive non-interventionism, and for a discussion of its application to Hong Kong's industrial development, see Yeung (1991). Writing as a representative of the Government's industry department, Yeung states: '[the positive non-interventionist] approach has been adopted for pragmatic rather than ideological reasons' (Yeung 1991: 49).

2. For a more elaborate discussion of this point, see Chapter 1.

3. This demand is epitomized in a statement by the vice-president of the Chinese Manufacturers' Association: 'Industrial expansion will require Government encouragement and help. I believe the time has come for Government to select a special territory to be developed as an industrial area... [as] haphazard industrial development, without a central directing force, will be of little or no avail' (Tat-chee 1953: 144–5).

4. As evidence, Chiu cites the Government's reluctance to supply industrial land at concessional prices and its refusal to set up an industrial bank to provide loans at reasonable interest rates to industrialists. He notes, for instance, the Government's practice of selling industrial land by public auction. This practice was opposed by the industralists, as it effectively raised the price of industrial land to the highest possible level. Chiu's point about governmental non-interventionism in industrial development is, however, open to debate. The discussion of the Government's public housing policy later in this chapter shows the Government to have played a more interventionist role than Chiu maintains was the case.

5. Some notable examples of state intervention in industrial development since the 1970s include the new land policy of 1973, under which land would be sold at concessional prices for the specific purpose of developing technology- and skill-intensive industries; the establishment of the Hong Kong Industrial Estates Corporation in 1977 to assist in the development and management of industrial estates; the founding of the Vocational Training Council in 1982 to upgrade labour skills; and the setting up of the Hong Kong Design Innovation Company in 1986 to provide industries with comprehensive product innovation, design, and development services. For more details on this point, see Yeung (1991) and Teresa Wong (1991). The political linkage between the state and industrial capitalists, and its impact on industrial policy, remain to be studied.

6. In public administration and organizational studies, there is a distinction between 'line' and 'staff'. 'Line' refers to those organizational personnel in charge of policy implementation, while 'staff' are those in charge of policy planning and formulation.

7. 'Incrementalism' is a conservative method of policy-making in that it seeks to introduce new policies through adjusting and slightly modifying existing policies in response to changing circumstances. In Scott's view, the Hong Kong government lacks the will and the ability to introduce path-breaking policies and has relied on incrementalism as a safe way to deal with problems.

8. This illustration of the cybernetic perspective is cited by A. W. F. Wong (1980: 53).

9. Wong castigates those who view Hong Kong's policy-making as manipulated by a capitalist ruling class or by a collusion of ruling or power élites made up of government bureaucrats and businessmen (A. W. F. Wong 1980: 61).

10. Scott views major policy changes in Hong Kong as attempts on the part

of the Government to resolve crises and to restore its legitimacy. See Scott (1989a, 1989b).

11. This enumerative definition of social welfare is based on Nelson Chow's broad conception of social welfare. See Chow (1985: 475).

12. There are, at the time of writing, five government housing subsidy schemes: the public rental housing programme, the Home Ownership Scheme, the Private Sector Participation Scheme, the Home Purchase Loan Scheme, and the housing scheme for the sandwich class. The first houses about 40 per cent of the population, while the other four together house about 8.7 per cent. In total, the public housing programme benefits nearly half of Hong Kong's population (Leung Wai-tung 1993: 269).

13. See Chapter 1, the sections on W. K. Chan's *The Making of Hong Kong Society* and Ian Scott's *Political Change and the Crisis of Legitimacy in Hong Kong*, for a more detailed discussion of these points.

14. The Government's concerns seemed justified, as the following incident illustrates. In an effort to control the bubonic plague afflicting the Colony around the turn of the century, the Government tried to induce public cooperation by offering two cents for every dead rat handed in. It was subsequently discovered that a sizeable proportion of the rats thus delivered had been imported from China just for the money (reported in Jones 1990: 133).

15. In this regard, Jones writes: 'Who gets what and who is subjected to what, by or from the Hong Kong Government, remains largely a matter of chance' (Jones 1990: 150), implying that there was no well-defined and principled social welfare policy in Hong Kong before the war.

16. For an account of the major voluntary agencies operating in Hong Kong at that time, and the welfare services they provided, see Chow (1990: 25–8).

17. The Government was referring to social welfare in the narrow sense of public assistance for the poor, special allowances and care for the elderly and the disabled, and the expansion of social and recreational facilities. See *Hong Kong Hansard Session* 1972/1973, 18 October 1972, pp. 13–14.

18. For a detailed account of the Government's expanded service provision regarding the 'four pillars', see Jones (1990, chap. 7) and Scott (1989a: 152–63).

19. Chow refers to the survey findings concerning the public's attitudes towards social welfare which were presented in Lau et al. (1991, 1993) and Tam and Yeung (1994). Chow concludes on the basis of these survey findings: 'There is no doubt that people in Hong Kong are increasingly looking to the government as the provider of social welfare' (Chow 1995: 406).

20. In 1973, Government-provided low-cost housing estates were renamed Public Housing Estates Type A; resettlement estates were renamed Public Housing Type B.

21. In 1972, three areas in the New Territories—Tsuen Wan, Castle Peak (renamed Tuen Mun in 1973), and Shatin—had already developed into new towns. Three other areas in the New Territories, namely Yuen Long, Tai Po, and Fan Ling/Sheung Shui, were officially named new towns in 1979.

22. The only year in which the Government had a budget deficit (in the amount of HK$379.9 million) was the financial year 1974–5. But this deficit was small in comparison with the huge surpluses in several subsequent years (for instance, HK$902.6 millions in 1976–7, HK$1,466.9 millions in 1978–9, and HK$6,696.8 millions in 1980–1).

23. The Private Sector Participation Scheme aims to make more use of the resources of the private sector to produce flats for sale at government-subsidized prices.

24. Quoted from 'Review of the Long Term Housing Strategy' (Internal Document, Housing Branch, Government Secretariat 1987; cited in Rebecca Chiu 1994:

349). Leung Wai-tung (1993: 267), a member of the Hong Kong Housing Authority, makes an almost identical statement when referring to the fundamental principles of the strategy.

25. For more details of this shortfall, see Leung Wai-tung (1993: 288–90).

26. Scott (1989a: chap. 6), for instance, considers the middle class to be the primary source of instability in Hong Kong since the mid-1980s. In this respect, he writes: '[the government] has sought to appease the middle class by promising improvements to the quality and quantity of services presently offered—a new university and a large number of places in tertiary educational institutions, more home-ownership schemes, and better medical facilities' (Scott 1989a: 246–7).

27. It is worth noting in this connection that Jones (1990) entitled her comprehensive study of social policy in Hong Kong, *Promoting Prosperity: The Hong Kong Way of Social Policy*.

28. Some notable examples are social policies in respect of the care of the elderly and of retired workers, the importation of workers from mainland China, and equal opportunity in employment. For details, see Henry T. K. Mok (1994) and Suen (1994).

7. Social Conflict and Social Movements

SOCIAL conflict is a comprehensive concept. In the present discussion, we use the term to refer to the struggle between social groups to gain access to, or control over, desired resources. Social movement, on the other hand, is used to refer to organized collective action undertaken on the basis of a belief to bring about or to resist change in a society. The study of social conflict and social movements is an investigation into the origins and process of confrontational collective action.

Despite its situation as a rapidly modernizing society under colonial rule, Hong Kong has been remarkably free from the turmoil and disorder that have plagued other countries in a similar situation. The 'unique' case of Hong Kong has been explained by and large in terms of the ethos and political culture of the indigenous population—the Chinese tradition of political apathy, the 'don't rock the boat' refugee mentality, and utilitarianistic familism (King 1981; Miners 1975; Lau 1982).[1] Such explanations only make more pressing the question of why in fact the territory has experienced a number of large-scale social conflicts, two of which (as our later discussion will illustrate) brought the administration and economy of the colony close to paralysis. These episodes of public disorder suggest that powerful factors instigated unrest in the society—and that these factors were compelling enough to provoke a normally quiescent population to militant collective action.

That instability and disorder have been rare in Hong Kong implies that sufficient instigating factors are operative only under special historical circumstances. The corollary of this supposition is that the territory's stability should be explained not only in terms of the population's social-political ethos, but also of the historical circumstances that have at most times rendered dormant or inoperative the factors that on occasion have incited the population to insurgency. In short, the study of social conflict is at the same time a contribution to our understanding of order and stability. The same viewpoint will inform our study of social movements in Hong Kong.

Theoretical Explanations of Social Conflict and Social Movements: A Brief Review

Social conflict and social movements have traditionally been explained by sociologists and political scientists as the outcome of defects in the social-political order. Typical examples of such defects include gross social inequality, rampant corruption, a lack of communication between government and people, and widespread unemployment. This theoretical approach, variously termed the classical model, the structural-functionalist model, or the breakdown model, summarily conceptualizes these defects as 'structural strain' which, according to the model, generates frustration and discontent.[2] This strain is held to provoke the aggrieved segments of the population to confrontational collective action such as protest, insurgency, and social movement.

The breakdown model has subsequently been challenged on the empirical grounds that social unrest typically occurs under improving social and economic conditions rather than in situations of abject deprivation. The theoretical approach developed from this critique is that of relative deprivation: rising expectations, or a discrepancy between what people want and what they actually get, are the cause of insurgent collective action.[3] What the breakdown model and the relative deprivation model have in common is the thesis that it is a psychological state of frustration and aggression which impels people to disruptive collective action.

More recent theoretical advances have questioned the role of social structural conditions and frustration/aggression as a direct cause of social unrest. The resource mobilization model, grounded in the writings of Anthony Oberschall (1973) and William Gamson (1968), and later developed and systematized in the works of John McCarthy and M. N. Zald (1973) and Charles Tilly (1978), holds that it is the capacity to articulate and mobilize social discontents that is most crucial in the genesis of confrontational collective action. This model views the organizational strength of a potential 'challenger group' as the prime determinant of insurgent uprising and argues, on the basis of empirical studies, that a challenger group will resort to confrontational action when it believes it can mobilize the resources (such as human power, material, and moral support) required for successful collective action. In contrast to the preceeding two models, the resource mobilization model sees social conflict and social movements as a calculated power contest between a challenger group and its opponent(s), not as an unplanned outburst of hostility fuelled by frustrations and discontent with the social establishment.

Another related theoretical advance, epitomized in Doug McAdam's (1982) political process model, locates the impetus of social conflict in the process of interaction between the challenger group and the larger social-political environment. The crucial variable in this view is the challenger group's estimation of the political opportunities afforded by the social-political environment for prospective confrontational action. This estimation is based primarily on an assessment of the power of the challenger group vis-à-vis that of its opponent(s). This model has an inherent historical dimension, for it implies that a challenger group will be inclined to collective action when changes in the social-political environment redress the existing balance of power in its favour. The model includes the additional factor that the challenger group will make use of these appropriate political opportunities when it can articulate a rationale, a justification for action—a process which McAdam terms 'cognitive liberation'. In short, the political process model views social conflict and social movements as the product of the confluence of three conditions: appropriate political opportunities, the challenger group's organizational capacity, and its cognitive liberation.

The cognitive dimension in the political process model acquires a new theoretical significance in Ron Eyerman and Andrew Jamison's (1991) interpretation of social movements as 'cognitive praxis'. A social movement, they argue, is in essence a process of articulating, promoting, and putting into practice (that is, praxis), a new belief or a new ideal (as a result of cognition) in place of an established one. The study of social movements has, therefore, to address first and foremost the sources and emergence of the ideology which motivates and joins together the movement participants in collective action. In this respect, Eyerman and Jamison highlight the important role of historical factors and the prevailing social and intellectual climate in generating the ideology, or what they call the 'cognitive cues', that precipitates a social movement.

In light of these theoretical positions, we may now proceed with our discussion of social conflict and social movements in Hong Kong. We begin with a descriptive account of the four major episodes of social conflict in Hong Kong—episodes which, in terms of duration, number of participants, and damage caused, rank as the most traumatic disturbances in the territory's history.[4] This account will be followed by a discussion of the trend of social conflict, and an analysis of social conflict in Hong Kong. Finally, we take a look at social movements, with the focus of our attention on the labour movement and student movement.

Major Episodes of Social Conflict: The Insurgencies

The General Strike-Boycott of 1925–1926[5]

The insurgency of the general strike and boycott lasted from June 1925 until October of the following year. Its impact on the Colony was later assessed by a historian: 'The strike-boycott was so effective that Hong Kong was almost totally incapacitated economically and financially' (see Chan Lau Kit-ching 1990: 169).

The strike-boycott did not originate from discontents within Hong Kong. Rather, it is more accurately seen as an off-shoot of the anti-imperialist movement of May 1925, which began in Shanghai and soon spread to other major cities in China, including Guangzhou (Canton). To extend this movement to Chinese compatriots under colonial rule, several Guangzhou labour leaders were dispatched to Hong Kong to mobilize a strike against British imperialism. The most influential labour union in Hong Kong at the time was the mechanics' union called the Hong Kong Engineering Institute. Under its leadership, the other labour unions in the Colony had successfully staged a number of strikes against their employers in the early 1920s. In particular, in the Mechanics' Strike of 1920 and the famous Seamen's Strike of 1922, many of the strikers left for Guangzhou, where they were looked after by the labour unions there. It was against this background that the Guangzhou labour unions in 1925 sought to mobilize Hong Kong workers in the anti-imperialist movement.[6]

The labour agitators from Guangzhou intially achieved little success. Chan Lau Kit-ching (1990), in her historical account of the episode, attributed this failure to 'the uncommitting attitude of the vast majority of the [Colony's labour] unions.... [M]any union leaders expressed doubt as to the feasibility of maintaining a large scale strike in the face of ... the intransigence of the Hong Kong government' (Chan Lau Kit-ching 1990: 180). The tide turned, however, when the minister for labour and finance of Guangzhou assured Hong Kong workers of all possible assistance in their anti-imperialist struggle. The strike-boycott in Hong Kong started with over one thousand seamen leaving their jobs on 19 June 1925, and other workers soon followed their example. As a condition for their return to work, the workers presented the Hong Kong government with a list of social and political demands, including equality before the law, popular election, labour legislation, and rent reduction (Chan Lau Kit-ching 1990: 179).

The budding struggle was then escalated by a tragic incident in Guangzhou: on 23 June 1925, 52 anti-imperialist demonstrators were killed and 117 seriously wounded by the British and French troops stationed on Shamian Island. The incident stirred the Hong Kong workers to a patriotic uprising. Many walked out of their jobs and began an exodus to Guangzhou. In Guangzhou the strikers, who at the peak of the exodus numbered over three hundred thousand, were provided food and lodging by the Guangzhou–Hong Kong strike-boycott committee. In addition, the strike committee set up a workers' college for the political training of union cadres and eight extramural schools for adult workers. Many workers were taught lessons on topics such as 'What is imperialism?', 'The history of the imperialist invasion of China', and 'The labour movement in China'. The strike committee also helped to enforce an embargo on Hong Kong and British shipping.

The strike-boycott eventually came to an end, not because of internal developments in Hong Kong but because of the progress of political events in China. In March 1926 the Northern Expedition, to be led by Generalissimo Chiang Kai-shek, was in active preparation in Guangzhou. As Chiang's attention would now be drawn towards waging battles with the warlords in the north, the Hong Kong government opportunely negotiated with the Guangzhou authorities for a settlement of the strike-boycott. The two sides agreed that the Guangzhou government would end the strike-boycott on condition that Britain acquiesced in China's imposition of a special consumption tax of 2.5 per cent on imports. In mid-September, the Guangzhou government announced that the strike-boycott in Hong Kong would end officially on 10 October. Chan comments aptly on the circumstances surrounding the demise of the insurgency in Hong Kong:

It was evident to everyone that the strike-boycott came to end because the Canton [Guangzhou] government saw to it that it did.... The lesson was difficult to forget. For the rest of [Governor Cecil] Clementi's term of office in Hong Kong, he acted with the conviction that, for the sake of the colony's well being, the goodwill of Canton had to be cultivated and maintained at all cost' (Chan Lau Kit-ching 1990: 218–9).

The 1956 Riots[7]

The 1956 riots were sparked by an apparently trivial incident in the Li Cheng Uk resettlement estate: the removal by a Resettlement Department staff member of Guomindang flags which were flying on a resettlement block on 10 October (the National Day of the Guomindang government) in violation of the Department's regulation. Throughout the 1950s, the Hong Kong government was vigilant about any event or sign that would precipitate an outbreak of hostility between the pro-Guomindang and pro-Communist factions, and so it had forbidden the flying of either faction's flags in public housing estates. The removal of the flag on this occasion, however, led to a hostile outburst from the residents of the estate, who demanded that the Department apologize for the incident and that portraits of Sun Yat-sen and Chiang Kai-shek be erected on the block, together with a large Guomindang flag. Some residents then broke into the estate's Resettlement Office and assaulted its staff, and the event escalated into a riot.

The rioting rapidly spread to two other resettlement estates, Tai Hang Tung and Shek Kip Mei. The reason for the speedy escalation of such a seemingly minor event into a major disturbance was hinted at in the Government's official report on the riots. It described the residents in the resettlement estates as 'predominantly in sympathy with the Nationalist [Guomindang] cause and opposed to the present government of China. ... [M]any are loosely organized in right wing labour unions and other bodies' (Hong Kong Government 1956: 2). The report also noted that triad members, many of whom were themselves of Guomindang persuasion, were exploiting the disturbance for criminal purposes: 'Triad members carrying Nationalist flags ... were seen inciting the crowd to yet further disorder' (Hong Kong Government 1956: 11).

This initial phase of the disturbance was followed by another hostile outburst on 11 October in the industrial area of Tsuen Wan where, according to the Government report's estimate, most of the workers were anti-Communist. The immediate cause of the Tsuen Wan rioting was again the flying of Guomindang national flags, although in this case it occurred in a factory dormitory. There was evidence that the events leading to the rioting were premeditated and orchestrated. The official report mentioned meetings of the factory's right-wing union members before 10 October to organize a confrontation with the factory management. Union representatives would demand that the management fly the Guomindang flag and that it dismiss all left-wing workers. Right-wing workers from other factories and triad members were to gather outside the factory in support.

The rioting lasted until 16 October, when the police restored order. The official report recorded 443 casualties, 59 of which were fatal. It described the riots as having the following characteristics: a degree of organization among the mobs, which were led by men with large Guomindang national flags; attacks on buildings housing Communist sympathizers and on their occupants; and the attempt to force factory management to dismiss left-wing workers and to replace them with people acceptable to the right-wing unions. Above all, the report's account of the property damage caused by the riots testifies to the political and partisan nature of the turmoil:

> In Kowloon, all but one of the small factories looted or burnt, and nearly all the thirty shops and private houses are believed to have displayed Chinese Communist flags or decorations on October 1st. Most of the stores which were looted had products from China on sale.... In Tsuen Wan all the union premises and nearly all the private property looted or set on fire were buildings used or occupied by left-wing sympathizers.... No attacks were made on the main administrative or business centres, whether on the mainland or on Hong Kong Island (Hong Kong Government 1956: 47, 52).

The 1966 Riots[8]

The 1966 riots originated in a peaceful protest demonstration against a fare increase by the Star Ferry Company. The events began with a lone demonstrator's hunger strike outside the Star Ferry terminal on 4 April. On the following day he was joined by a small crowd of supporters and was then arrested by the police for obstruction. The crowd soon increased to about four hundred people, who continued the protest that evening with a march through the streets of Kowloon. This demonstration led to a few more arrests, but otherwise the event proceeded in an orderly fashion.

According to the official report on the riots (Hong Kong Government 1967), the demonstration developed into a hostile outburst on the nights of 6 and 7 April, when the police attempted to break up the gathering crowd. The crowd members threw stones at the police and set fire to streetcars and nearby buildings and property. Rioting continued on a smaller scale on the night of 8 April, but by this time the police had taken control of the situation. By the morning of the following day, the riots were over.

The Government-appointed commission of inquiry subsequently discovered that the rioters' hostility did not seem to be directed at the Star Ferry Company, which in fact suffered no property damage during the disturbances. The commission further reported that most of the rioters had little understanding of the issue of the fare increase, most did not appear to harbour any specific grievance against the ferry company, and that the damage they inflicted was indiscriminate. It described their actions as spontaneous, uncoordinated, and lacking in central organization or control (Hong Kong Government 1967: 112). In the commission's report, the incident appears to be a case of issueless rioting generated by spontaneous and irresponsible crowd behaviour.[9]

In contrast, a different account of the riots was provided by Elsie Elliott in her autobiography, *Crusade For Justice* (Elliott 1981: 215–26). Elliot maintains that because of her attacks on police corruption, and because of her involvement in the initial peaceful phase of the Star Ferry protest demonstration, the police were making use of the occasion to frame her for instigating public disorder. In her account, it was the police who deliberately engineered the peaceful demonstration into rioting. She reports that she received a warning from a reliable source that the police had engaged gangsters to cause a riot and that they would put the blame on her by saying that she had paid them to riot. She writes: 'Later at the inquiry into this riot, the young people said that older and tougher demonstrators had been brought in by the police to urge them to riot, even putting stones into their hands...' (Elliott 1981: 215). The commission's report, in her view, was intended as a cover-up to protect the police and the authorities.

The 1967 Riots[10]

As with the 1925–6 strike-boycott, the 1967 riots were to a large extent repercussions of political events occurring in China. The context for the upheaval was the Cultural Revolution, which was gathering momentum throughout China in the mid-1960s. The Cultural Revolution was in essence a domestic power struggle with the ostensible aim of purging the society of recurrent bourgeois, bureaucratic consciousness and practices, but it had political overtones for international relations. Attacks by Chinese leaders on capitalist imperialism, descriptions of Western capitalist regimes as 'paper tigers', and slogans such as 'The East Wind is stronger than the West Wind', carried the message that overseas Chinese compatriots under colonial rule should rise up in struggle against capitalist imperialism. This political and ideological context made it possible in May 1967 for left-wing labour unions and Communist sympathizers in Hong Kong to escalate minor labour disputes rapidly into a territory-wide anti-colonial struggle which lasted until the end of the year.

The political bearing of the disturbances was evident even in the initial phase of the labour disputes. John Cooper (1970: 6) observed that upon their arrest by the police, the worker protesters shouted Communist slogans and some waved copies of Mao Zedong's quotations in defiance of the Hong Kong authorities. The left-wing organizations were quick to seize the opportunity to mobilize a large-scale confrontation against the established order. Under the auspices of the pro-Communist Federation of Trade Unions, these organizations established the All Trades Struggle Committee on 12 May and the All Circles Struggle Committee on 16 May to engineer and coordinate a territory-wide anti-colonial struggle. Within a few days, some 170 struggle committees were formed in schools, trade unions, banks, and other enterprises.

At the same time, moral support was coming from the mainland, raising the insurgents' hopes of intervention from the motherland on their behalf. On 15 May, China's Foreign Ministry issued a statement denouncing the 'fascist measures' of the Hong Kong government and expressing support for the Hong Kong compatriots. On 18 May, the Vice-Foreign Minister declared, 'Chinese care for the righteous struggle of the Chinese compatriots in Hong Kong.'[11] An editorial on 3 June in China's most influential newspaper, *The People's Daily*, called upon the Hong Kong compatriots 'to be ready at any time to respond to the call of the motherland, and smash the reactionary rule of British imperialism'. In response to the editorial, widespread rallies were held on the mainland, and the People's Liberation Army vowed to 'take our place in the forefront of the struggle against British imperialism' as soon as the motherland issued instructions.[12]

With these encouraging messages from China, the struggle committees in Hong Kong escalated the confrontation by launching a series of large-scale industrial actions: a joint strike (lasting 10–15 June), then a general strike (24–28 June), and finally a trade suspension (29 June–2 July). As the colonial government proved to be resilient to these measures, the insurgents resorted to terrorism and bomb attacks, which lasted roughly from August until December. Such tactics had the effect of turning the public against the left-wing faction. By September, the Cultural Revolution's leaders were shifting from a policy of confrontation to a policy of peaceful co-existence with Britain.[13] Under these circumstances, the anti-colonial struggle in Hong Kong ended in failure in December.

The Trends of Social Conflict in Hong Kong, 1950–1986

Two empirical studies (Benjamin K. P. Leung 1990b; Cheung and Louie 1991) provide a descriptive and analytic account of the trend of social conflict in Hong Kong. Benjamin K. P. Leung's study focuses on a particular form of social conflict—collective violence—in the period 1950 to 1986. Cheung Bing-leung and Louie Kin-sheun's inquiry, on the other hand, is a comprehensive study of various types of social conflict, including petitions to government, signature campaigns, press conferences, protests, and mass rallies in the period 1975 to 1986. This section draws from the information and analysis in these studies to throw light on the major factors that bear on the genesis as well as the pattern of social conflict in Hong Kong.

The most noteworthy finding in Leung's study relates to the magnitude of incidents of collective violence. Using the number of participants, the duration of the event, and the casualties involved to assess magnitude, Leung discovers that while Hong Kong experienced three large-scale incidents of collective violence (the 1956, 1966, and 1967 riots) in the first two decades of the period of study, the society was free from collective violence of such magnitude after 1970. What factors contributed to this change in the magnitude of collective hostile outbursts? We may here first consider Cheung and Louie's empirical findings on the trend of social conflict before examining Leung's explanation.

In concurrence with Leung's findings, Cheung and Louie observe that since 1975, 'among the various modes of [conflict] action taken, those of a peaceful and conciliatory nature . . . are predominant' (Cheung and Louie 1991: 51). Their findings also indicate, however, a rising trend in the frequency of social conflict, from 35 incidents in 1975, to 68 in 1980 and 136 in 1986 (Cheung and Louie 1991: 10, table 1). In other words, evidence from the two studies show that while the people of Hong Kong were increasingly disposed to resort to collective conflictual action to press for their demands, they also became less inclined to do so in a violent manner. Some changes in the society since the early 1970s must have had the effect of dampening collective violence while at the same time raising the frequency of social conflict. We may now return to Leung's study for an analysis of these changes.

Leung points out that the occurrence of social conflict is contingent primarily upon the capacity of potential challenger groups to mobilize themselves for collective action, rather than on the extent of social discontent among the population. In making this argument, he is borrowing from the insights of the resource mobilization model in his analysis of collective violence and social conflict in Hong Kong. The mobilizing capacity of a challenger group, he further observes, depends on its internal organization. A well-organized group means that it has strong leadership and can pull together its members' resources for collective action. In later studies (Benjamin K. P. Leung 1992, 1994b), Leung adds that a well-organized challenger group will resort to collective action against its opponent(s) when it finds the instigating cognitive cues and appropriate political opportunities for mounting an opposition. This is an important thesis both in the political process model and the cognitive model of social conflict and social movements. It is in the light of these theoretical perspectives that Leung (1990b, 1994b) conducts his analysis of social conflict in Hong Kong.

An Analysis of Social Conflict in Hong Kong

We begin our discussion of social conflict in Hong Kong with Leung's analysis (1990b, 1994b) of the major episodes of social conflict. Leung notes (1994b) that both the 1925–6 strike-boycott and the 1967 riots were instigated by political turmoils in China. In both cases, the cognitive cues for insurgency in Hong Kong were anti-colonialism and nationalism. While the 1925–6 insurgency was in essence an integral part of the anti-imperialist movement in China, the 1967 disturbances were to a large extent fuelled by the nationalist revolutionary fervour in the motherland. The insurgents in both incidents were reasonably well-organized collectivities. Labour unions and other established organizations of an anti-colonial orientation (the most noteworthy were the Canton-Hong Kong strike-boycott committee in 1925–6 and the Federation of Trade Unions in the 1967 riots) played a prominent role in mobilizing the insurgents and directing their struggle. Moral and material support for the insurgents was also forthcoming from China, and this substantially enhanced the prospect of their success. In other words, the political circumstances of the time offered the appropriate opportunities for the challenger groups to mount an opposition against the colonial and capitalist establishment.

The 1956 riots, on the other hand, were by and large a replica of partisan political rivalry between the Communists and the Guomindang in recent Chinese history. The Hong Kong government's report on the riots commented that 'people of Nationalist [Guomindang] persuasion joined in collaboration with Triad gangs to redress old scores and to attempt to win a dominant position in the labour world' (Hong Kong Government 1956: ii). Leung (1990b) observes that there was clear evidence of coordination and organization among the rioters. Further, the rioters looted and destroyed almost exclusively the property of Communist sympathizers, and targeted their attacks on left-wing trade unionists. Leung maintains that the presence of two rival partisan political factions in the territory was the context for the outbreak of the 1956 riots. The politically symbolic incident of flag-flying provided the Guomindang supporters the cognitive cue and the opportunity to launch an attack on their opponents.

Thus, of the four major insurgencies in Hong Kong, only the 1966 Star Ferry riots were of an uncoordinated and non-political nature. It is worth noting that in terms of duration, number of participants, and damage inflicted, these riots were of a much smaller magnitude than the other three insurgencies. This suggests that the largest episodes of social conflict in Hong Kong were contingent upon the challenger group's organizational and mobilizing capacity, and on the presence of politically charged cognitive cues for collective oppositional action. Leung's argument gains support by reference to John D. Young's comments on the 1925–6 and 1967 disturbances:

The impetus, the driving force, and the source of intellectual-emotional persuasions behind the outbursts was China. Whereas the local populace was unable to use local grievances as rallying points, they seemed to be more than ready to respond to the call of larger issues: anti-imperialism, nationalism, and world revolution. . . . Without China playing an active role, it would be inconceivable to witness disturbance of such magnitude and extensive action (Young 1981: 170–1).

It is on the basis of this thesis that Leung (1990b, 1994b) explains the absence of large-scale social turmoil since the early 1970s. China's policy of peaceful co-existence with the Western capitalist countries, and in particular its improving relationship with the British government in the 1970s and 1980s, were reflected in a less antagonistic and more cooperative relationship between the pro-China faction and the colonial government on the local scene. On the other hand, with regard to the pro-Guomindang faction, urban renewal in the past two decades has had the effect of breaking up the neighbourhood social networks of the Guomindang supporters, and rehousing and dispersing them in new housing estates. This relocation, together with the declining political strength and influence of the pro-Guomindang faction in the territory, accounts for the absence of large-scale hostile outbursts from this challenger group since the early 1970s.

We can similarly derive from the political process model and the cognitive model an explanation for the increasing frequency of social conflict in Hong Kong since the mid-1970s. The cognitive cues in this case can be attributed to the Government's vastly expanded role in social service provision. Cheung and Louie observe in their study: 'Matters which were previously considered as belonging to the "private" or "family" domain ... are now regarded as a proper "public" concern' (Cheung and Louie 1991: 50). In other words, the Government's greater involvement in the provision of social goods and services has had the effect of generating among the population the cognitive cue that the Government would be properly held responsible for catering to a vast range of their daily needs. This cognitive cue became the basis for mobilization for collective action. In this respect, Cheung and Louie (1991: 10) observe that social conflict in the period of their study increased most dramatically in the areas of housing, transport, environment, education, and politics.

Moreover, the rising trend of social conflict was also a consequence of the increasing organizational and mobilizing capacity of the protest participants. Cheung and Louie note that social conflict in the period was characterized by the growing involvement of students, political activists, community activists, and church groups, who played the role of organizing the masses for collective action. Thus, the number of incidents of social conflict with organizational backing or involvement increased from 26 in 1975 to 57 in 1980 and 137 in 1986 (Cheung and Louie 1991: 40). The writers comment:

Participants were getting more and more organized when involved in social conflicts. Creating a more solid organization and/or the involvement of the pre-existing social organizations in social conflicts have become a common feature of conflict articulation (Cheung and Louie 1991: 41).

These conflicts were typically small in scale and non-violent in nature, and we can explain this limitation in terms of the pertinent cognitive cue and the organizational strength of the challenger groups. We observed earlier that the territory's large-scale, violent confrontations were instigated by cognitive cues originating from Chinese politics and turbulances on the mainland, and that cognitive cues generated by indigenous conditions are unlikely to instigate large-scale mobilization among the local population.[14] Further, the organizational strength of the activist groups of the 1970s and 1980s paled in comparison with that of the left-wing and the right-wing factions of the previous two decades. In other words, the rising trend of social conflict, as well as the magnitude of conflict in the period 1975–86, can be explained primarily on the basis of the nature of the cognitive cue and the organizational capacity of the protest participants.

Social Movements in Hong Kong: A General Discussion

Social movements are collective actions organized in order to bring about or resist change in society. The genesis and career of social movements are thus contingent, in the last analysis, on the belief and orientation of the movement participants towards aspects of the social and political structure. Lui Tai-lok's study (1994) of popular protest movements in Hong Kong offers a historical-sociological analysis of such movements in terms of the changing political structure and climate of the society. Leung's writings (Leung and Chiu 1991; Benjamin K. P. Leung 1991b, 1992, 1994c), on the other hand, seek to throw light on the major political and ideological factors that spark and sustain social movements in Hong Kong through a detailed analysis of the history of the labour and student movements. In a larger sense, Lui's and Leung's studies of social movements contribute to our understanding of important aspects of the political process in Hong Kong.

The starting point of Lui's study (1994) is the 1966 and 1967 riots, which in his view provided the ideological context for the upsurge of popular protest movements[15] in the 1970s and early 1980s. These riots heightened awareness on the part of the Hong Kong Chinese of their national identity, and it drew their attention to the defects and discriminatory practices in the Colony. University students took the lead in articulating this budding social consciousness. The ensuing student movement was hence predominantly anti-colonial and nationalist in orientation, as was epitomized in the 'Make Chinese an Official Language' movement, the Tiao Yu Tai protest, and the anti-corruption campaign of the early 1970s. It was against this background of an emerging anti-colonial ethos, Lui maintains, that popular protest movements proliferated in the 1970s.

Lui adds that the upsurge of popular movements was also a consequence of the rising expectations, and hence the politicization, of the population concomitant with the Government's expanded role in social service provision. As institutionalized channels for communicating popular wishes to the Government were lacking in the undemocratic colonial system, the masses had to resort to protest movements to voice their demands. The resulting confrontation with the established authorities had the effect of accentuating the protest participants' dissatisfaction with the colonial government. Thus, while these protest movements were originally targeted at resolving immediate problems of livelihood, they eventually converged in the common larger objective of bringing about social and political reform. In this political context the pressure groups of the 1970s emerged and proliferated. By the end of the decade, pressure groups had become the principal articulator and organizer of popular protest movements. Lui writes:

Owing to the close nature of colonial rule, pressure groups ... became the force of opposition outside the political establishment.... They could rapidly mobilize the masses to support movements that challenged the legitimacy of the colonial government (Lui 1994: 73).

As popular movements since the late 1970s depended to a large extent on the leadership of pressure groups, the fate of the former hinged substantially on the career of the latter. This is the thesis which informs Lui's analysis of the decline of popular movements in the mid-1980s and after. The change came with the progressive opening up of Hong Kong's political system in the 1980s. As more and more of the pressure group leaders were absorbed through electoral politics into the formal political structure—the District Boards, the Municipal Councils, and the Legislative Council—popular movements were increasingly divided from their original objectives and direction. Instead of organizing the masses for confrontional politics, pressure groups now mobilized them for support in electoral politics. Since the mid-1980s, Lui observes, most popular movement organizations have evolved into political groups geared to electoral politics. With this redirection, the politics of opposition against the colonial establishment which fuelled and sustained the popular movements of the 1970s and early 1980s has been transformed into the politics of competition within the formal political system.

Social Movements as the Articulation of the Society's Concerns and Values

As collective actions guided by beliefs, social movements are a reflection of the cherished values and major concerns of the movement participants. The study of social movements which involve a significant portion of the population advances our understanding of the concerns and values that prevail in a society's collective consciousness. It is from this perspective that Leung (1991a, 1991b, 1992, 1994c) undertook his study of the labour movement and student movement in Hong Kong. His investigation was premised on the rationale that labour and students are members of two distinct social categories and so can be expected to have divergent concerns and values. Students are on the whole free from the mundane daily concerns of making a living, and they are inclined to the pursuit of higher values and ideals. In contrast, workers have more down-to-earth interests and perspectives related to wages and working conditions. A study of the student movement and the labour movement holds the promise of offering valuable insights into the most highly valued ideals of the society, as well as the dominant concerns of the majority of the working population. Leung's study covers the period from the end of the Second World War to the late 1980s. It aims to show how the historical and political contexts of Hong Kong impacted on the ideology and direction of the two social movements in question, and to use the movements' goals and ideals to throw light on the major concerns and cherished values of the society.

The Labour Movement

The strength of a labour movement is conventionally measured by the use of statistics on the labour union membership within the economic setting and by evaluation of the frequency of and level of participation in industrial strikes. The former index indicates the numerical strength of the labour movement; the latter reflects labour's capacity to undertake collective action against management. Taking into account changes in the size of the labour force, which has a bearing on the number of labour union members, Leung (1991b, 1994c) uses the adjusted index of labour union density (union membership as a percentage of total employees) to denote the numerical strength of the labour movement. The level of strikes, on the other hand, is assessed by the composite index of number of working days lost through strikes. This index is calculated as follows:

Number of working days lost =
Number of strikes × Duration of strikes × Number of strikers

To adjust for the size of the working population, Leung denotes the level of strikes as the number of working days lost per 1,000 workers (Benjamin K. P. Leung 1991b, 1994c). On the basis of these two indices, Leung constructs an historical profile of the labour movement in Hong Kong.

From the information given in Table 7.1 and its accompanying notes, Leung works out the main contours of the labour movement (Benjamin K. P. Leung 1994c: 93):

Periods of union growth	Periods of union stagnation
1946–50, 1970–6	1951–69, 1977–89
Periods of high level of industrial strikes	Periods of low level of industrial strikes
1946–50, 1967	1951–66, 1968–89

Several noteworthy features emerge from this historical profile of the labour movement. First, it is only in the period 1946–50 that union growth coincided with a high incidence of industrial strikes. The second period of union growth, 1970–6, was a period of relatively few industrial strikes. This finding suggests that in the case of Hong Kong, labour union strength is not necessarily conducive to the workers' propensity to strike. It also suggests that we should look for different explanations for the two aspects —labour unionism and industrial strikes—of the labour movement in Hong Kong. This observation is buttressed by the anomaly of 1967, the year of the highest industrial conflict in Hong Kong's post-war history and yet also a year falling in a period of union stagnation. Finally, there are the periods of 'coincidence or consistency' between union stagnation and low industrial strikes: 1951–66 and 1978–89 (Benjamin K. P. Leung 1994c: 94).

Leung's historical-sociological analysis of the labour movement (1991b, 1992, 1994c) offers clues to an understanding of the bewildering career of the movement. In his view, the high tide of the labour movement (seeing both union growth and a high incidence of strikes) in the immediate post-war years, 1946–50, was the outcome primarily of labour union politics. This observation needs to be understood against the background of the civil war between the Communists and the Guomindang in China in the second half of the 1940s, which had substantial repercussions on the labour movement in Hong Kong. The political struggle on the mainland was replicated in the rivalry between the pro-Communist and the pro-Guomindang workers in Hong Kong, culminating in the formation of the left-wing Federation of Trade Unions in 1947 and the right-wing Trades Union Council in 1948. The competition between these two rival labour factions for support and membership led to an upsurge of labour unionism.

In respect of strikes, the majority was instigated and organized by the left-wing labour faction, who apparently intended to match the success

Table 7.1 Trade Union Density and Level of Industrial Strikes in Hong Kong, 1946–1989

Year	Union Density	Number of working days lost per 1,000 workers
1946/7		2,385
1947/8		5,429
1948/9		433
1949/50		2,814
1950/1		48
1951/2		566
1952/3		2
1953/4		1,470
1954/5		30
1955/6		335
1956/7		69
1957/8		90
1958/9		13
1959/60		159
1960/1		127
1961/2		77
1962/3		98
1963/4		243
1964/5		123
1965/6		183
1966/7		99
1967/8	13.8	—
1968/9	13.5	33
1969/70	17.4	40
1972/3	18.6	77
1973/4	21.2	82
1974/5	22.0	18
1975	23.9	23
1976	25.2	6
1977	23.8	14
1978	22.6	37
1979	20.7	45
1980	18.5	22
1981	16.1	17
1982	16.4	21
1983	16.1	3
1984	16.1	3
1985	16.1	1
1986	15.7	6
1987	15.7	3
1988	15.7	3
1989	16.6	0.04

Notes continued on next page

Notes: 1. This table has been constructed on the basis on data provided in the annual reports of the Labour Department (Hong Kong Government). The Department did not provide information on the 'political' strikes of 1967–8, although industrial conflict in that year was at its highest level in post-war Hong Kong. 2. Data before 1975 cover financial years (1 April–31 March); data from 1975 cover calender years. 3. Data on union density before 1967–8 not available, but according to England's estimate (1979), 1946–50 was a period of union growth and 1951–69 was a period of union stagnation. 4. 'Workers' refers to employees in registered establishments.

of the Communists on the mainland with similar success in the Colony. The Commission of Labour at the time observed that most of the strikes were 'labour disputes where politics dominates economics', and that many of the behind-the-scenes advisers in the strikes 'were suspected to have been in touch as to policy with labour bodies in Canton [Guangzhou] and on the Chinese mainland generally' (Commissioner of Labour 1950: 49–50). Leung attributes the upsurge of the labour movement in the immediate post-war years to political events in China and their impact on the labour world in Hong Kong.

The tide of union activism in the territory gradually subsided when China entered into a new phase of development after the establishment of the People's Republic in 1949. The years 1951–66 (marked by union stagnation and a low incidence of strikes) was a period in which both Britain and China were keen to preserve the stability of the Colony. The left-wing labour unions by and large refrained from direct involvement in industrial disputes, guided as they were by the 'desire to maintain the economic stability of Hong Kong from which China derived a substantial proportion of her foreign exchange' (England 1979: 30). In the meantime, the two rival labour union factions were primarily occupied with consolidating their influence in the labour world and in the community, and attacking the militant industrial actions of the other faction as irresponsible and detrimental to the public interest.[16] This was a period when the two labour factions which controlled and directed the labour movement were preoccupied with mutual denigration and were apparently guided more by partisan political orientations than by a commitment to safeguarding the workers' interests against management. As a result, the workers became cynical about labour unionism and recoiled from union activities, a consequence reflected in union growth stagnation and low involvement in industrial strikes. China's Cultural Revolution, however, incited the Hong Kong left-wing workers to militant industrial action again in 1967.

The incidence of strikes dropped dramatically in the aftermath of the 1967 disturbances, and Hong Kong enjoyed a long period of industrial peace. In Leung's view (1991b), the major explanation for this hiatus was China's improved relations with the West after 1967. In 1969, the United States relaxed travel and trading restrictions with China, and a year later full ambassadorial meetings resumed between the two countries. This thaw in relations was followed by China's entry into the United Nations in 1971 and President Richard Nixon's visit to China in 1972. China's economic modernization and the open-door policy pursued since the late 1970s vastly expanded its economic ties with Hong Kong and the West. The left-wing labour unions, who had hitherto played the principal mobilizing role in industrial strikes, accordingly changed their orientation towards the colonial government and capitalist management, from one of antagonism to one of cooperation and mutual cordiality.

Labour union membership, however, as reflected in union density, exhibited a fluctuating trend of development in this period. The year 1970 saw the beginning of an upward climb, but after reaching a zenith in 1976 it moved in a downward direction. The upward trend was apparently connected with the aforementioned improvement in China's international status in the early 1970s, as evidence shows that union growth between 1970 and 1976 was due mainly to an increase in left-wing union membership.[17] The death of Mao and the fall of his successors, the Gang of Four, in 1976 had a negative impact on left-wing union membership, as these labour unions had in the past few years followed the policies of the discredited political faction. The effect was reflected in an overall drop in labour union density (Benjamin K. P. Leung 1994c).

Leung's study reveals that the nature and the career of the labour movement in Hong Kong was shaped to a significant extent by Chinese politics and the development of events in China. The 'China factor', as a number of writers (England 1989; Turner 1980; Levin and Jao 1988) have also observed, has split the labour movement into two rival factions and substantially weakened its strength. But the central message which Leung derives from his study is that the touchstone of China has constituted an important cognitive cue for the labour movement in Hong Kong. This suggests that larger issues and higher values—Chinese politics and nationalism—rather than the pragmatic concerns of wages and working conditions, have been the principal guiding force and the most effective mobilizing factor in Hong Kong's labour movement.

The Student Movement[18]

Hong Kong's student movement had a short life span, beginning in the late 1960s and fading towards the end of the 1970s. The event that precipitated the formation of the student movement was the 1967 riots. The strong anti-colonial and nationalist orientation of this turmoil awakened the university students from their habitual silence and indifference to politics. This awakening was evidenced in the student publication of the University of Hong Kong, *Undergrad*, which published a number of student commentaries on the riots, many with evocative titles such as 'Has Hong Kong a Future?' (13 July 1967) and 'The Riots, Public Opinion, and the Adoption of Chinese as an Official Language' (1 December 1967). Articles such as the above discussed the 1967 riots in terms of the national and cultural identity of the Hong Kong Chinese, and of the glaring inequality in the society and the lack of communication between the colonial government and the Chinese community.

The student movement itself started in February 1969, when students of the University of Hong Kong established the University Reform Movement, the principal objective of which was student participation in university administration. This episode was followed several months later by a two-day sit-in by university students outside the post-secondary Chu Hai College, in protest against the college's dismissal of twelve students who had allegedly attacked the college authorities in student publications. However, the one issue which generated the most momentum for the student movement, and which most profoundly shaped its development until the mid-1970s, concerned Chinese national interests. This was the issue, which arose in 1970, of the Tiao Yu Tai Islands, over which both the Chinese and the Japanese governments claimed territorial rights.

Against the background of Japan's invasion of China in the Second World War, Japan's territorial claim was to the students in Hong Kong a revival of Japanese militarism. The Tiao Yu Tai issue imbued the students with rampant nationalist sentiments, and students marched in protest against Japanese imperialism and in defence of the integrity of Chinese territory. In some of these protest demonstrations the students clashed with police, who resorted to brutal force against the student protesters. Such confrontations diverted the students' attention from the issue of Chinese interests to what they were then experiencing and which they viewed as colonial repression. As a result, nationalist feelings sparked by the Tiao Yu Tai issue broadened to encompass anti-colonialism. The Tiao Yu Tai protest movement faded by May 1972, but nationalist sentiments and their offshoot, anti-colonialism, continued to fuel the student movement for the next few years.

Nationalism in the student movement was given a further boost by China's advance in international status in the early 1970s. Many of the most committed student activists of the time were fervently looking forward to Hong Kong's reunion with the motherland, and they took on the responsibility of preparing the people of Hong Kong for this reunion through educating them about socialist China. To equip themselves for this self-appointed mission, student activists organized and undertook 'China tours', and set up China study groups for university and post-secondary students.

The mainstream of the student movement in the first half of the 1970s was strongly nationalist and pro-China in orientation. However, there was also a group of student activists who took a broader view of nationalism, which they did not consider to be necessarily equal to an identification with the Communist regime on the mainland. They expressed their nationalist sentiments in protests against injustices in the local colonial establishment and in offering help and services to their underprivileged compatriots in the Colony. These students attacked the pro-China faction as blindly accepting and following China's policies and putting their priority in socialist education to the neglect of the injustices and deprivations in Hong Kong.

The student movement, then, in its heyday was split between a pro-China faction and its rival, the Social Action Faction.[19] While pursuing their respective missions in the larger society, these two factions also battled with each other on university campuses to gain control of the student union and student publications. With the dominant pro-China faction seeking to purge their rivals, whom they considered to be renegades within the student body, the mainstream of the student movement was to some extent a miniature replica of the concurrent Cultural Revolution in China, and so it was little wonder that the demise of the Cultural Revolution and the fall of the Gang of Four dissipated the main drive of Hong Kong's student movement. As they had for a number of years identified with and supported the policies of the Cultural Revolution, the pro-China faction was now viewed by most students as having unwittingly misled the student movement. Disgraced and disoriented, the pro-China student activists receded from activity. With their rivals out of contention, the Social Action Faction soon also disintegrated, for it had been little more than a loosely organized group of students held together through opposition to the pro-China faction.

A number of social issues sustained the momentum of the student movement for a few more years after 1976. One noteworthy example was the Boat People Protest[20] issue of January 1979, in which university student activists backed up and supported the boat people in their demands to the Government to be resettled on land. In terms of the duration and intensity of student involvement, however, the Golden Jubilee Secondary School protests of 1978 were the most significant since the Tiao Yu Tai protest of the early 1970s.

The Golden Jubilee Secondary School was a Catholic secondary school run by the Precious Blood Order. The protest issue started in early 1977, when teachers at the school discovered irregularities in the school's financial accounts and reported them to the Education Department. The school's principal, Sister Leung, was subsequently found guilty of forgery and dismissed. In August 1977, the Precious Blood Order appointed a new principal, Miss Kwan, for the school. Shortly after taking over her position, Miss Kwan adopted a number of controversial measures, such as isolating new students from those teachers and students who had participated in exposing the school's financial mismanagement, temporarily banning student extra-curricular activities, and threatening to dismiss some of the dissident teachers. Opposition to Miss Kwan mounted, and on 9 May 1978, the dissenting teachers and students together with some of the students' parents, a group totalling about four hundred people, marched to Government House to petition Governor MacLehose to investigate the matter. At this point, student leaders from the universities and post-secondary colleges publicly declared their support for the protesting teachers and students.

The protest was exacerbated by the Education Department's announcement on 14 May of its decision to close the Golden Jubilee school from the next day, and to start in September another school on the old school's premises. The new school was to be named Saint Teresa's Secondary School, and would have Miss Kwan as its principal. Current students of the Golden Jubilee school could continue their schooling in the new institution, but the dissenting teachers would not be re-employed there. The Education Department's decision provoked a series of protest actions in which hundreds of university and post-secondary college students, together with the dissenting teachers and students of the Golden Jubilee school, held a number of sit-ins, march demonstrations, and a two-day hunger strike to demand a further investigation of the issue. An independent committee was subsequently appointed by the Governor to propose remedial measures. In July 1978, the committee issued its report, recommending the establishment of another school to accommodate the dissenting teachers and students. The teachers and students of the Golden Jubilee school could join either Saint Teresa's Secondary School or the new school proposed by the committee. The recommendation was accepted by both parties in the dispute and the Golden Jubilee school protest came to an end.

The 1980s and early 1990s were a period of drastic changes in Hong Kong, as the territory's political structure evolved in the course of the transition to 1997. It was also at this time, however, that the student movement declined into oblivion. This decline was caused in part by developments in the larger society and in part by internal developments within the student body. The emergence of professional politicians, concomitant with Hong Kong's development towards a representative government, and the gradual opening up of the political system had to a significant extent replaced the politics of protest with the politics of election. With this change the student movement, in essence a protest movement, was gradually eclipsed and superseded by the institutionalized, electoral politics of professional politicians.

There were in fact several notable episodes of student activism in the 1980s. During the 1982–4 Sino-British negotiations about Hong Kong's future, the members of the student union of the University of Hong Kong sent a letter to the British prime minister, Margaret Thatcher, expressing their views on Hong Kong's post-1997 political status. In July 1984, the Hong Kong Federation of Students publicly announced its strong preference for introducing direct elections into the selection process for the 1985 Legislative Council. From the mid-1980s to the end of the decade, the student unions of several local tertiary institutions expressed a series of opinions about the composition of the Basic Law Consultative Committee, as well as the contents of the Basic Law itself. Students also participated actively in the pro-democracy campaigns and demonstrations in connection with the 1989 gathering in Tiananmen Square and the June Fourth Incident of that year. Unlike the situation of the early 1970s, however, when students stood out as the pioneers and leaders of protest movements, the actions and voices of the students since the early 1980s have been overshadowed by the more comprehensive and effective mass mobilization tactics of politicians and political organizations. When the student movement lost its leading role in social and political action, it also lost much of its vitality and momentum.

The eclipse of the student movement can also be attributed to a weakening of solidarity within the student body itself, consequent upon the rapid expansion of the university student population beginning in the early 1980s. It has been argued (Hong Kong University Students' Union Journal 1988) that with this expansion, student interest associations in the territory's universities have proliferated, and interests and views within the student body have become more diversified. As a result, the student union has faced mounting difficulties in articulating a consensus and assuming leadership within the student body. At the same time, to manage efficiently the increasing volume of student affairs, the student union has developed into an increasingly bureaucratic and impersonal organization, with the result that student leaders have become more isolated from the majority of their constituents. The overall consequence has been a gross weakening of the student leaders' capacity to mobilize the student population for collective action.[21] This develpoment helps to explain why student activism since the early 1980s has generally been limited in scope, duration, and number of participants (Hong Kong University Students' Union Journal 1988: 39).

Conclusion

Athough a rapidly modernizing society under colonial rule, Hong Kong has been exceptional in having been spared the frequent turmoil and instability that have plagued other countries of a similar socio-economic and political status. Since they have not been a particularly salient feature of the society, social conflict and social movements have rarely been the subject of inquiry in studies of Hong Kong society. This chapter is an effort to fill that gap by trying to derive from the few studies of this neglected dimension insights about the factors and conditions that have provoked an otherwise quiescent community into occasional outbursts of opposition and hostility.

Our inquiry reveals that the major episodes of social conflict in Hong Kong were typically instigated not by indigenous conditions but rather by events and factors external to the society—most often Chinese politics and major political events on the mainland. Our discussion of Hong Kong's labour and student movements similarly testifies to the substantial impact of the China factor on the orientations, directions, and careers of these movements. In both cases, the nature, as well as the rise and fall of the movement, were closely related to Chinese politics and developments on the mainland. This, of course, is not to imply that the China factor is the only and sufficient explanation of social conflict and social movements in Hong Kong. There are, as we pointed out in the course of the discussion, other crucial variables, such as the organizational strength of the challenger groups and the availability of opportunities for oppositional collective action.

The main thesis in this chapter is that social conflict and social movements have to be understood as a political process in which the cause and the course of the participants' collective action are contingent on the presence of a motivating cognitive cue, and on their ability to mobilize resources for the struggle. In the Hong Kong context, the China factor has provided the cognitive cues for major episodes of collective action. These cognitive cues—particularly nationalism and its ramifications—were constituted by major ongoing or past political events in China. They provided the bearing on the basis of which the participants in insurgencies and in the labour and student movements located and sanctioned the targets of their collective action.

From this observation, we derive the corollary that Hong Kong's stability and instability are contingent to a significant extent on developments in China. The subject of stability in Hong Kong has often been studied in terms of social and political conditions indigenous to the society. The discussion in this chapter suggests the need to bring into perspective the role of China and Chinese politics when considering Hong Kong's stability and social conflict.

Notes

1. For a review of the explanations of order and stability in Hong Kong, see Lau (1982: chap. 1).
2. This theoretical approach is most clearly presented in Smelser (1963).
3. See, for instance, Gurr (1970).
4. The general strike-boycott of 1925–6, which at its height involved some 300,000 participants, is arguably one of the largest incidents of collective struggle in Hong Kong's history. For an assessment of the magnitude of episodes of social turmoil in Hong Kong from 1950 to 1985, see Benjamin K. P. Leung (1990). Leung identifies the three largest incidents of turmoil in this period to be the riots of 1956, 1966, and 1967.
5. The historical account in this section is based on Chan Lau Kit-ching (1990: 176–219) and Yuen (1988: 150–8).
6. For a more detailed account of the 1920 and 1922 strikes, see W. K. Chan (1991: 163–91) and Chan Lau Kit-ching (1990: 169–76).
7. The account in this section is based on Hong Kong Government (1956).
8. The account of the 1966 riots in this section is based on Hong Kong Government (1967) and Elliott (1981).
9. Two classic studies seek to explain the violent behaviour of crowds in terms of destructive instincts which allegedly surface in crowd situations. See Lebon (1960) and Freud (1945).
10. For a detailed description of these riots, see Cooper (1970). An extensive descriptive and analytic account of the events is available in Waldron (1976). For a succinct discussion, see Scott (1989a: 96–126).
11. United States Information Service, *Hong Kong Press Summary*, 19 May 1967; cited in Waldron (1976: 212).
12. Reported in *Survey of China Mainland Press*, 3959 (14 June 1967): 29.
13. John D. Young wrote: '[I]t became apparent that by the fall of 1967, the Cultural Revoluation leaders were intent on going back to a more peaceful relationship with China's neighbours.... By late September... China had already ceased its contribution to the strike fund.... In early October, the annual contract between China and Hong Kong for the sale of water was renewed' (Young 1981: 168).
14. In this connection, one may take note of the largest protest demonstrations to have taken place in Hong Kong: the march demonstrations in May and June 1989 in support of the pro-democracy movement in China. An estimated two to three million people in Hong Kong took part in these march demonstrations. While these were peaceful demonstrations and do not qualify as episodes of social conflict, they are a good illustration of the impact of the 'China factor' on collective action in Hong Kong.

15. Lui has not defined the concept of popular movements. He obliquely refers to these movements as 'protests . . . organized by people to make . . . claims to state provisions and to challenge the colonial political order' (Lui 1994: 67). As such, popular movements would refer primarily to protest movements in respect of housing, transport, social welfare, education, and the environment.

16. Leung cites the example of the 1954 strike of left-wing tramway workers as an illustration. The right-wing unions attacked the strike as serving only the selfish political interests of the left-wing union leaders and as detrimental to the interests of the workers. They declared: 'We are determined to stand firm in our dedication to lead the just and free Tramway workers to perform their duties responsibly. We will not take part in any action that for selfish motives would jeopardize the workers' employment' (*Wah Kiu Yat Po*, 10 October 1954; cited in Leung 1992: 22). The left-wing unions responded in a press report the next day: 'In the interests of the public, tramway workers have decided to resume work from today' (*Man Wui Po*, 11 October 1954; cited in Leung 1992: 23).

17. Declared membership in the left-wing Federation of Trade Unions increased from 114,387 in 1970 to 224,544 in 1976, while that in the right-wing Trades Union Council dropped from 36,280 to 33,931 in the same period (Registrar of Trade Unions; Hong Kong Government annual reports).

18. The account of the student movement in this section is based on Leung (1982, 1992, 1994c), who drew his empirical materials mainly from: the Hong Kong University Student Union, eds. (1978), *The Hong Kong Student Movement: Retrospect and Examination* (Hong Kong: The Hong Kong University Student Union); The Hong Kong Federation of Students, eds. (1983), *The Hong Kong Student Movement: A Retrospect* (Hong Kong: Wide Angle Press); and *The Undergrad* (student publication of the University of Hong Kong), various issues.

19. In Chinese, this faction was called Social Faction or Society Faction. The title Social Action Faction is used here to reflect the group's orientation. This group was also sometimes referred to as the Liberal Democratic Faction.

20. These 'boat people' were local people living in boats in the Yaumatei Typhoon Shelter. Their living conditions were deplorable, so, with the help of university students, they staged a number of demonstrations to persuade the Government to resettle them on land. They were subsequently rehoused in public housing blocks in Tuen Mun.

21. It is worth noting in this regard that in April 1995, an emergency general meeting called by the student union of the University of Hong Kong to discuss the issue of the appointment of the new Vice-Chancellor had to be called off because of the failure to obtain the required quorum.

8. The Development Towards a Representative Government

Hong Kong's development towards a representative government began in the early 1980s, with the introduction of electoral politics at the district level, and progressed towards the gradual opening of the legislature to democratic participation. The process has been accompanied by heated debates about the pace of political change and by the rise to prominence of political organizations and parties with divergent orientations and allegiances. This chapter is concerned with Hong Kong's evolving power configuration in the process of democratization, and about the factors that circumscribe and bear on this evolution. Some of these factors are the residues and by-products of the political make-up of the past, which we now briefly survey to set the stage for the main subject of our discussion.

The Background: The Administrative Absorption of Politics

A non-democratic colonial government faces the ominous prospect of opposition and rebellion from the colonized population: The administrative absorption of politics, according to Ambrose Y. C. King (1981b), defined the Hong Kong government's strategy to contain and neutralize potential opposition from the Chinese community through the absorption of members of their most prominent élites into the Government's administrative structure. In the nineteenth century and the first half of the twentieth century, this absorption took the form of co-opting Chinese notables, generally wealthy businessmen well known for their contributions to charitable and welfare services for the Chinese population, into the Executive and Legislative councils and other official consultative bodies.[1] Throughout much of the Colony's history, the Legislative Council, which is responsible for scrutinizing and enacting policies introduced by the Executive Council, consisted only of senior Government officials and members of the public appointed by the Governor. The latter category, referred to as unofficial or non-governmental members, has been comprised mostly of wealthy businesspeople and high-status professionals of both Chinese and other racial stocks. The Executive Council, on the other hand, has consisted entirely of Government officials and appointed unofficials. Until the introduction of indirect election to the Legislative Council in 1985, Hong Kong had no elected representatives in its two highest policy-making bodies and it was not a democracy. But the strategy of administrative absorption of politics resolved to some extent the problem of élite–mass integration, as the Chinese community could be expected to identify with their co-opted leaders and hence to comply with colonial rule. The system just described worked effectively on the whole for nearly one hundred years because the Hong Kong Chinese were politically passive and acquiescent, and disposed to self-reliance.

The reliance, however, on the co-option of members of the Chinese élites as an integrative strategy proved in the 1950s and 1960s to be outdated and inadequate. The mass of refugees who at the time made up a substantial portion of the local population knew little about these élites, let alone recognizing their members as legitimate leaders. Moreover, in the face of rapid population growth the charitable and welfare organizations which had been the basis of élite status and public recognition could cater to the needs of only a proportionally small clientele. The consequence was a drastic decline in the popularity and influence of the Chinese élites among the local population (Lau 1982: 141–2). Their members' ineffectiveness were starkly revealed during the 1967 riots, when they could neither forewarn the Government of the impending crisis nor mobilize popular support for the establishment. The Government subsequently attempted another strategy of élite–mass integration through launching the City District Officer (CDO) Scheme in 1968, under which ten City District Offices, to be administered entirely by Government officials, were to be established in the metropolitan area of Hong Kong.

The prime objectives of the CDO Scheme were to facilitate the interchange of information between government and people, and to provide government assistance in solving communal and individual problems in the districts.[2] The scheme was, in other words, a device to absorb politics at the grass-roots level through district administration without introducing democratic changes in the broader political system. It became evident after a few years of its operation that the scheme fell short of achieving its objectives. King's study of the performance of the CDO in Kwun Tong, for instance, led him to the conclusion that 'despite its efforts to reach people in the street, it has thus far not been very successful in penetrating the masses' (King 1981b: 142). It soon became clear to the Government that for the purpose of maintaining political stability through community-building, the CDO Scheme had to be supplemented by a broader and more penetrating social network of integration. The addition took the form of a three-tier community participatory structure, officially launched in 1973, which consisted of City District Committees, Area Committees, and Mutual Aid Committees.

This three-tier structure was an improvement over the CDO Scheme in that it incorporated community leaders into the district administrative bodies. At the top of the structural hierarchy was the City District Committee, chaired by the city district officer (of the CDO Scheme) and composed of representatives from various Government departments and appointed local leaders. Under each City District Committee were a number of Area Committees, whose members similarly consisted exclusively of Government representatives and appointed local leaders. The organizational link between these two administrative levels was the chairperson of the Area Committee, who was *ipso facto* a member of the City District Committee. The Mutual Aid Committees, at the bottom of the structure, were each constituted on the basis of individual residence blocks and consisted entirely of representatives elected by those residents. The work of this singular, democratically constituted body within the participatory structure was, however, restricted to the maintenance of sanitation and security within the pertinent residence block, and it was coordinated and monitored by a steering committee within the Government.

In short, the community participatory structure was in essence an extension of the administrative absorption of politics at the grass-roots level. On these grounds, Cheung Bing-leung (1989) critiques the political reasoning underlying the scheme:

This structure was in a vantage position to neutralize through political absorption the community's opposition to the government, and to forge a re-integration of the ruler and the ruled. In instituting the government's role in district affairs, it facilitated the monitoring of the public mood, and strengthened the government's influence and control over the masses (Cheung Bing-leung 1989: 49).

Moreover, the Government was particularly concerned that community participation was not to become the prelude to political reform:

While community building is clearly socio-political in nature, one must assume in Hong Kong's circumstances that it is not to lead to any basic political (i.e. constitutional) reform, and that community involvement and participation is not to develop into representative government (Secretary for Home Affairs, Hong Kong Government 1977: 8).

To forestall such development, the Government-sponsored participatory bodies excluded from their membership those grass-roots activists whose demands for reforms, piecemeal though they were, nevertheless posed a threat to the operational principle of the three-tier participatory structure. Deprived of an institutionalized channel for political participation, these activists formed pressure groups, on the basis of which they mobilized the grass roots to communicate their demands to the Government through protest and disruptive actions (Joe C. B. Leung 1990: 46–7). The proliferation of pressure groups and the increasing prevalence of social protests through the 1970s signalled to the Government that pressure group activities carried 'the risk of very serious consequences for stability and security' (Home Affairs Branch, Hong Kong Government 1980: 1) and that a system had to be instituted to absorb such confrontational political activism.[3]

The product of that concern was a new scheme of district administration introduced in 1981, under which a District Management Committee and a District Board were to be formed in each of eighteen districts in the urban area and the New Territories. These two bodies were to work in coordination within their district. The District Management Committee was to be composed entirely of senior Government officers, while the District Board would be comprised of Government representatives, appointed members, and popularly elected members—the last category constituting one-third of the District Board membership. By embracing an elected element to appease and accommodate the pressure group activists, and yet retaining an overwhelmingly strong pro-Government presence in its composition, the District Board was apparently instituted as another mechanism for the administrative absorption of politics rather than as a prelude to more fundamental political reform.

The Sino-British negotiations in the early 1980s and the ensuing Joint Declaration of 1984 were to change the subsequent course of the territory's political development. The colonial government had to arrange for the relinquishing of political power to the indigenous population in preparation for Hong Kong's post-1997 status as a Special Administrative Region with a high degree of autonomy under the sovereignty of China. Accordingly, the District Board was reconstituted in 1985 to comprise only unofficial members, two-thirds of whom were to be elected; it was further reconstituted in 1994 to comprise (until the transfer of sovereignty in 1997) only elected members. More significantly, the Legislative Council was reformed to include indirectly elected members from 1985, and directly elected members from 1991.

The first District Board election took place in 1982—the beginning of a political contest between the conservatives, already well-established through their work in the Government-sponsored participatory structure, and the pressure group activists who had to that point been excluded from institutionalized political participation and whose political resources lay mainly in their capacity to mobilize grass-roots support. Hong Kong's competitive electoral politics began in the context of these residues and legacies of the past. The contest was to become more acute, and to involve more groups of more diverse political persuasions, in the course of the territory's development towards a representative government, the parameters of which have been prescribed jointly by the Chinese and the British governments. To these parameters we now turn before examining the dynamics of electoral politics in Hong Kong.

The Parameters of Political Development

The Hong Kong government's policy on the development towards a representative government was explained and justified in its 1988 White Paper on the subject. The document recommended progressive but gradual evolution from the existing system 'to meet the growing needs and expectations of society, while maintaining political stability, economic prosperity and effective administration' (Hong Kong Government 1988: 3). Implicit in this recommendation was the Government's apprehension that too rapid a pace of democratization might be disruptive of the territory's stability and prosperity. Hong Kong's special circumstances, 'its status as a non-sovereign territory . . . and its position as a major business and financial centre', the White Paper points out (Hong Kong Government 1988: 3), warrant a cautious and gradual approach to democratization. These considerations set the parameters of Hong Kong's political development in the 1980s and early 1990s. Their validity and their implications for Hong Kong's political future are the subject of Benjamin K. P. Leung's analysis in his paper (1990c) 'Political Development: Prospects and Possibilities'.

The experiences of a number of contemporary developing societies suggest that a possible outcome of democratization is political instability, characterized by widespread political violence, frequent *coups d'état*, or even civil war.[4] The issue Leung investigates is whether Hong Kong's development towards a representative government would likely entail such dire political consequences and, by extension, whether the Hong Kong government's proposed rate of change is justifiable. Leung observes, with reference to Seymour Martin Lipset's (1981) empirically grounded thesis, that there is a positive relationship between the level of economic development and stable democratic processes. A study by Larry Diamond (1980), for instance, found that in 1974 some 76 per cent of the economically well-developed countries (with a per capita GNP of between US$2,380 and US$7,870) were stable democracies; the figure dropped to only 8 per cent in the case of the economically under-developed countries (with a per capita GNP of US$70–US$150). As Hong Kong's per capita GNP (at constant 1973 market prices) in 1980 was around US$2,384 (Youngson 1982: 8), the evidence suggests that Hong Kong has a high potential for developing into a stable democracy.

Leung finds further support for this contention from Robert Dahl's data (1971: 67) on the major socio-economic characteristics of democratic societies. Hong Kong compares favourably with these societies in terms of those socio-economic features deemed to be conducive to democratic stability, such as the percentage of the working population employed in industry and the proportion of the general population enrolled in various levels of education.[5] As the Hong Kong government's proposed conservative approach to democratization does not seem to be justified in terms of the territory's socio-economic characteristics, Leung turns to examine the bearing of Hong Kong's 'special circumstances' on political development.

The White Paper's allusion to Hong Kong's status as 'a non-sovereign territory', in Leung's view, reflects the circumscribing influence of the Chinese government on Hong Kong's political development before and after the transfer of sovereignty in 1997. Citing arguments articulated by Lau Siu-kai (1987), Leung lists some of the major reasons why China might be opposed to a thoroughgoing democracy in the territory. In the first place, democratization might lead to a transfer of power to political groups either hostile to China or disposed to place the interests of Hong Kong before those of China. Moreoever, the Chinese government appears to be wary that democratic forces in Hong Kong may eventually be subversive of political order on the mainland by sheer demonstration effects and by their promotion of Western-style democracy in China. In addition, China may be concerned that democratization would be detrimental to Hong Kong's capitalist economy by scaring away local and foreign capital.

The last point cited here makes the connection with Hong Kong's position as 'a major business and financial centre', and by extension, the paramount role of the territory's capitalists in sustaining its economic prosperity. In this respect, the aversion of Hong Kong's bourgeoisie to democratization[6] renders them China's most powerful allies both economically and politically. This is the bearing of Hong Kong's status as a non-sovereign territory and business centre on its political development:

The former status implies political dependence on China, the latter economic dependence on the bourgeoisie, both of whom are joined in their aversion to democratization in Hong Kong (Benjamin K. P. Leung 1990c: 40).

It is against the backdrop of such political and economic circumstances that we can comprehend the conservative schedule and arrangements prescribed by the British and Chinese governments for Hong Kong's political development. The 1982–5 Legislative Council was composed entirely of civil servants and unofficials appointed by the Governor. Indirect election to the Legislative Council through functional constituencies, the District Boards, the Urban Council, and the Regional Council was introduced in 1985, but these elected members filled only twenty-four of the total fifty-seven seats in the Legislative Council. In 1988–91, the Legislative Council had two additional indirectly elected members; the remainder was composed of civil servants (eleven) and appointed unofficials (twenty). It was not until 1991 that direct election on the basis of geographical constituencies was introduced to fill eighteen of the sixty seats in the Legislative Council; twenty-one seats were allocated to members indirectly elected through functional constituencies, seventeen to appointed unofficials, and four to civil servants. The 1995–9 Legislative Council will be composed entirely of elected members: twenty directly elected, thirty indirectly elected through functional constituencies, and ten indirectly elected by an election committee.

It may be seen that the electoral arrangements described above were biased in favour of the business and professional sectors. In the 1991 indirect election, for instance, the functional constituencies were so constituted that most of the pertinent seats in the Legislative Council went to businesspeople and professionals associated to varying degrees with conservative and pro-China organizations (Scott 1992: 10–11).[7] The election committee was similarly designed to give a competitive edge to conservative business and professional voices (Cheng 1990: 57).[8] Governor Chris Patten's political reforms in 1994 subsequently enlarged the electorate for the functional constituencies to cover the entire working population, and set up an election committee composed of directly elected District Board members, but the Chinese government has attacked Patten's reforms as 'side-tracking', and made clear that these reforms will not last beyond 1997. Such, then, have been the parameters within which various political forces in Hong Kong contested for a niche within the democratizing political system.

Electoral Politics and the Emergence of the Political Market: The 1982 District Board Elections

Political elections resemble the operation of an economic market. They have sellers, buyers, and products. Politicians, political groups, and political parties promote and sell their products—ideas, platforms, and candidates—to potential buyers who constitute the electorate. The process involves capital, which includes organizational resources, labour power, social networks, and political experiences and reputation. With reference to this analogy, Stephen Tang Lung-wai (1993) conducted his study of the emergence and evolution of the political market in Hong Kong since the introduction of District Board elections in 1982.[9] Tang's work offers a comprehensive conceptual framework for analysing the politicians' strategies, resources, and changing fortunes, the electorate's preferences and orientations, and the factors that impinge on Hong Kong's electoral politics, in the course of the territory's development towards a representative government.

The evolution of the political market in the New Territories, Tang observes, has been different from that in urban Hong Kong. A limited political market had existed in the New Territories before the 1980s, as there was a tradition of elections—with the franchise confined to indigenous males—to seats on the rural committees and the Heung Yee Kuk (the Rural Council). This market, however, was controlled by the gentry class, whose support and patronage were essential for a political novice to succeed in rural politics. In urban Hong Kong, a portion of the seats on the Urban Council had been filled by elections since the 1950s, but the franchise was so restricted that eligible voters seldom exceeded 2 per cent of the urban population. Thus, when District Board elections were introduced in 1982, a political market scarcely existed in urban Hong Kong, while that in the New Territories was highly parochial and élitist.

The results of the 1982 District Board elections reflected the state of the political markets. In the New Territories, candidates with the support of established rural organizations and élites won a substantial number of seats (Lau and Kuan 1983: 13). A caveat has to be registered here, however, for their electoral success also owed much to their opportune filling of the power vacuum in the new towns, where recent migrants from the urban area were just beginning to establish their roots and social networks in the new environment. A challenge to the traditional rural forces emerged later, when the residents of the new towns had become a more settled community. In urban Hong Kong, electoral competition, which was far from enthusiastic, occurred largely on an individual basis (Lau and Kuan 1983: 13). The community leaders in previous Government-sponsored bodies and traditional communal organizations, apparently on account of their experience and credentials, attained a moderate victory: twenty-nine of the total seventy-six seats were captured by candidates associated with Mutual Aid Committees and Kaifong Associations (Joe C. B. Leung 1990: 50). The 'activist' pressure groups, on the other hand, lacked both the will and the mobilizing capacity to compete successfully in elections (Tang 1993: 258; Joe C. B. Leung 1990: 49–50).

In short, while the rural established forces were quick to seize the 1982 District Board elections as an opportunity to consolidate their power, the urban candidates had yet neither the organizational strength nor the motivation to forge collective political identities or interests through the elections. In this sense, the urban political market in the immediate aftermath of the 1982 elections remained unstructured. The Sino-British negotiations in the following two years, however, and the signing of the

Joint Declaration in 1984, were to drastically change the territory's political markets.

New Entrants to the Political Market: The 1985 and 1988 District Board Elections

The Sino-British Joint Declaration's promise to the people of Hong Kong that the territory would enjoy self-rule in the post-1997 period had the effect of enhancing the political significance of the District Boards. District politics was now perceived by the territory's intending politicians as the preparatory ground for self-government. Its importance was further boosted by the Government's announcement in the 1984 *White Paper on Representative Government* (Hong Kong Government 1984) that the proportion of District Board seats to be filled by direct election would be increased from one-third to two-thirds in 1985, and that at the same time ten of the seats in the Legislative Council would be filled by election among District Board members. These developments attracted a cohort of new entrants to the political market. The pressure groups, meanwhile, had evolved into 'groups of political commentary' during the period of Sino-British negotiations and were now consolidating themselves into 'groups of political participation' (Louie 1991). The 1985 District Board elections bore the imprint of their political ascendance.

The prime operating territories of the pressure-group activists were the public housing estates in the urban areas and in the New Territories new towns. Their principal campaign strategy was to mobilize grass-roots support through pressuring the Government for environmental improvement in the new towns and massive public housing redevelopment in the urban areas. They soon emerged as crusaders on behalf of the grass roots in the new towns, an image which in comparison relegated the established rural élites to the status of 'merely the clients of the colonial bureaucrats' (Tang 1993: 260). In the urban areas, they established themselves as young and enterprising 'socially conscious actors', while the Kaifong Association and Mutual Aid Committee leaders in contrast appeared to be 'old, conservative and status-conscious' hangers-on (Tang 1993: 261). The pressure-group activists capitalized as well on their experience of community organization and on the grass-roots networks they had built up since the early 1970s. In consequence, the activists scored a landslide victory in the 1985 District Board elections. Tang provides this assessment of the activists' impact on the distribution of power in electoral politics: 'Their entries made the local political markets more diverse, structured, and competitive' (Tang 1993: 262).

Meanwhile, the ongoing debates about the territory's political development were carving out a political demarcation between the so-called liberals, pressure-group activists who advocated a faster pace of democratization, and the conservatives, led by the gentry and their allies in the New Territories and wealthy businesspeople in the urban areas who considered the existing moderate rate of change to be commensurate with Hong Kong's 'special circumstances'. The results of the 1985 District Board elections indicated that the liberals were emerging as the territory's popular leaders. The Chinese government subsequently appeared to recognize that it was in its interest to play a more purposive role in Hong Kong's district politics than that of a concerned bystander. Under its encouragement and patronage, the territory's pro-China forces soon became a potent power bloc in the evolving political markets, cooperating with the rural gentry and the urban business élites in political competition with a common antagonist: the liberals.

The strengthening of connections between the rural gentry, members of the business élites, and the Chinese government occurred at a time when the conservatives were adopting new strategies to rebuild their political strength. In the New Territories, the traditional rural élites revitalized the conservative camp through recruiting and grooming a cohort of young leaders with closer connections with the grass roots. They also sought to enhance their political image and appeal by gradually shedding their pro-Government stance and deploying the mass mobilization tactics of the liberals. In the urban areas, the conservatives banked on the influence and connections they had built up under past colonial patronage to set up political organizations and to canvass support for their candidates in the forthcoming 1988 elections.[10] At the same time, they consolidated their links with China through business investments on the mainland, through serving as advisors in local pro-China organizations, and by adopting a sympathetic stance on issues endorsed by China (Tang 1993: 266–9).

With the active political involvement of pro-China forces, and their alliance with the conservatives in joint opposition against the liberals, a new dimension surfaced in district politics on the eve of the 1988 elections. In addition to the issues of people's livelihood and environmental improvement which had prevailed in the past two elections, orientations towards China and the pace of constitutional change in Hong Kong were now to have a significant bearing on election results. In other words, district politics was no longer concerned simply with the affairs of the pertinent neighbourhood, but was also an arena where the participants contested on the issues of the Hong Kong–China relationship and of the nature of the territory's future political system.

The liberals outperformed their opponents in the 1988 District Board elections, but the conservative and pro-China forces nevertheless succeeded in winning a sizeable portion of the seats. These election results, after all, have to be viewed in terms of the comparatively late entry of the urban business conservatives and the pro-China faction into the political market. After the 1988 elections, in preparation for future contests, both the liberals and the conservatives organized themselves into political parties. With this development, the political market became still more structured and distinctly polarized into two ideologically opposing camps. The real showdown, it seemed, was to come in the 1991 elections—the more so as they would include for the first time direct election to the Legislative Council.

The Political Market on the Eve of the 1991 Elections

If a balance of power between the opposing political factions in Hong Kong was in the making in the wake of the 1988 elections, that balance

The Development Towards a Representative Government

was decisively tilted in favour of the liberals under the impact of the events that occurred on 4 June 1989 in Beijing's Tiananmen Square. The events so alienated the Hong Kong people from the Chinese government that the territory's pro-China groups nearly lost their credibility entirely among the local population. They also tarnished the image of the conservatives on account of their pro-China orientation and their political alliance with pro-China forces. In contrast, the liberals, by virtue of their pro-democracy stance and the leading role they had played in the territory's mass demonstrations in connection with the June Fourth Incident, gained substantial political support. The 1991 elections, consisting of elections to the District Boards, the two Municipal Councils (that is, the Urban Council and the Regional Council), and the Legislative Council, took place against this background.

The nature of the political market on the eve of the 1991 elections posed a number of intriguing questions about voter preferences. Foremost was the question of the extent to which the population's orientation towards China in the aftermath of the June Fourth Incident would shape the voters' choices. There was also the question of whether the voters in making their choices would take account of each candidate's party affiliation. Lastly, there was the issue of how far the traditional rural forces, in the context of the liberals' mounting challenge, could still influence the voting preferences of New Territories residents. In short, in what way would the structure of the political market—in respect of the political cleavage between the pro-China conservative forces and the liberal democrats, of parties and political groups competing with each other and with the independents, and of indigenous rural forces in contest with the urban newcomers—impact on the election results?

The China Syndrome and Its bearing on the Political Market: The 1991 Elections

The liberals scored a landslide victory in the 1991 direct elections, evidenced most dramatically in the Legislative Council elections where sixteen of the eighteen directly elected seats were won by candidates affiliated with liberal political organizations (twelve seats went to the United Democrats of Hong Kong, three to the Meeting Point, and one to the Hong Kong Association for Democracy and People's Livelihood). Why did the electorate vote overwhelmingly for the liberals? We have the answer from several pertinent studies which also throw light on the way the voters' preferences were shaped by their attitudes towards the Chinese government.

Lee Ming-kwan's study (1993) addresses the fundamental issue of to what degree the liberals' victory can be explained in terms of their positions regarding the territory's social and welfare policies and the pace of political change, and to what degree it was a referendum on Hong Kong–China relations. Corresponding to these two factors, he constructs a 'liberalism' index and a 'pro-China' index,[11] on the basis of which he compares the political platforms of the liberals and the pro-China candidates in the Legislative Council direct election. His findings show that there was no significant difference between the liberal candidates and the pro-China candidates in respect of 'liberalism'. On the other hand, the pro-China candidates did score very high, and the liberal candidates very low, on the 'pro-China' index. Lee concludes that the so-called conservative pro-China forces were defeated in the 1991 elections not because they were less liberal than were the liberals, but because they advocated a conciliatory approach to Hong Kong–China relations and were perceived by the electorate as supporters of China's policies. Other studies lend support to Lee's inference.

Tsang Wing-kwong's (1993) survey study of the characteristics of those voters who supported the liberals in the 1991 Legislative Council direct election provides some illuminating information. Part of his study tries to find out in what way support for liberal candidates was related to the voter's opinions on certain major issues regarding the Hong Kong–China relationship. These issues included whether the Hong Kong government should dissolve the Hong Kong Alliance in Support of Patriotic Democratic Movements in China, and whether China has the right to examine those policies of the Hong Kong government that extend beyond 1997. His findings show that those who opposed such stances were far more likely to have voted for the liberals than those who adopted a pro-China position. Tsang's other findings also reveal that the pro-liberal voters were more likely to have participated actively in the mass demonstrations and rallies in response to the June Fourth Incident, and tended to favour candidates who were critical of the Chinese government. The liberals' success in the 1991 elections, Tsang contends, was due predominantly to a prevalent political disposition which he calls 'the China complex'.

What made up this so-called 'China complex', and in what way did it affect the voters' perception of the pro-China candidates? These are the underlying questions in Leung Sai-wing's study (1993) of the dramatic failure of the pro-China candidates in the 1991 Legislative Council direct election. Beginning with his survey findings that only 12 per cent of the registered voters in his territory-wide sample said they would vote for a pro-China candidate, whereas 43 per cent said they would not, Leung sought to find out what accounted for this lack of support for the pro-China faction. He discovered from his findings on the respondents' perception of the pro-China candidates that the voters in fact did not hold entirely negative views of such candidates. Over one-third of the respondents, for instance, described the pro-China candidates as patriots, contributing to China's modernization, and facilitating Hong Kong's communication with China. Yet, side by side with these positive images, many respondents also perceived such candidates negatively, as 'China's running dogs', and hence as too 'committed to China' and not sufficiently 'committed to Hong Kong'. Leung's further analysis reveals that in making their voting decisions, the voters took into account primarily the pro-China candidates' negative attributes. Leung went on to explore the reasons for this singularity in voting consideration.

Leung's survey findings show that it was the June Fourth Incident which turned the voters against the pro-China candidates. More than three-fourths of the respondents in his study said that they opposed the Chinese government's handling of the incident, while less than 4 per cent supported it. It was also this 'defiant' majority, the findings show, who were most likely to denounce the pro-China candidates as 'China's running dogs' and as 'not committed to Hong Kong'. Leung contends that the June Fourth Incident had implanted among the Hong Kong population a pervasive attitude of distrust and defiance towards the Chinese government, and that it was this 'anti-China syndrome' (Leung Sai-wing 1993: 217) which eroded support for the pro-China candidates. The pro-China candidates lost because 'they were just joining an election battle in the wrong place at the wrong time' (Leung Sai-wing 1993: 197).

Political Parties and the Rural-Urban Cleavage in the 1991 Elections

The 1991 elections were a turning point in the evolution of Hong Kong's political market in that they involved for the first time the active participation of political parties in the territory's electoral politics. This observation prompted Louie Kin-sheun to undertake an investigation (Louie 1993) of the extent to which parties influenced voting choices in the Legislative Council direct elections.[12] Louie calls 'core party identifiers' those who voted for a particular candidate because he or she was affiliated with a political party of their preference. His findings show that such voters made up only 14.1 per cent of the electorate. Another category, whom Louie calls the 'peripheral party identifiers', consisted of those who had no firm or consistent preference for any party and yet chose to vote for a candidate of a particular party affiliation in the election. These 'peripheral party identifiers' made up 20.5 per cent of the electorate. Louie concludes:

The number of party-identifiers, especially the core-identifiers, was still too small to have a substantial impact on the outcome of the election. Therefore, viewed as a whole, the 1991 Legco election could not be considered as determined by the effect of party-identification (Louie 1993: 181).

One needs here to note that Louie's findings also show that the voters' acceptance or rejection of a party was determined primarily by its attitudes towards the Chinese government (Louie 1993: 167). This finding implies that party identification was contingent mainly on Tsang's 'China complex', and that the effect of parties on electoral choice would have been even weaker if events in China in the preceding few years had not generated such concern and controversy among the Hong Kong population.

The impact of the 'China complex' on electoral politics was subsumed under the rural–urban cleavage in the New Territories, where the political market on the eve of the 1991 elections was characterized primarily by a contest between the conservative pro-China rural forces and the liberal urban newcomers. The extent to which voting choice was made on the basis of this rural–urban dichotomy was the subject of Li Pang-kwong's study (1993) of the 1991 District Board elections in Tuen Mun and Yuen Long—two areas where the contest between the rural forces and the liberal faction was particularly acute. Li's findings show that the success of the conservative rural candidates in the elections varied directly, while the success of the liberals varied inversely, with the proportion of rural residents in the respective constituencies in the two areas. Li points out further that seven of the total twenty-eight constituencies were uncontested, and all these uncontested seats went to conservative candidates. The mean proportion of rural residents in these seven constituencies was 52 per cent (Li 1993: 322), and Li infers from this statistic that a constituency with a high proportion of rural residents would tend to return uncontested conservative candidates. In other words, the 'urban' liberals surrendered such constituencies, for they knew that rural residents would vote predominantly for conservative rural candidates.

This pattern of voting among the rural residents in the New Territories, in Li's view, was attributable to their perceived threat of an urban liberal encroachment on their traditional rural interests and way of life. He observes:

Stategically, it is very natural and logical for the conservative leaders to mobilize electoral support along the line of rural and non-rural (urban) differences. Thus, at least in the local elections, the rural–urban cleavage has been politicized and has served as the basis of electoral division (Li 1993: 327).

Towards a New Balance of Power? Preliminary Observations on the 1994 District Board Elections and the 1995 Legislative Council Elections

The defeat of the conservative pro-China forces in the 1991 elections was due largely to historical circumstances beyond their control. The June Fourth Incident tarnished their image in the minds of the Hong Kong people; the pro-democracy movement in the Soviet Union and the subsequent collapse of the Soviet communist regime had the effect of enhancing the popular appeal of Hong Kong's liberal–democratic faction. But as Joseph Y. S. Cheng (1994) aptly observes, given the substantial resources of the pro-China united front (which embraces business interests, professional associations, as well as grass-roots organizations) and its increasing influence on the mass media, and in the context of the fading memory of the June Fourth Incident, this potent power bloc holds the promise of a successful comeback in forthcoming elections. Cheng points out further that Hong Kong's people adopt a utilitarian approach to democracy and 'do not have a firm commitment to democracy and are unwilling to sacrifice for it' (Cheng 1994: 312).[13] To the extent that the liberals have been labelled by the Chinese government as subversive, their political appeal is likely to be increasingly compromised by the local people's apprehension that confrontation with the future sovereign political master will have dire consequences for the territory's future. The 1994 District Board elections took place in this context of this apprehension.

About half of the 346 District Board seats were won by candidates with party backgrounds. The liberal camp captured 111 seats, most of which (75 seats) went to the Democratic Party (a merger of the United Democrats of Hong Kong and the Meeting Point) and the Hong Kong Association for Democracy and People's Livelihood (28 seats). The pro-China parties captured 49 seats, of which 37 went to the Democratic Alliance for the Betterment of Hong Kong. The business-oriented and conservative Liberal Party secured only 18 seats (*Ming Pao*, 20 and 21 September 1994). In short, the liberal parties scored a distinct victory over the pro-China and pro-business parties in the 1994 District Board elections. However, the election results also show that the pro-China parties were making clear headway in electoral politics. Indeed, the success of the liberals is seen as far from overwhelming if we take into account that one-half of the District Board seats were won by independent candidates.

About one-half of these independents, according to the analysis of a leading Hong Kong newspaper (*Ming Pao*, 21 September 1994), were either members of or closely connected with pro-China associations. Many were advisors on Hong Kong affairs or advisors on district affairs appointed by the Chinese government; some were members of the Federation of Trade Unions; a substantial number were members of residents' associations and rural groups that had a close relationship with the pro-China parties. Taking into consideration the seats won by political parties and by the independents, *Ming Pao* estimates that there is an even balance of power between the liberals and the pro-China camp in the 1994–7 District Boards. At the end of 1994, the pro-China united front seemed to have made a successful comeback in local politics.

The liberals, however, again scored an impressive victory in the 1995 Legislative Council elections. Their achievement was most remarkable in the direct elections based on geographical constituencies, where the Democratic Party won twelve seats and the Hong Kong Association for Democracy and People's Livelihood captured two of the twenty seats in contention. In contrast, the pro-China Democratic Alliance for the Betterment of Hong Kong won two seats and the pro-business Liberal Party won only one. The remaining three seats went to independents, two of whom were liberals. The liberals' electoral performance in the elections based on functional constituencies and on the election committee (composed of elected members of the District Boards) was circumscribed by the pertinent electoral arrangements. They won twelve seats (the Democratic Party winning seven, the Hong Kong Association for Democracy and People's Livelihood two, and liberal independents three) of the forty seats. The remaining places went to pro-China and pro-business candidates and other politically unaffiliated candidates. We shall examine in a later section how Hong Kong's existing and future political system constrains the electoral performance of the liberals.

The Emerging Political Configuration: Parties, Politicians, and Civil Servants

The emerging political configuration in Hong Kong in the course of the territory's development towards a representative government has to be examined not only in terms of the power contest in direct elections, for these constitute but one route to political power in the territory. The civil bureaucracy, by virtue of its representation through senior civil servants on the Legislative Council, remains a major power in Hong Kong's politics. Moreover, as laid down in the Basic Law, the legislature until 2003 (see Table 8.1) will be made up of three types of members: members returned

Table 8.1 Composition of the Hong Kong Legislature Towards 1997 and Beyond

	1995–9	1999–2003	2003–7
Selected from functional constituencies	30	30	30
Selected by direct election	20	24	30
Indirect election by an election committee	10	6	0
Total number of seats	60	60	60

by geographical constituencies through direct elections, members returned by an Election Committee[14] of 800 members representing various socio-economic sectors, and members returned by functional constituencies. A number of writers have identified several problems in Hong Kong's emerging political configuration in the light of such multiple bases of political power.

The change in the composition of the Legislative Council concomitant with the development towards a representative government, in some writers' view (Cheek-Milby 1989; Louie 1992), has generated confrontation and conflict between the official members (that is, the Government's representatives) and the elected members in the legislature. The conflict is based in the differing responsibilities of the two groups: while the initiation of policies and policy-making are the primary responsibility of the civil bureaucracy, the enactment of policies is the role of the Legislative Council. To the extent that the elected members of the Legislative Council have to be accountable to their constituencies, they perceive their role as that of defending and representing the interests of the public against those of the Government. The official members are in the minority in the Legislative Council, and so this gives rise to an anomalous political situation of 'governing without a majority' (Louie 1992: 73). The former Chief Secretary, Sir David Ford, described the difficulties faced by the Government in such a situation:

We all recognize that it may not always be easy to gain the support of a majority of the Members of the Legislative Council because under our present system there is no organized party support for the Government in the Legislative Council, or in the media or in the community as a whole.... We must be careful therefore not to drift into a series of situations in which the Government is isolated because it has no built-in support. There is a real danger of this because there is a perception in Hong Kong that, to be popular, a politician must sometimes be seen to be openly critical of the Administration (address in the Legislative Council, 6 November 1991; cited in Louie 1992: 73–4).

The resulting fragmentation in political leadership between bureaucrats and politicians in the legislature will persist beyond 1997, as the government of the Special Administrative Region (SAR) will continue to be led by an executive branch. Moreover, in the views of Lau (1990) and Louie (1991, 1992), there are additional factors that will aggravate the problem of political leadership in post-1997 Hong Kong.

The Chief Executive of the SAR government, Lau notes, will be elected by an Election Committee in which socio-economic élites will predominate. This selection procedure, together with the requirement that the Chief Executive be appointed by the Chinese government after the election, means that the attainment of this top governmental position is contingent on the support of the territory's élites and the Chinese government. Furthermore, the powers bestowed on the Chief Executive—in particular the power to appoint and dismiss members of the SAR Executive Council—render it possible for individuals to reach the top echelons of the power structure through appointment by the Chief Executive. In other words, the socio-economic élites and the pro-China faction can attain the territory's most important political positions without submitting to a process of popular election.

Indirect elections to the legislature through the Election Committee and functional constituencies, Lau further points out, are similarly biased in favour of the socio-economic élites, as the electorates in both cases are constituted predominantly from the privileged sectors of the community. Direct elections through geographical constituencies will, therefore, remain the only channel to attain political leadership on the basis of general public support, but until the year 2007, directly elected members will make up no more than 50 per cent of the legislature. In short, grass-roots interests are not likely to have a strong representation in the SAR government. Moreover, in Lau's view, the multiple channels of leader recruitment—appointments to administrative positions, patronage by the Chinese government, indirect elections, and direct elections—will lead to the fragmentation of political leadership, as leaders with different bases of legitimacy are accountable to different sources of political support. 'The structural configuration of the new political system of Hong Kong', Lau observes, 'is not favourable to the production of strong political leadership' (Lau 1990: 17).

Nor is the emerging political system conducive to the development of strong political parties. The expansion and strengthening of political parties, Louie (1991) aptly observes, depend on the development of mass elections and the capability of parties to influence the policy-making process. To the extent that mass elections contribute fewer than one-half of the seats in the legislature in the years before 2003, the political influence of parties is severely restricted, and the incentive for party development is correspondingly reduced. The representatives of functional constituencies, on the other hand, are accountable to an electorate with specific, well-defined interests and as such have to be loyal to their respective particular interest groups rather than to a political party. For this reason, a party has great difficulty in recruiting members from those elected through functional constituencies.

One can apply the same argument to the Election Committee and its elected representatives. In this sense, no matter how successful a party is in direct elections, its influence on policy-making will be significantly reduced by the arrangements prescribed for the future political system. Louie concludes:

> The political structure of the future SAR as defined in the Basic Law seems to be designed in such a manner that parties will not be able to play a major role in it.... They can only expect to play a subsidiary role... without much possibility of dictating the course of policy-making. The chance that a single party may become the majority in the legislature almost does not exist (Louie 1991: 74).

Louie's conclusion implies that despite the widespread popular support for the Democratic Party in recent years, it cannot realistically expect to play a dominant political role in the SAR government. In a recent article (Sonny S. H. Lo 1995), Sonny S. H. Lo holds a similar view and argues in addition that in light of the political system prescribed for post-1997 Hong Kong, and of China's support for the pro-China and the pro-business politicians, the Democratic Alliance for the Betterment of Hong Kong and the Liberal Party are likely to emerge as Hong Kong's major political forces:

> While the present... democratization period is characterized by the relative success and increasing influence of the popularly supported Democratic Party, the post-1997 Hong Kong polity will be at least for some time characterized by the inevitable dominance of the Democratic Alliance for the Betterment of Hong Kong [and] the rejuvenation of the Liberal Party under political patronage (Sonny S. H. Lo 1995: 66).

Conclusion

The development towards a representative government in Hong Kong has proceeded in the context of heated debates about the pace and scope of the pertinent political reforms. Such debates have defined the main contours of political competition in the territory's democratization, culminating in the emergence and consolidation of two major opposing political factions: the conservatives and the liberal–democrats. Their political contest carried the imprint of the 'China factor', because the stance of the conservatives towards the pace of democratization was close to that of the Chinese government. Attitudes towards the Chinese government and towards Hong Kong's relationship with China soon became the main identifying feature of Hong Kong's rival political factions.

The political fortunes of the liberals and the conservatives were thus closely bound up with the Hong Kong people's view of China. For this reason, the dramatic success of the liberals in the 1991 elections is to a large extent attributable to the June Fourth Incident which alienated a substantial portion of the Hong Kong public from the Chinese government. However, in the context of fading memories of the incident, and in view of the growing strength of the pro-China united front, the liberals are facing a mounting political challenge from their rivals.

Mass support is, however, only one basis of power in Hong Kong's emerging political configuration. The political system prescribed for the Special Administrative Region is such that socio-economic élites, especially those favoured by China, can attain influential political positions without submitting to direct mass elections. Hong Kong's emerging representative government, at least until a few years after the transfer of sovereignty, will in all probability remain biased in favour of the socio-economically privileged and the pro-China segments of the community.

Notes

1. King writes: 'The wealthy Chinese have demonstrated extreme adaptive capacity in creating high-power associations of various kinds for the purposes of mutual assistance and self-advancement in a rapidly urbanized settlement under alien rule. The Tung Wah Group of Hospitals, the Po Leung Kuk and the Kaifongs are all indigenously developed. The key figures in these Chinese associations are civic-minded men of achievement respected by their community. They have developed an informal system of power and influence parallel to the formal system of the British' (King 1981b: 135).

2. For details, see Secretary for Chinese Affairs (1969: 12, 18, 21).

3. There were 188 cases of urban social protests in the decade 1970–9, more than five times the number (31 cases) in the preceding decade. In particular, urban social protests increased substantially in the second half of the 1970s, reaching an average of 29 per year. For details, see Lui and Kung (1985: 62–3). The Government's coping strategy is reflected in the following proposal from its Standing Committee on Pressure Groups: 'At times, it is possible to divert some of the group's efforts into more useful channels by bringing active members into contact with or even directly on existing boards and committees. This brings the individual and the group into the established system, helps them to obtain a more balanced picture of the Government and its policies, and can remove them from extremist influence' (Home Affairs Branch 1980: 10).

4. For the relevant empirical evidence, see the classic study by Huntington (1968). The explanation in this respect is that democratization entails a rising level of mass participation in politics. Given the possibility that the masses in developing societies are politically unsophisticated and oriented to the pursuit of parochial or sectional interests, their political participation may generate political fragmentation, disorder, or even authoritarian politics.

5. For example, for the democratic countries in Dahl's study, 20 per cent of the working population were employed in industry and 62 per cent of the population aged 5–19 years were enrolled in primary and secondary education. The corresponding figures for Hong Kong in 1986 were 50 per cent and 91 per cent, respectively. For more comparative statistics, see Benjamin K. P. Leung (1990c: 33, table 2.2). Leung highlights Hong Kong's comparatively high rate of enrolment in education and clarifies the implication of this for democratic stability by quoting Lipset: 'Education presumably broadens a man's outlook, enables him to understand the need for norms of tolerance, restrains him from adhering to extremist doctrines, and increases his capacity to make rational electoral choices.... The higher one's education, the more likely one is to believe in democratic values and support democratic practices' (Lipset 1981: 39–40).

6. As evidence of this aversion, Leung cites press reports in *The South China Morning Post* and a report in the *Far Eastern Economic Review* (16 April 1987, p. 44) which states: '[Chairman of World-Wide Shipping] Sohmen said he is

convinced democracy would damage Hong Kong.... Sohmen's stance is echoed by many whose clout straddles corporate and political life. They say they are wary of "free-lunchers" and the "riff-raff" holding office, voting for all kinds of social spending'.

7. For a complete listing of the functional constituencies and the size of the respective electorates in 1991, see Scott (1992: 11, table 1.3). Most of the seats were allotted to the business (commercial, industrial, financial, real estate, and construction functional constituencies) and professional (medical and health care, legal, engineering and architectural, and accountancy functional constituencies) sectors. In contrast, labour had only two of the total twenty-one seats. The Government made it clear that this bias was designed to safeguard the territory's stability and prosperity in the process of development towards a representative government: 'Full weight should be given to representation of the economic and professional sectors of Hong Kong which are essential to future confidence and prosperity. Direct elections would run the risk of a swift introduction of adversarial politics, and would introduce an element of instability at a critical time' (Hong Kong Government, *Green Paper: The Further Development of Representative Government in Hong Kong*: 9; cited in Scott 1992: 26).

8. The Basic Law stipulates that the election committee is to be composed of 800 members with 200 from the industrial, commercial, and financial sectors; 200 from the professions; 200 from labour, social services, religious, and other sectors; and 200 from members of the Legislative Council, representatives of district-based organizations, Hong Kong deputies to the National People's Congress, and Hong Kong representatives to the National Committee of the Chinese People's Political Conference. Cheng comments: 'This system will facilitate the domination of conservative political forces' (Cheng 1990: 57).

9. It is worth noting at this juncture that the Hong Kong people's participation rate in public elections over the years has been moderate. The rate has varied between a low of 17.6 per cent (1989 Municipal Councils elections) to a high of 39.1 per cent (1991 Legislative Council direct election) of registered voters. The voter registration rate (that is, registered voters as a percentage of eligible voters), on the other hand, has varied between a low of 32.4 per cent (1982 District Board election) to a high of 61.8 per cent (1994 District Board election). If we consider voter turnout with reference to eligible voters, then the highest rate is 20 per cent (1991 Legislative Council direct election). For more detailed information on this point, see Louie and Sum (1995: 267, app. 3).

10. The most active and influential member of the conservative camp in this respect was arguably Maria Tam, a former appointed member of the Executive and Legislative councils. Tang (1993: 270–2) describes Tam as a power broker working to forge liaisons among the conservatives and between the conservatives and the pro-China forces.

11. Lee constructed the 'liberalism' index from six indicators including, for example, the candidate's stances on tax rates, the welfare budget, labour rights, and the pace of political reforms. The 'pro-China' index was constructed mainly on the basis of whether the candidate advocated a conciliatory approach to Hong Kong–China relations and avoidance of confrontation with China. For details on this subject, see Lee (1993: 240–1).

12. Louie adopted a loose definition of 'political party' to include organizations fielding candidates in a political election. Parties contesting in the 1991 Legislative Council election included the United Democrats of Hong Kong, Meeting Point, Liberal Democratic Federation, Hong Kong Association for Democracy and People's Livelihood, New Hong Kong Alliance, Hong Kong Democratic Foundation, Hong Kong Citizen Forum, Hong Kong Civic Association, Reform Club, Hong Kong Federation of Trade Unions, and Association for

the Stabilization of Hong Kong (Louie 1993: 182–3). As many of these groups did not really qualify as full-fledged political parties in the strictest sense, one can construe Louie's study as an investigation of the impact of political organizations, or embryonic political parties, on electoral choice.

13. For the pertinent empirical studies, see the section on political attitudes in Chapter 3.

14. Annex 1 of the Basic Law stipulates that the Election Committee after 1997 shall be composed of 800 members. The Election Committee of 1996, however, is composed of 400 members.

References

* Abbas, Agber, 1992. 'The Last Emporium: Verse and Cultural Space', in Leung Ping-kwan (ed.), *City at the End of Time*, Hong Kong: Twilight Books, pp. 2–18.
Anderson, Michael, 1980. *Approaches to the History of the Western Family, 1500–1914*, London: Macmillan.
Ashby, Ross, 1952. *A Design for a Brain*, New York: Wiley.
Association for the Advancement of Feminism, 1993. *The Hong Kong Women File*, Hong Kong: Association for the Advancement of Feminism.
Barnett, K. M. A., 1961. *The Census and You*, Hong Kong: The Government Press.
Barnett, K. M. A., 1969. *Hong Kong Statistics 1947–1967*, Hong Kong: Census and Statistics Department.
Berkowitz, Leonard, 1962. *Aggression: A Social-Psychological Analysis*, New York: Free Press.
Carr, Neil, 1973. 'Employer Attitude Survey in a Hong Kong Engineering Company', *The Journal of Industrial Relations*, 15(1): 56–67.
Castells, Manuel, et al., 1988. *Economic Development and Housing Policy in the Asian Pacific Rim: A Comparative Study of Hong Kong, Singapore, and Shenzhen Special Economic Zone*. Monograph 37, Berkeley: Institute of Urban and Regional Development, University of California.
Census and Statistics Department (Hong Kong Government), 1960. *Pilot Census*, Hong Kong: Government Printer.
Census and Statistics Department (Hong Kong Government), 1979. *Crime and Its Victims in Hong Kong 1978*, Hong Kong: Government Printer.
Census and Statistics Department (Hong Kong Government), 1982. *Crime and Its Victims in Hong Kong 1981*, Hong Kong: Government Printer.
Census and Statistics Department (Hong Kong Government), 1987a. *Crime and Its Victims in Hong Kong 1986*, Hong Kong: Government Printer.
Census and Statistics Department (Hong Kong Government), 1987b. *Hong Kong Social and Economic Trends 1976–1986*, Hong Kong: Government Printer.
Census and Statistics Department (Hong Kong Government), 1990. *Crime and Its Victims in Hong Kong 1989*, Hong Kong: Government Printer.
Census and Statistics Department (Hong Kong Government), 1992. *Hong Kong 1991 Population Census: Main Report*, Hong Kong: Government Printer.
Census and Statistics Department (Hong Kong Government), 1993. *Hong Kong's Development in the Past 25 Years*, Hong Kong: Government Printer. Text in Chinese.
Chan Hoi-man, 1993. 'Popular Culture and Democratic Culture: Outline of a Perspective on the 1991 Legislative Council Election', in Lau Siu-kai and Louie Kin-shuen (eds.), *Hong Kong Tried Democracy*, Hong Kong: Hong Kong Institute of Asia-Pacific Studies, The Chinese University of Hong Kong, pp. 346–68.
* Chan Hoi-man, 1995. 'Popular Culture and Political Society: Prolegomena on Cultural Studies in Hong Kong', in Elizabeth Sinn (ed.), *Culture and Society in Hong Kong*, Hong Kong: Centre of Asian Studies, University of Hong Kong, pp. 23–50.

Chan Kai-cheung, 1991. 'The Media and Telecommunications', in Sung Yun-wing and Lee Ming-kwan (eds.), *The Other Hong Kong Report: 1991*, Hong Kong: The Chinese University of Hong Kong, pp. 447–76.
Chan Kai-cheung, 1995. 'The Establishment of an Indigenous Hong Kong Culture and the Role of the Television', in Elizabeth Sinn (ed.), *Culture and Society in Hong Kong*, Hong Kong: Centre of Asian Studies, University of Hong Kong, pp. 80–8. Text in Chinese.
Chan Lau Kit-ching, 1990. *China, Britain, and Hong Kong, 1895–1945*, Hong Kong: The Chinese University Press.
Chan, Wai-kwan, 1991. *The Making of Hong Kong Society*, New York: Oxford University Press.
Chaney, David, 1971. 'Job Satisfaction and Unionization', in Keith Hopkins (ed.), *Hong Kong: The Industrial Colony*, Hong Kong: Oxford University Press, pp. 261–70.
Chaney, David, and Podmore, David, 1973. *Young Adults in Hong Kong: Attitudes in a Modernizing Society*, Hong Kong: Centre of Asian Studies, The University of Hong Kong.
Chau, Larry L. C., 1989. 'Labour and Labour Market', in Henry C. Y. Ho and Larry L. C. Chau (eds.), *The Economic System of Hong Kong*, Hong Kong: Asian Research Service, pp. 169–89.
Cheek-Milby, Kathleen, 1989. 'The Civil Servant as Politician: The Role of the Official Member of the Legislative Council', in Kathleen Cheek-Milby and Miron Mushkat (eds.), *Hong Kong: The Challenge of Transformation*, Hong Kong: Centre of Asian Studies, University of Hong Kong, pp. 256–94.
Cheng, Joseph Y. S., 1990. 'The Basic Law: Messages for Hong Kong People', in Richard Y. C. Wong and Joseph Y. S. Cheng (eds.), *The Other Hong Kong Report: 1990*, Hong Kong: The Chinese University Press, pp. 29–64.
Cheng, Joseph Y. S., 1994. 'Hong Kong's Legislative Council Elections: Review of 1991 and Planning for 1995', in Benjamin K. P. Leung and Teresa Y. C. Wong (eds.), *25 Years of Social and Economic Development in Hong Kong*, Hong Kong: Centre of Asian Studies, University of Hong Kong, pp. 291–316.
Cheung Bing-leung, 1988. 'The New Middle Class: Its Rise and Political Influence', in Cheung Bing-leung et al., *Class Analysis and Hong Kong*, Hong Kong: Ching Man Publisher, pp. 9–26. Text in Chinese.
Cheung Bing-leung, 1989. 'The Pattern of District Administration: A Political-Structural Analysis', in Joseph Y. S. Cheng (ed.), *Hong Kong in Transition*, Hong Kong: Joint Publishing Co., pp. 38–66. Text in Chinese.
Cheung Bing-leung, and Louie Kin-sheun, 1991. 'Social Conflicts in Hong Kong, 1975–1986: Trends and Implications', Occasional Paper no. 3, Hong Kong: Hong Kong Institute of Asia-Pacific Studies, The Chinese University of Hong Kong.
Cheung Bing-leung, et al., 1988. *Class Analysis and Hong Kong*, Hong Kong: Ching Man Publisher. Text in Chinese.
Cheung, M. K., 1985. 'Some Social Correlates of Juvenile Misbehaviour in Hong Kong', Senior Thesis, Department of Sociology, The Chinese University of Hong Kong.
Cheung, Yuet-wah, and Ng, Agnes, 1988. 'Social Factors in Adolescent Deviant Behaviour in Hong Kong: An integrated Theoretical Approach', *International Journal of Comparative and Applied Criminal Justice*, 12(1) and 12(2)(Spring/Winter): 27–45.
Chiu, Rebecca, 1994. 'Housing Intervention in Hong Kong: From Laissez Faire to Privatization', in Benjamin K. P. Leung and Teresa Y. C. Wong (eds.), *25 Years of Social and Economic Development in Hong Kong*, Hong Kong: Centre of Asian Studies, University of Hong Kong, pp. 336–56.

Chiu, Stephen, 1992. 'The State and the Financing of Industrialization in East Asia', Ph.D. Dissertation, Princeton University, Princeton, N. J.

Choi Po-king, 1990. 'Popular Culture', in Richard Y. C. Wong and Joseph Y. S. Cheng (eds.), *The Other Hong Kong Report: 1990*, Hong Kong: The Chinese University of Hong Kong, pp. 537–64.

Chow, Nelson W. S., 1985. 'Welfare Development in Hong Kong: The Politics of Social Choice', in Jao Yu-ching et al. (eds.), *Hong Kong and 1997: Strategies for the Future*, Hong Kong: Centre of Asian Studies, University of Hong Kong, pp. 475–91.

Chow, Nelson W. S., 1990. *The Ideology and System of Social Welfare*, Hong Kong: Chung Wah Books Publishing Company. Text in Chinese.

Chow, Nelson W. S., 1991. *Social Welfare Policy in Hong Kong: A Critical Analysis*, Hong Kong: Cosmos Books. Text in Chinese.

Chow, Nelson W. S., 1994. 'Welfare Development in Hong Kong: An Ideological Appraisal', in Benjamin K. P. Leung and Teresa Y. C. Wong (eds.), *25 Years of Social and Economic Development in Hong Kong*, Hong Kong: Centre of Asian Studies, University of Hong Kong, pp. 321–35.

Chow, Nelson W. S., 1995. 'Social Welfare: The Way Ahead', in Joseph Y. S. Cheng and Sonny S. H. Lo (eds.), *From Colony to SAR: Hong Kong's Challenges Ahead*, Hong Kong: The Chinese University of Hong Kong, pp. 393–412.

Chow, Nelson W. S., et al., 1985. *A Study of the Values, Leisure, Behaviour, and Misbehaviour of the Youth in Tsuen Wan and Kwai Chung*, Hong Kong: Tsuen Wan District Board.

Chow, Nelson W. S., et al., 1987. *A Comparison of Delinquent Youth and Non-delinquent Youth on the Aspects of Parental Supervision and Schooling*, Hong Kong: Kwai Chung and Tsing Yi District Board and Tsuen Wan District Board.

Clifford, William, 1973. *Development and Crime*, Chichester: Barry Rose.

Clifford, William, 1974. *An Introduction to African Criminology*, London: Oxford University Press.

Clinard, Marshall, and Abbott, David, 1973. *Crime in Developing Countries*, New York: Wiley.

Clinard, Marshall, 1964. 'The Relation of Urbanization and Urbanism to Criminal Behaviour', in E. Burgess and D. Bogue (eds.), *Contributions to Urban Sociology*, Chicago: The University of Chicago Press, pp. 541–59.

Commissioner for Resettlement (Hong Kong Government), 1955. *Annual Report*, Hong Kong: Government Printer.

Commissioner of Labour (Hong Kong Government), 1950. *Annual Report*, Hong Kong: Government Printer.

Cooper, John, 1970. *Colony in Conflict*, Hong Kong: Swindon.

Dahl, Robert, 1971. *Polyarchy: Participation and Opposition*, New Haven, Ct.: Yale University Press.

Dahrendorf, Ralf, 1959. *Class and Class Conflict in Industrial Society*, Stanford, Ca.: Stanford University Press.

Diamond, Larry, 1980. 'The Social Foundations of Democracy: The Case of Nigeria', Ph.D. Dissertation, Stanford University, Stanford, Ca.

Dobinson, Ian, 1994. 'The Measurement of Crime', in Mark S. Gaylord and Harold Traver (eds.), *Introduction to The Hong Kong Criminal Justice System*, Hong Kong: Hong Kong University Press, pp. 15–28.

Drakakis-Smith, D., 1979. *High Society: Housing Provision in Metropolitan Hong Kong 1954–1979: A Jubilee Critique*, Hong Kong: Centre of Asian Studies, University of Hong Kong.

Elliott, Elsie, 1981. *Crusade For Justice*, Hong Kong: Heinemann Education Books.

Endacott, G. B., 1973. *A History of Hong Kong* (2nd ed.), Hong Kong: Oxford University Press.
England, Joe, 1979. 'Trade Unionism and Industrial Disputes in Hong Kong: An Explanatory Framework', in The Japan Institute of Labour (ed.), *Social Tensions and Industrial Relations Arising in the Industrialization Processes of Asian Countries*, Japan: Institute of Labour, pp. 79–104.
England, Joe, 1989. *Industrial Relations and Law in Hong Kong*, Hong Kong: Oxford University Press.
England, Joe, and Rear, John, 1975. *Chinese Labour under British Rule*, Hong Kong: Oxford University Press.
Eyerman, Ron, and Jamison, Andrew, 1991. *Social Movements: A Cognitive Approach*, Cambridge: Polity Press.
Farber, B., 1975. 'Bilateral Kinship: Centripetal and Centrifugal Types of Organization', *Journal of Marriage and the Family*, 37(November): 871–89.
Freud, Sigmund, 1945. *Group Psychology and the Analysis of the Ego*, London: The Hogarth Press.
Friedman, Milton, 1980. *Free to Choose*, Hammondsworth: Penguin.
Galle, O. R., et al., 1972. 'Population Density and Pathology: What are the Implications for Man', in *Science*, 176: 23–30.
Gamson, William, 1968. *Power and Discontent*, Homewood, Ill.: Dorsey.
Gaylord, Mark S., 1991. 'Commercial Crime', in Harold Traver and Jon Vagg (eds.), *Crime and Justice in Hong Kong*, Hong Kong: Oxford University Press, pp. 70–82.
Giddens, Anthony, 1993. *Sociology* (2nd ed.), Oxford: Polity Press.
Goode, William, 1963. *World Revolution and Family Patterns*, New York: Free Press.
Gramsci, Antonio, 1971. *Selections from the Prison Notebooks*, London: Lawrence and Wishart.
Gurr, Ted Robert, 1970. *Why Men Rebel*, Princeton, N.J.: Princeton University Press.
Hall, C., 1982. 'The Butcher, the Baker, and the Candlestickmaker: The Shop and the Family in the Industrial Revolution', in E. Whiteless et al. (eds.), *The Changing Experience of Women*, Oxford: Martin Robertson, pp. 149–63.
Haralambos, Michael, and Holborn, Martin, 1991. *Sociology: Themes and Perspectives* (3rd ed.), London: Collins Educational.
Hareven, T., 1991. 'The Home and the Family in Historical Perspective', *Social Research*, 58(1): 254–85.
Ho Kwok-leung, 1989. 'The Political Economy of Public Housing in Hong Kong: A Sociological Analysis', M.Phil. Thesis, University of Hong Kong.
Hoadley, Stephen, 1970. 'Hong Kong is the Life-boat: Notes on Political Culture and Socialization', *Journal of Oriental Studies*, 8: 206–18.
Hodge, Peter, 1981. 'The Politics of Welfare', in T. Khoo (ed.), *Aspects of Mental Health Care in Hong Kong*, Hong Kong: Mental Health Association of Hong Kong, pp. 24–35.
Home Affairs Branch (Hong Kong Government), 1980. 'Information Paper for Chief Secretary's Committee, Monitoring of Pressure Group Activities', mimeograph copy, Hong Kong: Government Printer.
Hong Kong Government, 1948. *Annual Report*, Hong Kong: Government Printer.
Hong Kong Government, 1956. *Report on the Riots in Kowloon and Tsuen Wan, 1956*, Hong Kong: Government Printer.
Hong Kong Government, 1965. *Aims and Policy for Social Welfare in Hong Kong*, Hong Kong: Government Printer.
Hong Kong Government, 1967. *Commission of Inquiry on Kowloon Disturbances, 1966*, Hong Kong: Government Printer.

Hong Kong Government, 1984. *White Paper on Representative Government*, Hong Kong: Government Printer.
Hong Kong Government, 1988. *White Paper: The Development of Representative Government: The Way Forward*, Hong Kong: Government Printer.
Hong Kong Hansard, 1950, Hong Kong: Government Printer.
Hong Kong Hansard, 1972, Hong Kong: Government Printer.
Hong Kong Hansard, 1977, Hong Kong: Government Printer.
Hong Kong University Students' Union, 1988. *Union Journal 1988*, Hong Kong: Hong Kong University Students' Union.
Hong Kong Young Women's Association, 1984. 'Research Report on the Lives of Full-time Housewives', Hong Kong: Hong Kong Young Women's Association.
Hopkins, Keith, 1971. 'Housing the Poor', in Keith Hopkins (ed.), *Hong Kong: The Industrial Colony*, Hong Kong: Oxford University Press, pp. 271–338.
Huntington, Samuel, 1968. *Political Order in Changing Societies*, London: Yale University Press.
Inkeles, Alex, 1960. 'Industrial Man: The Relation of Status to Experience, Perception and Value', *American Journal of Sociology*, 66(1): 1–31.
Jary, David, and Jary, Julia, 1991. *Collins Dictionary of Sociology*, London: Harper Collins.
Jones, Catherine, 1990. *Promoting Prosperity: The Hong Kong Way of Social Policy*, Hong Kong: The Chinese University Press.
Kerr, C., et al., 1960. *Industrialism and Industrial Man*, Cambridge, Mass.: Harvard University Press.
Keung, John K., 1985. 'Government Interventions and Housing Policy in Hong Kong', in *Third World Planning Review*, 7(1): 23–44.
King, Ambrose Y. C., 1980. 'An Institutional Response to Corruption: The ICAC of Hong Kong', in Leung Chi-keung et al. (eds.), *Hong Kong: Dilemmas of Growth*, Canberra: Research School of Pacific Studies, Australian National University, and the Centre of Asian Studies, University of Hong Kong, pp. 115–42.
King, Ambrose Y. C., 1981a. 'The Political Culture of Kwun Tong: A Chinese Community in Hong Kong', in Ambrose Y. C. King and Rance P. L. Lee (eds.), *Social Life and Development in Hong Kong*, Hong Kong: The Chinese University Press, pp. 147–68.
King, Ambrose Y. C., 1981b. 'Administrative Absorption of Politics in Hong Kong: Emphasis on the Grass Roots Level', in Ambrose Y. C. King and Rance P. L. Lee (eds.), *Social Life and Development in Hong Kong*, Hong Kong: The Chinese University Press, pp. 127–46.
Kuan Hsin-chi, 1981. 'Anti-Corruption Legislation in Hong Kong: A History', in Rance P. L. Lee (ed.), *Corruption and Its Control in Hong Kong*, Hong Kong: The Chinese University Press, pp. 15–44.
Lang, Olga, 1946. *Chinese Family and Society*, New Haven, Ct.: Yale University Press.
Laslett, Peter, 1972. 'Mean Household Size in England since the Sixteenth Century', in Peter Laslett (ed.), *Household and Family in Past Time*, Cambridge: Cambridge University Press, pp. 54–68.
Laslett, Peter, 1977. *Family Life and Illicit Love in Earlier Generations*, Cambridge: Cambridge University Press.
Lau Chong-chor, and Lee, Rance P. L., 1981. 'Bureaucratic Corruption and Political Instability in Nineteenth-Century China', in Rance P. L. Lee (ed.), *Corruption and Its Control in Hong Kong*, Hong Kong: The Chinese University Press, pp. 105–32.
Lau Siu-kai, 1981. 'Utilitarianistic Familism: The Basis of Political Stability', in Ambrose Y. C. King and Rance Lee (eds.), *Social Life and Development in Hong Kong*, Hong Kong: The Chinese University Press, pp. 195–216.

Lau Siu-kai, 1982. *Society and Politics in Hong Kong*, Hong Kong: The Chinese University Press.
Lau Siu-kai, 1983. 'Social Change, Bureaucratic Rule, and Emergent Political Issues in Hong Kong', *World Politics*, 35(4): 562–73.
Lau Siu-kai, 1987. 'Decolonization Without Independence: The Unfinished Reforms of the Hong Kong Government', Centre for Hong Kong Studies, The Chinese University of Hong Kong.
Lau Siu-kai, 1990. 'Decolonization Without Independence and the Poverty of Political Leaders in Hong Kong', Occasional Paper no. 1, Hong Kong: Hong Kong Institute of Asia-Pacific Studies, The Chinese University of Hong Kong.
Lau Siu-kai, 1991. 'Institutions Without Leaders: The Hong Kong Chinese View of Political Leadership', HKIAPS Reprint Series No. 1, Hong Kong: Hong Kong Institute of Asia-Pacific Studies, The Chinese University of Hong Kong.
Lau Siu-kai, 1992. 'Political Attitudes', in Lau Siu-kai et al. (eds.), *Indicators of Social Development: Hong Kong 1990*, Hong Kong: Hong Kong Institute of Asia-Pacific Studies, The Chinese University of Hong Kong, pp. 129–57.
Lau Siu-kai, et al. (eds.), 1991. *Indicators of Social Development: Hong Kong 1988*, Hong Kong: Hong Kong Institute of Asia-Pacific Studies, The Chinese University of Hong Kong.
Lau Siu-kai, et al. (eds.), 1992. *Indicators of Social Development: Hong Kong 1990*, Hong Kong: Hong Kong Institute of Asia-Pacific Studies, The Chinese University of Hong Kong.
Lau Siu-kai, and Kuan Hsin-chi, 1983. 'The District Board Elections in Hong Kong', Occasional Paper no. 3, Hong Kong: Centre for Hong Kong Studies, The Chinese University of Hong Kong.
Lau Siu-kai, and Kuan Hsin-chi, 1985. 'The 1985 District Board Election in Hong Kong: The Limits of Political Mobilization in a Dependent Polity', Occasional Paper no. 8, Hong Kong: Centre for Hong Kong Studies, The Chinese University of Hong Kong.
Lau Siu-kai, and Kuan Hsin-chi, 1986. 'The Changing Political Culture of the Hong Kong Chinese', in Joseph Y. S. Cheng (eds.), *Hong Kong in Transition*, Hong Kong: Oxford University Press, pp. 26–51.
Lau Siu-kai, and Kuan Hsin-chi, 1988. *The Ethos of the Hong Kong Chinese*, Hong Kong: The Chinese University Press.
Lau Siu-kai, and Kuan Hsin-chi, 1989. 'The Civic Self in a Changing Polity: The Case of Hong Kong', in Kathleen Cheek-Milby and Miron Mushkat (eds.), *Hong Kong: The Challenge of Transformation*, Hong Kong: Centre of Asian Studies, University of Hong Kong, pp. 91–115.
Lau Siu-kai, and Kuan Hsin-chi, 1990. 'Public Attitudes Toward Laissez Faire in Hong Kong', *Asian Survey*, 30(8): 766–81.
Lau Siu-kai, and Wan Po-san, 1987. *A Preliminary Report on Social Indicators in Hong Kong*, Hong Kong: Centre for Hong Kong Studies. Text in Chinese.
Lau Siu-kai, Kuan Hsin-chi, and Wan Po-san, 1991. 'Political Attitudes', in Lau Siu-kai et al. (eds.), *Indicators of Social Development: Hong Kong 1988*, Hong Kong: Hong Kong Institute of Asia-Pacific Studies, The Chinese University of Hong Kong, pp. 173–205.
Lebon, Gustave, 1960. *The Crowd*, New York: Viking Press.
Lee, C. T., 1990. *Notes on Hong Kong Movies of the 1980s* (2 vols.), Hong Kong: Chong Kin Publishing. Text in Chinese.
Lee, J. P., 1988. 'Management–Labour Relationships: Dialogue, Cooperation and Public Policy Consultation', in Y. C. Jao et al. (eds.), *Labour Movement in a Changing Society: The Experience of Hong Kong*, Hong Kong: Centre of Asian Studies, University of Hong Kong, pp. 67–76.

Lee Ming-kwan, 1982. 'Emergent Patterns of Social Conflict in Hong Kong Society', in Joseph Y. S. Cheng (ed.), *Hong Kong in the 1980s*, Hong Kong: Summerson Eastern Publishers Ltd.

Lee Ming-kwan, 1987a. 'The Hong Kong Family: Organization and Change', in Lee Ming-kwan, *Hong Kong: Politics and Society in Transition*, Hong Kong: The Commercial Press. pp. 153–78. Text in Chinese.

Lee Ming-kwan, 1987b. 'Government Policy and the Structure of the Family', in Lee Ming-kwan, *Hong Kong: Politics and Society in Transition*, Hong Kong: The Commercial Press, pp. 179–90. Text in Chinese.

Lee Ming-kwan, 1987c. *Hong Kong: Politics and Society in Transition*, Hong Kong: The Commercial Press. Text in Chinese.

Lee Ming-kwan, 1991. 'Family and Social Life', in Lau Siu-kai et al. (eds.), *Indicators of Social Development: Hong Kong 1988*, Hong Kong: Hong Kong Institute of Asia-Pacific Studies, The Chinese University of Hong Kong, pp. 41–66.

Lee Ming-kwan, 1992. 'Family and Gender Issues', in Lau Siu-kai et al. (eds.), *Indicators of Social Development: Hong Kong 1990*, Hong Kong: Hong Kong Institute of Asia-Pacific Studies, The Chinese University of Hong Kong, pp. 1–31.

Lee Ming-kwan, 1993. 'Issue-Positions in the 1991 Legislative Council Election', in Lau Siu-kai and Louie Kin-sheun (eds.), *Hong Kong Tried Democracy*, Hong Kong: Hong Kong Institute of Asia-Pacific Studies, The Chinese University of Hong Kong, pp. 237–48.

Lee Ming-kwan, and Ng, C. H., 1991. 'Class, Family and Social Life in Hong Kong, 1950–1980'. Research Report presented to the Hong Kong Polytechnic Research Sub-committee.

Lee, Rance P. L., 1981. 'Incongruence of Legal Codes and Folk Norms', in Rance P. L. Lee (ed.), *Corruption and Its Control in Hong Kong*, Hong Kong: The Chinese University of Hong Kong Press, pp. 75–104.

Lethbridge, Henry, 1980. 'The "Management" of Social Information During Periods of Growth: The Problem of Sexual Violence in Hong Kong', in Leung Chi-keung et al. (eds.), *Hong Kong: Dilemmas of Growth*, Canberra: Research School of Pacific Studies, Australian National University, and the Centre of Asian Studies, University of Hong Kong, pp. 561–86.

Lethbridge, Henry, 1985. *Hard Graft in Hong Kong*, Hong Kong: Oxford University Press.

Leung, Benjamin K. P., 1982. 'Who Protests: A Developmental Profile of the Student Activist', Ph.D. Dissertation, York University, Toronto, Canada.

Leung, Benjamin K. P., 1990a. 'Power and Politics: A Critical Analysis', in Benjamin K. P. Leung (ed.), *Social Issues in Hong Kong*, Hong Kong: Oxford University Press, pp. 13–26.

Leung, Benjamin K. P., 1990b. 'Collective Violence: A Social-Structural Analysis', in Benjamin K. P. Leung (ed.), *Social Issues in Hong Kong*, Hong Kong: Oxford University Press, pp. 143–63.

Leung, Benjamin K. P., 1990c. 'Political Development: Prospects and Possibilities', in Benjamin K. P. Leung (ed.), *Social Issues in Hong Kong*, Hong Kong: Oxford University Press, pp. 27–42.

Leung, Benjamin K. P., 1991a. *Social Sciences: A Foundation Course—Sociology 2, Units 13 and 14* (chap. 4), Hong Kong: Open Learning Institute of Hong Kong.

Leung, Benjamin K. P., 1991b. 'Political Process and Industrial Strikes and the Labour Movement in Hong Kong, 1946–1989', *Journal of Oriental Studies*, 29(2): 172–206.

Leung, Benjamin K. P., 1992. 'Social Movement as Cognitive Praxis: The Case of the Student and Labour Movements in Hong Kong', Occasional Paper no. 9, Hong Kong: Social Sciences Research Centre and the Department of Sociology, University of Hong Kong.
Leung, Benjamin K. P., 1993. 'The Significance of Social Class in Hong Kong Society', *Hong Kong Economic Journal Monthly*, 190(January): 53–6. Text in Chinese.
Leung, Benjamin K. P., 1994a. 'Class and Politics', in Benjamin K. P. Leung and Teresa Y. C. Wong (eds.), *25 Years of Social and Economic Development in Hong Kong*, Hong Kong: Centre of Asian Studies, University of Hong Kong, pp. 203–16.
Leung, Benjamin K. P., 1994b. 'Social Inequality and Insurgency in Hong Kong', in Benjamin K. P. Leung and Teresa Y. C. Wong (eds.), *25 Years of Social and Economic Development in Hong Kong*, Hong Kong: Centre of Asian Studies, University of Hong Kong, pp. 177–98.
Leung, Benjamin K. P., 1994c. 'The China Factor and Hong Kong's Student and Labour Movements', *Hong Kong Journal of Social Sciences* 4(Autumn): 79–102. Text in Chinese.
Leung, Benjamin K. P., 1994d. '"Class" and "Class Formation" in Hong Kong Studies', in Lau Siu-kai et al. (eds.), *Inequalities and Development: Social Stratification in Chinese Societies*, Hong Kong: Hong Kong Institute of Asia-Pacific Studies, The Chinese University of Hong Kong, pp. 47–72.
Leung, Benjamin K. P., 1995. 'Women and Social Change: The Impact of Industrialization on Women in Hong Kong', in Veronica Pearson and Benjamin K. P. Leung (eds.), *Women in Hong Kong*, Hong Kong: Oxford University Press, pp. 22–46.
Leung, Benjamin K. P., and Chiu, Steven, 1991. 'A Social History of Industrial Strikes and the Labour Movement in Hong Kong, 1946–1989', Occasional Paper no. 3, Hong Kong: Social Sciences Research Centre and Department of Sociology, University of Hong Kong.
Leung Chi-keung, 1980. 'Urbanization and New Towns Development', in Leung Chi-keung et al. (eds.), *Hong Kong: Dilemmas of Growth*, Camberra: Research School of Pacific Studies, Australian National University, and Centre of Asian Studies, University of Hong Kong, pp. 289–308.
Leung, Joe C. B., 1990. 'Problems and Changes in Community Politics', in Benjamin K. P. Leung (ed.), *Social Issues in Hong Kong*, Hong Kong: Oxford University Press, pp. 43–66.
Leung, N., 1990. 'The Long Goodbye to the China Factor', in C. Li (ed.), *The China Factor in Hong Kong Cinema*, Hong Kong: The Urban Council, pp. 71–6.
Leung Sai-wing, 1993. 'The "China Factor" in the 1991 Legislative Council Election: The June Fourth Incident and Anti-Communist China Syndrome', in Lau Siu-kai and Louie Kin-sheun (eds.), *Hong Kong Tried Democracy*, Hong Kong: Hong Kong Institute of Asia-Pacific Studies, The Chinese University of Hong Kong, pp. 187–236.
Leung Wai-tung, 1993. 'Housing', in Choi Po-king and Ho Lok-sang (eds.), *The Other Hong Kong Report: 1993*, Hong Kong: The Chinese University Press, pp. 265–98.
Levin, David, 1990. 'Work and Its Deprivations', in Benjamin K. P. Leung (ed.), *Social Issues in Hong Kong*, Hong Kong: Oxford University Press, pp. 85–113.
Levin, David, and Jao, Y. C., 1988. 'Introduction', in Y. C. Jao et al. (eds.), *Labour Movement in a Changing Society: The Experience of Hong Kong*, Hong Kong: Centre of Asian Studies, University of Hong Kong, pp. 1–23.

Li Pang-kwong, 1993. 'An Exploratory Study of the Rural–Urban Cleavage in the 1991 Elections', in Lau Siu-kai and Louie Kin-sheun (eds.), *Hong Kong Tried Democracy*, Hong Kong: Hong Kong Institute of Asia-Pacific Studies, The Chinese University of Hong Kong, pp. 317–30.

Lilley, Rozanna, 1993. 'Claiming Identity: Film and Television in Hongkong', *History and Anthropology*, 6(2–3): 261–92.

Lipset, Seymour Martin, 1981. *Political Man* (2nd ed.), Baltimore, Md.: The Johns Hopkins University Press.

Lo, Sonny S. H., 1995. 'Legislative Cliques, Political Parties, Political Groupings and Electoral System', in Joseph Y. S. Cheng and Sonny S. H. Lo (eds.), *From Colony to SAR: Hong Kong's Challenges Ahead*, Hong Kong: The Chinese University of Hong Kong, pp. 51–70.

Lo, T. Wing, 1993. *Corruption and Politics in Hong Kong and China*, Buckingham: Open University Press.

Louie Kin-sheun, 1991. 'Political Parties', in Sung Yung-wing and Lee Mingkwan (eds.), *The Other Hong Kong Report: 1991*, Hong Kong: The Chinese University Press, pp. 55–76.

Louie Kin-sheun, 1992. 'Politicians, Political Parties and the Legislative Council', in Joseph Y. S. Cheng and Paul C. K. Kwong (eds.), *The Other Hong Kong Report: 1992*, Hong Kong: The Chinese University Press, pp. 53–78.

Louie Kin-sheun, 1993. 'The "Party-Identification" Factor in the 1991 Legislative Council Election', in Lau Siu-kai and Louie Kin-sheun (eds.), *Hong Kong Tried Democracy*, Hong Kong: Hong Kong Institute of Asia-Pacific Studies, The Chinese University of Hong Kong, pp. 157–86.

Louie Kin-sheun, and Sum Kwok-cheung (eds.), 1995. *A Collection of Materials on Elections in Hong Kong*, Hong Kong: Hong Kong Institute of Asia-Pacific Studies, The Chinese University of Hong Kong. Text in Chinese.

Lui Tai-lok, 1988a. 'The New Middle Class in Hong Kong: Its Characteristics and Future', in Cheung Bing-leung et al., *Class Analysis and Hong Kong*, Hong Kong: Ching Man Publisher, pp. 27–48. Text in Chinese.

Lui Tai-lok, 1988b. 'The Political Role of Hong Kong's New Middle Class', in Cheung Bing-leung et al., *Class Analysis and Hong Kong*, Hong Kong: Ching Man Publisher, pp. 77–90. Text in Chinese.

Lui Tai-lok, 1990. 'The Social Organization of Outwork: The Case of Hong Kong', in Elizabeth Sinn (ed.), *Between East and West: Aspects of Social and Political Development in Hong Kong*, Hong Kong: Centre of Asian Studies, University of Hong Kong, pp. 187–215.

Lui Tai-lok, 1992a. 'Work Orientations and Values: Social Indicators and Labour Studies in Hong Kong', in Lau Siu-kai et al. (eds.), *The Development of Social Indicators Research in Chinese Societies*, Hong Kong: Hong Kong Institute of Asia-Pacific Studies, The Chinese University of Hong Kong, pp. 205–16. Text in Chinese.

Lui Tai-lok, 1992b. 'Work and Work Attitudes', in Lau Siu-kai et al. (eds.), *Indicators of Social Development: Hong Kong 1990*, Hong Kong: Hong Kong Institute of Asia-Pacific Studies, The Chinese University of Hong Kong, pp. 105–28.

Lui Tai-lok, 1993. 'Hong Kong's New Middle Class: Its Formation and Politics', in Michael Hsin-huang Hsiao (ed.), *Discovery of the Middle Classes in East Asia*, Taipei: Institute of Ethnology, Academia Sinica, pp. 247–71.

Lui Tai-lok, 1994. 'The Disintegration of Hong Kong's Popular Movements in a Rapidly Changing Political Environment', *Hong Kong Journal of Social Sciences*, 4(Autumn): 67–78. Text in Chinese.

Lui Tai-lok, and Chan, T. W., 1987. 'The Predicament of the White-Collar Worker in Hong Kong', *Ming Pao Monthly*, 264: 51–5. Text in Chinese.

Lui Tai-lok, and Kung Kai-sing, 1985. *The City in Perspective: The Residents Movement in Hong Kong and the Study of Urban Politics*, Hong Kong: Wide Angle Publisher. Text in Chinese.
Luk Hung-kei, 1995. 'Hong Kong History and Hong Kong Culture', in Elizabeth Sinn (ed.), *Culture and Society in Hong Kong*, Hong Kong: Centre of Asian Studies, University of Hong Kong, pp. 64–79. Text in Chinese.
Lukes, Steven, 1974. *Power: A Radical View*, London: Macmillan.
Mann, Michael, 1986. 'Work and the Work Ethic', in R. Jowell et al. (eds.), *British Social Attitudes: The 1986 Report*, Aldershot: Gower, pp. 162–75.
McAdam, Doug, 1982. *Political Process and the Development of Black Insurgency, 1930–1970*, Chicago, Ill.: The University of Chicago Press.
McCarthy, John, and Zald, M. N., 1973. *The Trend of Social Movements* Morristown, N.J.: General Learning.
Miliband, Ralph, 1969. *The State in Capitalist Society*, New York: Basic Books.
Miller, K., 1976. 'Modern Experience, the Family and Fertility in Six Nations', Ph.D. Dissertation, Stanford University, Stanford, Ca.
Mills, C. Wright, 1956. *The Power Elite*, New York: Oxford University Press.
Miners, N. J., 1975. 'Hong Kong: A Case Study in Political Stability', *Journal of Commonwealth and Comparative Politics*, 13(1): 26–39.
Mitchell, Robert E., 1969. *Family Life in Urban Hong Kong*, Hong Kong: Project of the Urban Family Life Survey.
Mok, B. H., 1985. 'Problem Behaviour of Adolescents in Hong Kong: A Sociocultural Perspective', Occasional Paper no. 7, Hong Kong: Centre of Hong Kong Studies, The Chinese University of Hong Kong.
Mok, Henry T. K., 1994. 'Elderly in Need of Care and Financial Support', in Donald H. McMillen and Man Si-wai (eds.), *The Other Hong Kong Report*, Hong Kong: The Chinese University Press, pp. 315–30.
Morris, Jan, 1989. *Hong Kong*, New York: Vintage Books.
Munro, Donald, 1969. *The Concept of Man in Early China*, Stanford, Ca.: Stanford University Press.
Ng, Agnes, 1975. *Social Causes of Violent Crime Among Young Offenders*, Hong Kong: Social Research Centre, The Chinese University of Hong Kong.
Ng, Agnes, 1980. 'Family Relationships and Delinquent Behaviour', Ph.D. Dissertation, Columbia University, New York.
Ng, Agnes, 1994. 'Delinquency Trends in Socio-Economic Perspective', in Benjamin K. P. Leung and Teresa Y. C. Wong (eds.), *25 Years of Social and Economic Development in Hong Kong*, Hong Kong: Centre of Asian Studies, University of Hong Kong, pp. 390–409.
Ng Chung-hung, 1989. 'Family Crisis, Whose Crisis?', *Ming Pao Monthly*, 1: 3–10. Text in Chinese.
Ng Chung-hung, 1991. 'Family Change and Women's Employment in Hong Kong', in Fanny M. Cheung et al. (eds.), *Selected Papers of Conference on Gender Studies in Chinese Societies*, Hong Kong: Hong Kong Institute of Asia-Pacific Studies, The Chinese University of Hong Kong, pp. 43–54.
Ng Chung-hung, 1993. 'Popular Culture and the Domestic Ideal', in Sze Man-hung and Ng Chung-hung (eds.), *Hong Kong Popular Culture Studies*, Hong Kong: Joint Publishing Co., pp. 109–31. Text in Chinese.
Ng Chung-hung, 1994. 'Power, Identity, and Economic Change: 25 Years of Family Studies in Hong Kong', in Benjamin K. P. Leung and Teresa Y. C. Wong (eds.), *25 Years of Social and Economic Development in Hong Kong*, Hong Kong: Centre of Asian Studies, University of Hong Kong, pp. 94–110.
Ng Chung-hung, 1995. 'Bringing Women Back In: Family Change in Hong Kong', in Veronica Pearson and Benjamin K. P. Leung (eds.), *Women in Hong Kong*, Hong Kong: Oxford University Press, pp. 74–100.

Ng-Quinn, Michael, 1991. 'Bureaucratic Response to Political Change: Theoretical Use of the Atypical Case of the Hong Kong Police', Occasional Paper no. 2, Hong Kong: Hong Kong Institute of Asia-Pacific Studies, The Chinese University of Hong Kong.

Oberschall, Anthony, 1973. *Social Conflict and Social Movements*, Englewood Cliffs, N.J.: Prentice-Hall.

Parsons, Talcott, 1943. 'The Kinship System of the Contemporary United States', *American Anthropologist*, 45: 22–38.

Parsons, Talcott, and Bales, R. F., 1955. *Family, Socialization and Interaction Process*, Glencoe, Ill.: The Free Press.

Podmore, David, 1971. 'The Population of Hong Kong', in Keith Hopkins (ed.), *Hong Kong: The Industrial Colony*, Hong Kong: Oxford University Press, pp. 21–54.

Podmore, David, and Chaney, David, 1974. 'Family Norms in a Rapidly Modernizing Society: Hong Kong', *Journal of Marriage and the Family*, 36: 400–7.

Rabushka, A., 1979. *Hong Kong: A Study in Economic Freedom*, Chicago, Ill.: The University of Chicago Press.

Rear, John, 1971. 'One Brand of Politics', in Keith Hopkins (ed.), *Hong Kong: The Industrial Colony*, Hong Kong: Oxford University Press, pp. 55–140.

Redding, S. Gordon, 1991. 'Weak Organizations and Strong Linkages: Managerial Ideology and Chinese Family Business Networks', in Gary Hamilton (ed.), *Business Networks and Economic Development in East and Southeast Asia*, Hong Kong: Centre of Asian Studies, The University of Hong Kong, pp. 30–47.

Reidel, J., 1973. *The Hong Kong Model of Industrialization*, Dusternbrooker: Weltwirtschaftliches Archiv, Institut für Weltwirtschaft.

Republic of China, Council for Economic Planning and Development, 1993. *Taiwan Statistical Data Book 1993*, Taiwan: Council for Economic Planning and Development.

Rosen, Sherry, 1976. *Mei Foo Sun Chuen: Middle Class Chinese Families in Transition*, Taipei: Orient Cultural Service.

Salaff, Janet, 1981. *Working Daughters of Hong Kong*, Cambridge: Cambridge University Press.

Salaff, Janet, 1995. *Working Daughters of Hong Kong* (2nd ed.), New York: Columbia University Press.

Scott, Ian, 1986. 'Policy-Making in a Turbulent Environment: The Case of Hong Kong', *International Review of Administrative Sciences*, 52: 447–69.

Scott, Ian, 1987. 'Policy Implementation in Hong Kong', *South-East Asian Journal of Social Science*, 15(2): 1–19.

Scott, Ian, 1989a. *Political Change and the Crisis of Legitimacy in Hong Kong*, Hong Kong: Oxford University Press.

Scott, Ian, 1989b. 'Administration in a Small Capitalist State: The Hong Kong Experience', in *Public Administration and Development*, 9: 185–99.

Scott, Ian, 1992. 'An Overview of the Hong Kong Legislative Council Elections of 1991', in Rowena Kwok et al. (eds.), *Votes Without Power: The Hong Kong Legislative Council Elections 1991*, Hong Kong: The Hong Kong University Press, pp. 1–30.

Scott, Ian, and Cheek-Milby, Kathleen, 1986. 'An Overview of Hong Kong's Social Policy-Making Process', *Asian Journal of Public Administration*, 8(2): 166–76.

Secretary for Chinese Affairs (Hong Kong Government), 1969. 'The City District Officer Scheme', Hong Kong: Government Printer.

Secretary for Home Affairs (Hong Kong Government), 1977. 'Development Plan on Community Building', mimeograph copy, Hong Kong: Government Printer.

Shively, Stan, 1972. 'Political Orientations in Hong Kong: A Social-psychological Approach', Hong Kong: Social Research Centre, The Chinese University of Hong Kong.
Singapore, Ministry of Information and the Arts, 1994. *Singapore 1994*, Singapore: Singapore Ministry of Information and the Arts.
Sinn, Elizabeth, 1989. *Power and Charity*, Hong Kong: Oxford University Press.
Sit, Victor, and Wong Siu-lun, 1989. *Small and Medium Industries in an Export-oriented Economy: The Case of Hong Kong*, Hong Kong: Centre of Asian Studies, University of Hong Kong.
Sit, Victor, et al., 1979. *Small Scale Industry in a Laissez-Faire Economy: A Hong Kong Case Study*, Hong Kong: Centre of Asian Studies, University of Hong Kong.
Smelser, N. J., 1963. *Theory of Collective Behaviour*, New York: Free Press.
Smith, Adam [1776] 1963. *An Inquiry into the Nature and Causes of the Wealth of Nations*, Homewood: Irwin.
So, Alvin Y., 1993. 'Western Sociological Theories and the Hong Kong New Middle Class', in Michael Hsin-huang Hsiao (ed.), *Discovery of the Middle Classes in East Asia*, Taipei: Institute of Ethnology, Academia Sinica, pp. 219-45.
Steinmo, Sven, et al. (eds.), 1992. *Structuring Politics: Historical Instrumentalism in Comparative Analysis*, Cambridge: Cambridge University Press.
Stoodley, Bartlett, 1967. 'Normative Family Orientations of Chinese College Students in Hong Kong', *Journal of Marriage and the Family*, 29(4): 773-82.
Suen Wing, 1994. 'Labour and Employment', in Donald H. McMillen and Man Si-wai (eds.), *The Other Hong Kong Report*, Hong Kong: The Chinese University Press, pp. 149-64.
Szczepanik, Edward, 1958. *The Economic Growth of Hong Kong*, London: Oxford University Press.
Sze Man-hung, 1994. 'Hong Kong's Television Culture towards the End of the Century', *Ming Pao Monthly*, 29(1): 52-5. Text in Chinese.
Tam, S. K. Tony, and Yeung Sum, 1994. 'Community Perception of Social Welfare and Its Relations to Familism, Political Alienation, and Individual Rights: The Case of Hong Kong', *International Social Work*, 37: 47-60.
Tang, Stephen Lung-wai, 1993. 'Political Markets, Competition, and the Return to Monopoly: Evolution amidst a Historical Tragedy', in Lau Siu-kai and Louie Kin-sheun (eds.), *Hong Kong Tried Democracy*, Hong Kong: Hong Kong Institute of Asia-Pacific Studies, The Chinese University of Hong Kong, pp. 249-96.
Tat-chee, U., 1953. 'Promotion of Hong Kong's Industry', *Far Eastern Economic Review* 30 (July): 144-5.
Tilly, Charles, 1978. *From Mobilization to Revolution*, Reading, Mass.: Addison-Wesley Publishing Company.
Ting Chau, Theodora, and Ng Sek-hong, 1983. 'Labour Mobility: A Study of Garment-Making and Electronics Workers', in Ng Sek-hong and David Levin (eds.), *Contemporary Issues in Hong Kong Labour Relations*, Hong Kong: Centre of Asian Studies, University of Hong Kong, pp. 103-15.
Traver, Harold, 1980. 'Crime and Socio-Economic Development in Hong Kong', in Leung Chi-keung et al. (eds.), *Hong Kong: Dilemmas of Growth*, Canberra: Research School of Pacific Studies, Australian National University, and Centre of Asian Studies, University of Hong Kong, pp. 527-60.
Traver, Harold, 1984. 'Crime and Development: The Case of Hong Kong', *International Annals of Criminology*, 22: 151-72.
Traver, Harold, 1991. 'Crime Trends', in Harold Traver and Jon Vagg (eds.), *Crime and Justice in Hong Kong*, Hong Kong: Oxford University Press, pp. 10-24.

Traver, Harold, 1994. 'The Royal Hong Kong Police', in Mark S. Gaylord and Harold Traver (eds.), *Introduction to the Hong Kong Criminal Justice System*, Hong Kong: Hong Kong University Press, pp. 29–50.

Traver, Harold, and Gaylord, Mark S., 1991. 'The Royal Hong Kong Police', in Harold Traver and Jon Vagg (eds.), *Crime and Justice in Hong Kong*, Hong Kong: Oxford University Press, pp. 98–110.

Tsang Wing-kwong, 1993. 'Who Voted for the Democrats? An Analysis of the Electoral Choice of the 1991 Legislative Council Election', in Lau Siu-kai and Louie Kin-sheun (eds.), *Hong Kong Tried Democracy*, Hong Kong: Hong Kong Institute of Asia-Pacific Studies, The Chinese University of Hong Kong, pp. 115–56.

Tsang Wing-kwong, 1994. 'Behind the Land of Abundant Opportunities: A Study of Class Structuration in Hong Kong', in Benjamin K. P. Leung and Teresa Y. C. Wong (eds.), *25 Years of Social and Economic Development in Hong Kong*, Hong Kong: Centre of Asian Studies, University of Hong Kong, pp. 8–75.

Tuen Mun District Board, 1991. *The Needs of Married Women in Tuen Mun, 1990*, Hong Kong: Tuen Mun District Board. Text in Chinese.

Turner, H. A., et al. 1980. *The Last Colony: But Whose?*, Hong Kong: Cambridge University Press.

Vagg, Jon, 1991. 'Policing Hong Kong', *Policing and Society*, 1: 235–47.

Vagg, Jon, 1994. 'Crime and Its Control in Hong Kong: Recent Developments and Future Prospects', in Benjamin K. P. Leung and Teresa Y. C. Wong (eds.), *25 Years of Social and Economic Development in Hong Kong*, Hong Kong: Centre of Asian Studies, University of Hong Kong, pp. 357–78.

Waldron, Stephen, 1976. *Fire on the Rim: A Study in Contradictions in Left-wing Political Mobilization in Hong Kong, 1967*, Ann Arbor, Mich.: University Microfilms International.

Webb, Paul, 1977. 'Voluntary Social Welfare Services', in *Chung Chi College Twenty-Fifth Anniversary Symposium*, Hong Kong: Chung Chi College, pp. 123–44.

Wong, A. W. F., 1980. 'Non-Purposive Adaptation and Administrative Change in Hong Kong', in Leung Chi-keung et al. (eds.), *Hong Kong: Dilemmas of Growth*, Canberra: Research School of Pacific Studies, Australian National University, and the Centre of Asian Studies, University of Hong Kong, pp. 49–94.

Wong Chi-wah, 1995. 'Works of Social Satire and Social Realism in Cantonese Popular Songs: Their Social Significance and Artistic Value', in Elizabeth Sinn (ed.), *Culture and Society in Hong Kong*, Hong Kong: Centre of Asian Studies, University of Hong Kong, pp. 169–229. Text in Chinese.

Wong, F. M., 1972. 'Modern Ideology, Industrialization and Conjugalism: The Case of Hong Kong', *International Journal of Sociology of the Family*, 2: 139–50.

Wong, F. M., 1975. 'Industrialization and Family Structure in Hong Kong', *Journal of Marriage and the Family*, 37: 985–1000.

Wong, F. M., 1979. 'Family Structure and Processes in Hong Kong', in Lin Tzongbiau et al. (eds.), *Hong Kong: Economic, Social and Political Studies in Development*, New York: M. E. Sharpe, pp. 95–121.

Wong, F. M., 1981. 'Effects of the Employment of Mothers on Marital Role and Power Differentiation in Hong Kong', in Ambrose Y. C. King and Rance P. L. Lee (eds.), *Social Life and Development in Hong Kong*, Hong Kong: The Chinese University of Hong Kong, pp. 217–34.

Wong, Gilbert, 1991. 'Business Groups in a Dynamic Environment: Hong Kong, 1976–1986', in Gary Hamilton (ed.), *Business Networks and Economic Development in East and Southeast Asia*, Hong Kong: Centre of Asian Studies, University of Hong Kong, pp. 126–54.

Wong Jim, 1995. 'Popular Songs and the Hong Kong Culture', in Elizabeth Sinn (ed.), *Culture and Society in Hong Kong*, Hong Kong: Centre of Asian Studies, University of Hong Kong, pp. 160–8. Text in Chinese.

Wong Siu-lun, 1985. 'The Chinese Family Firm: A Model', *The British Journal of Sociology*, 36: 58–72.

Wong Siu-lun, 1988a. *Emigrant Entrepreneurs*, Hong Kong: Oxford University Press.

Wong Siu-lun, 1988b. 'The Applicability of Asian Family Values to Other Sociocultural Settings', in Peter L. Berger and Michael Hsiao Hsin-Huang (eds.), *In Search of an East Asian Development Model*, New Brunswick, N.J.: Transaction Books, pp. 134–52.

Wong Siu-lun, 1991. 'Chinese Entrepreneurs and Business Trust', in Gary Hamilton (ed.), *Business Networks and Economic Development in East and Southeast Asia*, Hong Kong: Centre of Asian Studies, University of Hong Kong, pp. 13–29.

Wong Siu-lun, 1993. 'Business and Politics in Hong Kong during the Transition', in One Country Two Systems Economic Research Institute (ed.), *Hong Kong in Transition*, Hong Kong: One Country Two Systems Economic Research Institute, pp. 489–514.

Wong Siu-lun, and Yue, Shirley, 1991. 'Satisfaction in Various Life Domains', in Lau Siu-kai et al. (eds.), *Indicators of Social Development: Hong Kong 1988*, Hong Kong: Hong Kong Institute of Asia-Pacific Studies, The Chinese University of Hong Kong, pp. 1–24.

Wong, Teresa Y. C., 1991. 'A Comparative Study of the Industrial Policy of Hong Kong and Singapore in the 1980s', in Edward K. Y. Chen et al. (eds.), *Industrial and Trade Development in Hong Kong*, Hong Kong: Centre of Asian Studies, University of Hong Kong, pp. 256–96.

Wong, Thomas W. P., 1988. 'Class and Social Analysis', in Cheung Bing-leung et al., *Class Analysis and Hong Kong*, Hong Kong: Ching Man Publisher, pp. 125–70. Text in Chinese.

Wong, Thomas W. P., 1991. 'Inequality, Stratification and Mobility', in Lau Siu-kai et al. (eds.), *Indicators of Social Development: Hong Kong 1988*, Hong Kong: Hong Kong Institute of Asia-Pacific Studies, The Chinese University of Hong Kong, pp. 145–72.

Wong, Thomas W. P., 1992a. 'Discourses and Dilemmas: 25 Years of Subjective Indicators Studies in Hong Kong', in Lau Siu-kai et al. (eds.), *Indicators of Social Development: Hong Kong 1990*, Hong Kong: Institute of Asia-Pacific Studies, The Chinese University of Hong Kong, pp. 239–68.

Wong, Thomas W. P., 1992b. 'Personal Experience and Social Ideology: Thematization and Theorization in Social Indicators Studies', in Lau Siu-kai et al. (eds.), *Indicators of Social Development: Hong Kong 1990*, Hong Kong: Institute of Asia-Pacific Studies, The Chinese University of Hong Kong, pp. 205–38.

Wong, Thomas W. P., 1993. 'The New Middle-Class in Hong Kong: Class in Formation?', in Michael Hsiao Hsin-Huang (ed.), *Discovery of the Middle Classes in East Asia*, Taiwan: Institute of Ethnology, Academia Sinica, pp. 273–306.

Wong, Thomas W. P., and Lui Tai-lok, 1992a. 'From One Brand of Politics to One Brand of Political Culture', Occasional Paper no. 10, Hong Kong: Hong Kong Institute of Asia-Pacific Studies, The Chinese University of Hong Kong.

Wong, Thomas W. P., and Lui Tai-lok, 1992b. 'Reinstating Class: A Structural and Developmental Study of Hong Kong', Occasional Paper no. 10, Hong Kong: Social Sciences Research Centre and Department of Sociology, University of Hong Kong.

Wong, Thomas W. P., and Lui Tai-lok, 1993. 'Morality, Class and the Hong Kong Way of Life', Occasional Paper no. 30, Hong Kong: Hong Kong Institute of Asia-Pacific Studies, The Chinese University of Hong Kong.

Working Group on Juvenile Crime (Hong Kong Government), 1981. *Report of the Working Group on Juvenile Crime*, Hong Kong: Government Printer.

Yang, C. K., 1959. *Chinese Communist Society: The Family and the Village*, Cambridge, Mass.: M.I.T. Press.

Yeung, K. Y., 1991. 'The Role of the Hong Kong Government in Industrial Development', in Edward K. Y. Chen et al. (eds.), *Industrial and Trade Development in Hong Kong*, Hong Kong: Centre of Asian Studies, University of Hong Kong, pp. 48–56.

Yiu Yiu, 1983. 'The Development of Hong Kong's Popular Culture: A Retrospective Examination', in Lui Tai-lok (ed.), *Popular Culture in Hong Kong*, Hong Kong: Wide Angle Publisher, pp. 10–20. Text in Chinese.

Young Men's Christian Association, 1986. 'The Pattern of Participation in Billiard Rooms of Youth in the Central and Sheung Wan Districts', Hong Kong: Young Men's Christian Association. Text in Chinese.

Young Women's Christian Association, 1986. 'Sex Knowledge, Behaviours, and Attitudes of Outreaching Youth: A Research Report', Hong Kong: Young Women's Christian Association. Text in Chinese.

Young, John D., 1981. 'China's Role in Two Hong Kong Disturbances: A Scenario For the Future?', *Journal of Oriental Studies*, 19(1): 158–73.

Youngson, A. J., 1982. *Hong Kong: Economic Growth and Policy*, Hong Kong: Oxford University Press.

Yuen Kin-bon, 1988. *A Short History of Hong Kong*, Hong Kong: Chung Lau Publishers. Text in Chinese.

Index

ADMINISTRATIVE ABSORPTION OF POLITICS, *see* Political stability
Ann Tse-kai, 48
Area Committees, 163, 164

BASIC LAW, 16, 27, 158, 180, 181; and political development, 175–8; and social welfare development, 128
Basic Law Consultative Committee, 158
Basic Law Drafting Committee, 27, 42, 48
Bureaucratic polity, 12, 13, 19, 20, 26, 39; and Chinese community, 15–17

CAPITALIST CLASS: and crime, 106–9; as a social-political force, 39–43, 45, 47; and social policy, 17, 118, 135
Capitalists, 4, 17, 25, 40–2, 44, 108, 123, 130; commercial or mercantile, 24, 39, 117; financial, 39, 117; industrial, 39, 116
Chan Hoi-man, 70, 71
Chan Lau Kit-ching, 142, 160
Chan Wai-kwan, 2–4, 10, 25, 26
Chaney, David, 55, 58, 78
Cheek-Milby, Kathleen, 115, 176
Cheung Bing-leung, 31, 146, 148, 149, 164
China's open-door policy, 6, 42, 68, 155
Chinese community, 3, 13–17; and Chinese culture, 49–51; class structure of, 45; and co-option of élites, 163; and *laissez-faire* social policy, 116
Chinese labourers, 1–4
Chinese People's Political Consultative Conference, 48
Chiu, Stephen, 116–17, 122–3, 136
Choi Po-king, 71, 72, 74

Chow, Nelson W. S., 111, 124, 126–8, 137
Christian Industrial Committee, 127
City District Committees, 163, 164
City District Offices, 16, 163
City District Officer (CDO) Scheme, 22, 163
Clansmen Associations, 15, 16, 124
Class, 2–4, 13–14, 24–5, 72, 109; conflict, 4, 5, 29, 30, 33, 72, 107, 108; consciousness, 2, 3, 10, 17, 30, 31, 34, 38, 45, 72, 108; debates on, 29–32; formation, 2, 4, 10, 34–6, 38, 45, 47; and life chances, 34, 46, 47; orientations and actions, 32–4; and politics, 39–45; and social mobility, 34–6; *see also* Capitalist class, Middle class, Social inequality, Working class
Collective action, 26–39, 43–5, 139, 141, 147, 159; confrontational, 140, 164; the basis of mobilization for, 34, 44, 45, 59, 107, 147, 149, 151
Community Involvement Plan, 22
Cooper, John, 145, 160
Co-option of Élites, *see* Political stability
Corruption, 106–9, 113, 114, 139; Chinese norms regarding, 108, 109, 113, 114; civil service, 106–8, 114; class perspective on, 106–8, 110; and commercial crime, 110, 113
Crime, 95, 102–5, 109; and industrialization, 94, 95, 99, 110; property crime, 94–8, 104, 105, 110, 111; and relative deprivation, 95, 97, 98; reporting of, 101–5, 110; violent crime, 94–8, 105, 111
Crime rates, 95–100, 103–5, 111, 112; and police corruption, 103, 104; and police–triad alliance, 102, 103, 110

Crime trend, 94, 95, 97, 98, 102, 104, 105, 113; and Government's victimization surveys, 105, 113; and social-control policies, 102–6, 110
Cultural Revolution, 22, 44, 134, 145, 146, 154, 157, 160
Culture, 49; of affluence, 70–2; and Confucian values, 49, 50, 51, 64, 65; of deliverance, 70–2; of survival, 70–2; traditional Chinese culture and the Hong Kong experience, 49, 53, 72; *see also* Popular culture

DELINQUENCY, *see* Juvenile crime and delinquency
Democracy, 18, 20, 61, 74, 128, 162, 166; level of education and stability of, 179; understanding of, 61–3
Democratic Alliance for the Betterment of Hong Kong, 174, 175, 178
Democratic Party, 174, 175, 178
Democratization, 18, 20, 166, 178, 179; and capitalist class, 42; and economic prosperity, 165–7; and expanded social service provision, 118, 128; and increased control over the police, 104; and middle class, 37; pace of, 63, 162, 165, 169, 178; and political stability, 62, 165, 166
Depoliticization, 14, 15, 19, 26, 32, 33, 39, 72, 81, 116
Development, 37, 49, 86; economic, 4, 6, 7, 9, 24, 105, 166; political, 18, 38, 41, 62, 63, 103, 162, 165, 166; socio-economic, 63, 95, 110; socio-political, 22, 31; *see also* Crime, Family
Deviance, 101, 110; definition of, 94; *see also* Juvenile crime and delinquency, Social control
District Watch Committee, 3, 26
District Boards, 23, 28, 92, 150, 164, 165, 167, 174, 175
District Management Committee, 164

EDUCATION DEPARTMENT, 157
Educational attainment, 10, 11
Elections, 18, 20, 23, 142, 168, 170, 175, 180; District Board, 18, 165, 167–71, 173–5, 180; influence of June Fourth Incident on, 171, 172, 174, 178; Legislative Council, 167, 171, 172, 174, 175, 180; Municipal Council, 167, 171, 180; Regional Council, 167, 171; Urban Council, 167, 171; *see also* Representative government
Election Committee, 18, 176, 177, 181
Electoral politics, 38, 42, 150, 162, 165, 167; and 'anti-China syndrome', 171, 173; 'China complex', 172, 174; rural–urban cleavage in, 173, 174; *see also* Representative government
Élites, 28, 92, 162, 168–70; Chinese, 13, 16, 163; co-option of, 21, 39–44; and masses, 16, 51, 163; *see also* Political stability
Elliot, Elsie, 144, 145, 160
Emigration, 24
England, Joe, 5, 58, 59, 87
Entrepôt, 4, 6, 8, 21, 24, 117, 124, 125
Entrepreneurs, 5, 6, 41, 60, 64, 92
Executive Council, 13, 117, 162; co-option of élites into, 15, 21, 39–44; and masses, 16, 51, 163; *see also* Political stability

FAMILISTIC ETHOS, 10, 39, 45, 51, 80, 90
Family, 14, 52, 75–8, 85, 86, 133; decision-making within, 79; division of labour within, 78, 79; industrialization and its impact on, 76, 77, 79, 82, 84–6, 89; and modern domestic ideal, 84, 85; modified centripetal, 81–3, 90; patriarchal, 82–4; and political stability, 14; public housing policies and the size of, 77; *see also* Utilitarianistic familism
Family firm, 9, 41, 80, 86; model of, 89; and entrepreneurial familism, 87, 89, 90; and nepotism, 87, 88; and paternalistic management, 87, 88; and personal trust in business, 87, 92
Family or household strategies, 59, 86, 90
Fight Violent Crime campaign, 103; Functional constituencies, *see* Representative government

GENDER INEQUALITY AND
DISCRIMINATION, 82, 83, 90
Government's Working Group on
Juvenile Crime, 111
Gross Domestic Product, 7

HEUNG YEE KUK (RURAL COUNCIL),
168
Hong Kong Alliance in Support of
Patriotic Democratic Movements in
China, 172
Hong Kong Association for
Democracy and People's
Livelihood, 171, 174, 175, 180
Hongkong Bank, 40, 48
Hong Kong Club, 2
Hong Kong Engineering Institute,
141
Hong Kong Federation of Trade
Unions, 145, 152, 161, 175,
180
Hong Kong Federation of Students,
158
Hong Kong Television Broadcasts,
48
Hopkins, Keith, 129
Housing Authority, 91, 137
Housing policy, 115, 126, 129, 134,
136; economic objectives of
Government's, 118, 129, 130; and
Home Ownership Scheme, 130,
132, 134, 137; and Home Purchase
Loan Scheme, 132, 135, 137; and
Housing Scheme for Middle-
income Families, 133; and Long
Term Housing Strategy, 132, 134,
137; and Private Sector Participation
Scheme, 132, 137; and Ten Year
Housing Programme, 23, 126, 130,
134; and Temporary Housing
Areas, 132

INDEPENDENT COMMISSION AGAINST
CORRUPTION (ICAC), 22, 23, 103,
104, 106, 109, 114
Industrialization, 4–6; and family,
76–80, 90; and industrial policy,
116, 117; and small-scale industrial
firms, 3–9; and social discontents,
21; see also Crime, Family
Inequalities, see Social inequality
Instrumentalism, see Work
Interlocking directorships, 40, 41

JOB SATISFACTION, 58
Jones, Catharine, 124–6, 134, 137,
138
June Fourth Incident (1989), 38, 158
Juvenile crime and delinquency,
99–101, 111; and change in
family structure, 99; effect of
Government's New Towns Policy
on, 99–101; and family
relationships, 98, 100; and informal
social control, 98, 101, 110;
influence of delinquent associates
on, 101, 110; 'path model' of, 100,
101; social control perspective on,
98, 99; and socio-economic
development, 98; and system of
schooling, 98–101

KAIFONG ASSOCIATIONS, 15–16, 125,
168, 169
King, Ambrose Y. C., 39, 92, 109,
113, 162–3, 179
Kuan Hsin-chi, 18, 38, 46, 50, 53, 55,
60–2, 73–4

LABOUR MOBILITY, see Mobility
Labour movement, 141, 142, 151,
152, 154, 155, 159; and Chinese
politics, 154, 155, 159; and labour
union politics, 152; and union
membership, 151, 155; see also
Strikes
Labour unions, 4, 43, 142, 143, 147,
152, 154
Lau Siu-kai, 26, 45, 90, 116, 177; on
class, 30; critique of, 32–3; on
family, 79–81; on Hong Kong
ethos, 50–4; on politics, 17–19, 39,
60–3, 177; on social structure,
12–17
Lee Ming-kwan: on class, 29–30; on
family, 77–8, 85–6, 39–90, 93; on
political elections, 171–2
Lee, Rance P. L., 108, 109
Legislative Council, 15, 28, 117;
Chinese élites in, 13, 15; co-option
of élites into, 2, 3, 21, 39; functions
of, 26; political configuration
within, 175–6; and political
elections, 23, 158, 165, 167, 169–75
Legitimacy, 13, 15, 20–5; and
housing policy, 134; and protest
movements, 150

Lethbridge, Henry, 102, 106
Leung, Benjamin K. P., on class, 39–42, 44–5; on labour movement, 151–5, 161; on political development, 166–7, 179; on social conflict, 146–51; on student movement, 155–9
Levin, David, 73
Liberal Party, 175, 178
Life chances, 34; inequalities in, 46, 59; *see also* Class
Lilley, Rozanna, 70, 74
Lo, T. Wing, 106–9, 113
Louie Kin-sheun, 146, 148, 149, 173, 176–8, 180
Lui Tai-lok: on class, 31–4, 37–8; on social mobility, 34–6; on social movements, 149–51, 161; on work attitudes, 59–60

MACLEHOSE, GOVERNOR MURRAY, 107, 109, 126, 130, 157
Manual workers, *see* Workers
Meeting Point, 171, 174, 180
Merchants, 1, 25, 50, 117, 124; British, 1–3, 21, 28; Chinese, 2–4, 28, 51, 124, 125
Mitchell, Robert E., 55, 56, 57
Mobility, 47; intergenerational, 34; labour, 9, 10, 17, 43; opportunities, 30, 34, 35, 47, 55, 57, 72; social, 29, 31, 34, 45, 47, 55, 56; upward, 30, 35, 55, 56
Municipal Councils, 150
Mutual Aid Committees, 22, 103, 163, 164, 168, 169

NATIONAL PEOPLE'S CONGRESS, 48, 180
New China News Agency, 28
New Territories Administration, 131
Ng, Agnes, 98–101, 111
Ng-Quinn, Michael, 103, 104

OFFICIAL LANGUAGES ACT, 23
Opportunities: economic, 49, 59, 80; equality of, 35, 70, 72; job, 1

PATTEN, GOVERNOR CHRIS, 167
People's Association for Public Housing, 127
Po Leung Kuk, 124, 179
Podmore, David, 55, 78

Political apathy, 14, 19, 50, 60, 63, 73, 81, 116, 139
Political attitudes, 18, 60, 63
Political participation, 25, 38, 164, 165, 169, 179; different types of, 61, 73; instrumental or utilitarian orientation towards, 18–20, 60–2, 73; middle class, 24, 31
Political stability, 13, 14, 20, 24, 46, 102, 131, 163; and administrative absorption of politics, 39, 92, 162–4; and co-option of élites, 3, 15, 21, 24, 39, 162, 163; and influence of China's politics, 148, 149, 160; and economic prosperity, 23, 49, 121–3, 126, 133, 135, 165; and familial absorption of politics, 81, 90; *see also* Riots, Strikes
Political trust, 19, 20, 41
Popular culture, 49, 63, 64, 70–3; and 1997, 68, 69; and 'Ah Charn' syndrome, 68, 69; Chineseness in, 64, 65, 67, 68; and Hong Kong ethos, 69–72; and Hong Kong identity, 67–9; indigenization of, 66, 67; Western influence on, 63, 65
Population, 1, 5, 75; Chinese, 3, 50, 64, 124, 126, 162; working, 7, 11, 151, 152, 179
Positive non-interventionism, 15, 106, 115, 116, 118, 122, 135, 136; *see also* Social policy
Preparatory Committee, 42, 43
Pressure groups, 150, 151, 164, 165, 169, 179
Public housing policy, *see* Housing policy

RACIAL SEGREGATION, 2, 4, 49
Redding, S. Gordon, 92
Refugees: and family, 76, 79–81; and Hong Kong culture, 51, 63–5; and industrialization, 5–6, 8–9, 90; and welfare policy, 125–6
Refugee mentality, 5, 11, 55, 58, 139
Regional Council, 28
Representative government, 20, 165–7, 176, 178; and electoral politics, 18, 162; and functional constituencies, 18, 23, 28, 167, 175, 177, 180; and middle class, 36–8

Index

Riots: 1956 riots, 22, 43–4, 143–4, 147–8, 160; 1966 riots, 22, 44, 144–5, 148; 1967 riots, 22, 44, 145–8

SALAFF, JANET, 47, 78, 82–4, 90, 92
Scott, Ian, 28, 32, 123, 180; on housing policy, 131; on legitimacy crises, 20–5; on social policy, 115–20
Sino-British Joint Declaration, 18, 27, 165, 169
Sino-British negotiations, 23, 127, 158, 165, 168
So, Alvin Y., 36, 37
Social class, *see* Class
Social conflict, 30, 43, 50, 70, 139–41, 146, 147, 159; and collective violence, 146, 147; definition of, 139; anti-colonialism and nationalism in, 145–8; four major episodes of, 141–6; and the political rivalry between Communists and Guomindang, 44, 143, 147, 148; *see also* Riots, Strikes
Social control, 3, 108–10; definition of, 94; formal, 94, 98; informal, 94; *see also* Crime trends, Juvenile crime and delinquency
Social inequality, 12, 21, 22, 55–7, 70; and class, 24, 25, 45, 72; perception of, 56; and social conflict, 56, 140
Social mobility, *see* Mobility
Social movement, 43, 139–41, 149, 151, 159; cognitive model of, 141, 147, 148; as 'cognitive praxis', 141; definition of, 139; political process model of, 140, 147, 148; resource mobilization model of, 140, 147; structural-functionalist model of, 140; *see also* Labour movement, Student movement
Social policy, 115, 119–22, 133, 138; capitalist state approach to, 118–20; definition of, 115; *laissez-faire*, 52–4, 80, 115–18, 135; non-interventionist, 20, 52, 60, 116, 117, 122; as non-purposive adaptation, 120–2, *see also* Positive non-interventionism

Social stability, 19, 33, 36, 55, 56, 62, 63, 132; and ideology of abundant opportunities, 55–8, 69, 71, 72; and the Hong Kong Dream, 57, 60, 70, 72; *see also* Political stability
Social structure, 2, 4, 6, 29, 32, 33, 46
Social Welfare Department, 126, 128
Social welfare policy, 52, 115, 123, 137; development of, 124–9; role of Chinese merchants and missionaries in pre-War, 124, 125; and the golden era of voluntary welfare activity, 125, 126; the emergence of the 'politics of social choice' in, 127, 129
Special Administrative Region (SAR), 16, 17, 20, 27, 42, 128, 165, 177, 178; Chief Executive of, 177
Special Administrative Region's Preparatory Working Committee, 48, 179
State, 110, 113, 117; capitalist, 106, 108, 118; relative autonomy of, 108, 113, 118, 120, 123; *see also* Social policy
Strikes, 142, 146, 152, 161; incidence and level of industrial, 43, 48, 73, 90, 151–3; General Strike-Boycott of (1925–26), 26, 141, 142, 145, 147, 148, 160; Mechanics' Strike (1920), 141; Seamen's Strike (1922), 4, 141
Student movement, 37, 141, 155–61; nationalism in, 156, 157; pro-China faction and Social Action Faction in, 156, 157, 161; the eclipse of, 158
Subcontracting, 9, 27
Sze, Stephen Man-hung, 71, 72

TANG, STEPHEN LUNG-WAI, 168
Television Broadcasts Company (TVB), 66
Trade unions, 17, 44, 145, 148
Trade Unions Council, 152, 161
Traver, Harold, 94, 95, 111, 112
Tung Wah Hospital, 3, 26, 124, 179
Turner, H. A., 58, 59, 73, 88

UNITED DEMOCRATS OF HONG KONG, 171, 174, 180
Urban Council, 28

Urban Council Ward, 16
Utilitarianistic familism or Utilitarian familism, 14, 32, 51, 55, 90; critique of, 93; decline of, 52; and political stability, 79–81
Utilitarian or egoistic individualism, 52–5, 81

VAGG, JON, 102, 106, 112

WOMEN: educational attainment of, 83; employment opportunities of, 76, occupational status of, 83, and work, 83, 91, *see also* Family
Wong, Fai-ming, 75–8, 81, 89, 91
Wong, Gilbert, 41, 48
Wong, Siu-lun, 9, 56; on capitalist class, 41–2; on family firms, 86–8, 90, 93

Wong, Thomas W. P., 15, 46, 47; on attitudes towards social mobility, 54–7; on class, 31–4, 38–9, 45
Work, 54, 59, 63, 142; attitudes towards, 57–60, 72, 87, 88; and instrumentalism, 54, 57–60
Workers, 10–12, 73, 161; attitudes towards work, 57–9; and labour movement, 151–5; and riots, 142–6; manual, 12, 35, 36, 43
Working class, 10; family, 85–6; and riots, 22–3; as a social-political force, 43–5; and social mobility, 35–6

YOUNG, JOHN D., 148, 160
Young Men's Christian Association (YMCA), 101, 112
Young Women's Christian Association (YWCA), 101, 112